# ABOUT THE AUTHOR

argaret Urwin (née Kelly) has worked with Justice for the For-
tten, the organisation representing the families and survivors of
Dublin and Monaghan bombings, since 1993 and, for more
an a decade, with the families of victims of other cross-Border
mbings. Justice for the Forgotten affiliated with the Pat Finu-
ae Centre in December 2010.

A native of Ballymitty, County Wexford, Margaret is a graduate
of the Open University and has an MA (Hons) in Local History
rcm NUI Maynooth.

Her publications include:

'The Effects of the Great Famine (1845–9) in the County Wexford Parish of Bannow/Ballymitty', *The Journal of the Wexford
Historical Society*, 1996

*County Wexford Family in the Land War: The O'Hanlon Walshs
of Knocktartan* (Four Courts Press, Dublin, 2001)

The Murder of Charles Daniel Boyd', in F. Sweeney (ed.),
*Hanging Crimes* (Mercier Press, Cork, 2005)

Counter-gangs: A history of undercover military units in
Northern Ireland 1971–1976', Spinwatch website, 2013

# A STATE IN DENIAL

## British Collaboration with Loyalist Paramilitaries

### MARGARET URWIN

 JFF

**Justice for the
Forgotten**

MERCIER PRESS

IRISH PUBLISHER – IRISH STORY

MERCIER PRESS

Cork

www.mercierpress.ie

ISBN: 978 1 78117 462 3

10 9 8 7 6 5 4 3 2 1

A CIP record for this title is available from the British Library

Printed and bound in the EU.

# CONTENTS

# ABBREVIATIONS

| | |
|---|---|
| ACC | Assistant Chief Constable |
| AP | Arrest policy |
| AUS | Army Under-Secretary |
| BGS | Brigade General Staff |
| CESA | Catholic Ex-Servicemen's Association (also CEA) |
| CID | Criminal Investigation Department, RUC |
| CGS | Chief of the General Staff |
| CLF | Commander of Land Forces, Northern Ireland |
| DOW | Down Orange Welfare |
| DPP | Director of Public Prosecutions |
| DS10 | Defence Secretariat 10 of the MoD |
| DUP | Democratic Unionist Party |
| DUS | Deputy Under-Secretary |
| ECHR | European Commission of Human Rights |
| ECtHR | European Court of Human Rights |
| FCO | Foreign and Commonwealth Office |
| FRU | Force Research Unit |
| GOC | General Officer Commanding |
| HET | Historical Enquiries Team |
| HMG | Her Majesty's Government |
| HQNI | British Army Headquarters Northern Ireland |
| ICO | Interim Custody Order |
| INC | Irish National Caucus |
| INLA | Irish National Liberation Army |
| IPU | Information Policy Unit, British Army Headquarters |
| IRA | Irish Republican Army |

| | |
|---|---|
| IRSP | Irish Republican Socialist Party |
| JFF | Justice for the Forgotten |
| LCC | Loyalist Coordinating Committee |
| MoD | Ministry of Defence |
| MRF | Military Reaction Force |
| NAI | National Archives of Ireland |
| NAUK | National Archives UK |
| NIAC | Northern Ireland Advisory Commission |
| NIO | Northern Ireland Office |
| NUPRG | New Ulster Political Research Group |
| OIRA | Official Irish Republican Army |
| OV | Orange Volunteers |
| PAB | Public Affairs Branch, NIO |
| PAD | Public Affairs Division, NIO |
| PAF | Protestant Action Force |
| PD | People's Democracy |
| PFC | Pat Finucane Centre |
| PIRA | Provisional Irish Republican Army |
| PONI | Police Ombudsman for Northern Ireland |
| PRONI | Public Records Office Northern Ireland |
| PSF | Provisional Sinn Féin |
| PSNI | Police Service of Northern Ireland |
| PsyOps | Psychological Operations |
| PUL | Protestant Unionist Community |
| PUP | Progressive Unionist Party |
| PUS | Permanent Under-Secretary |
| RHC | Red Hand Commando |
| RID | Republic of Ireland Department, Foreign and Commonwealth Office |
| RSR | Review Summary Report of Historical Enquiries Team |

| | |
|---|---|
| RUC | Royal Ulster Constabulary |
| RUCR | RUC Reserve |
| SAS | Special Air Service |
| SDLP | Social Democratic and Labour Party |
| SLR | Self-loading rifle |
| SMG | Sub-machine gun |
| SitRep | Situation Report |
| TAVR | Territorial Army Volunteer Reserve |
| UAC | Ulster Army Council |
| UCD | University College Dublin |
| UDA | Ulster Defence Association |
| UDR | Ulster Defence Regiment |
| UFF | Ulster Freedom Fighters |
| ULDP | Ulster Loyalist Democratic Party |
| USC | Ulster Special Constabulary |
| USCA | Ulster Special Constabulary Association |
| UUP | Ulster Unionist Party |
| UUUC | United Ulster Unionist Council |
| UVF | Ulster Volunteer Force |
| UWC | Ulster Workers' Council |
| VCP | Vehicle checkpoint |
| VPP | Volunteer Political Party |
| YCV | Young Citizen Volunteers |

# ACKNOWLEDGEMENTS

This publication is the result of years of collaborative research by the Pat Finucane Centre (PFC) and Justice for the Forgotten (JFF) (now part of the PFC) at the National Archives in both London and Dublin, the National Library of Ireland, the University College Dublin Archives, the Linen Hall Library in Belfast and the London School of Economics.

I would like to thank my colleagues, Anne Cadwallader, Sara Duddy and Alan Brecknell, for their assistance in plundering the archives and for their helpful suggestions. Thanks also to PFC board members Paddy Hillyard, Stuart Ross and Robin Percival for their crucial editorial input. I particularly wish to acknowledge the enormous contribution of PFC Director Paul O'Connor. His guidance, advice and suggestions throughout the project were invaluable. I am also grateful to London-based journalist Tom Griffin for helping with the London end of the research and Raymond Walker for his assistance. The final product is the collective responsibility of the editorial board of the PFC/JFF.

I wish also to thank those families who kindly agreed to allow details from their case files to be included. A special thank you to Ian Knox for creating a cartoon for the picture section.

Finally, I hope that even those who disagree profoundly with me will take the time to examine the evidence and reflect on the conclusions.

# FOREWORD

In 1989 the deputy head of the Royal Ulster Constabulary (RUC) Special Branch, Brian Fitzsimons, submitted two documents to the Stevens investigation, which had been set up to examine allegations of collusion between the British Army, the RUC and loyalist para-militaries.[1] These documents, reproduced in the de Silva Report, summarised intelligence reports on collusion between the security forces and loyalist paramilitaries in the mid-1980s.[2] In a cover note an unnamed official commented: 'the overall picture seems to be one of RUC collusion and links with the loyalists which is similar in scale (if not greater in some respects) to that of the UDR [Ulster Defence Regiment].' Since the UDR was a British Army infantry regiment, the primary purpose of which was to aid the RUC, this shows just how deep the relationship between the RUC and loyalist organisations was thought to be.

The declassified official documents discussed in this book show more than a decade of official toleration, and at times encourage-ment, of loyalist paramilitaries throughout the 1970s, which would have horrifying results. According to *Lost Lives: The Stories of the Men, Women and Children Who Died as a Result of the Northern Ire-land Troubles*, between 1969 and the signing of the Good Friday Agreement in 1998, in all but two years, more Catholic civilians than Protestant civilians died each year.[3] There were only two years – 1978 and 1987 – when this deadly trend was reversed. Loyalist paramilitaries were responsible for the majority of Catholic civilian deaths.[4]

This is not to trump one community's suffering over another –

the entire conflict was a desperate waste of human life and clearly the high level of casualties, including those of serving and retired members of the RUC and UDR, had a profound and devastating effect on the Protestant and unionist community.

But it is important to remember that the main focus of the Ulster Defence Association (UDA) and the Ulster Volunteer Force (UVF) assassination campaign was the Catholic civilian population. As this was happening, the British government, the RUC, the British Army and the criminal justice system were living in a state of denial about the true extent of the assassination campaign and who was carrying out these assassinations – the fictional Ulster Freedom Fighters (UFF) or the still-legal UDA, as well as the illegal UVF.[5] Perhaps the greatest state of denial – a phrase coined by sociologist Stan Cohen[6] – was the fiction that collusion, if it existed at all, was limited to a few bad apples. The evidence shows that successive British governments turned a blind eye and sometimes encouraged the actions of the UDA and UVF. Church leaders were too often silent. Senior unionist political figures from 1969 onwards flirted with the 'men of violence' as it suited them, and abandoned them just as quickly.

This is not to overlook the fact that there were many decent officers in the RUC who were not engaged in collusion, and who sought to uphold the rule of law and put loyalist paramilitaries behind bars. But all too often Special Branch, army intelligence and the Security Service, MI5, withheld vital intelligence from the RUC's Criminal Investigation Department (CID) officers on the ground. As a result, many investigations were doomed from the outset.

It is possible that many within the RUC wished to see the UDA proscribed, but it was a chief constable, John Hermon, who opposed this in the early 1980s, as did secretaries of state and the mandarins in the Northern Ireland Office (NIO). It is sometimes argued that the emerging evidence of state collusion with republicans through British agents working undercover, as in the case of the man code-named 'Stakeknife', somehow balances the equation.[7] This is to miss the point. Collusion with loyalists was intended to help defeat the IRA by increasing the effectiveness of loyalist groups. The infiltration of agents into the IRA, and ignoring their involvement in murder, had the same goal – weakening and ultimately defeating the IRA.

It is clear that the evidence presented in this book is only one part of the tragic story that led to the loss of so many lives. As our colleague Anne Cadwallader wrote in *Lethal Allies* (a previous PFC publication), 'not for one moment should anyone suggest that the agony was restricted to one community'.[8] During the period covered in this book, the IRA and other republican organisations killed and maimed hundreds of members of the security forces, both on and off duty. Some were killed in front of their families. IRA and Irish National Liberation Army (INLA) attacks also led to a shocking loss of civilian lives. Many survivors are still struggling to come to terms with horrific injuries. To negate this would be a form of denial as repugnant as the denial that still exists in the face of overwhelming evidence of a collusive relationship between loyalist paramilitaries and the state. But the state is still with us and the state is still in denial, as evidenced by the refusal to grant an independent public inquiry into the murder of Pat Finucane and to release documents relating to the Dublin and Monaghan bombings.[9]

The declassified documents discussed within these pages paint an extraordinary picture. Where *Lethal Allies* explored the extent of collusion during a specific time in a specific area, *A State in Denial* peeps behind the doors of Whitehall and Stormont in the 1970s and early 1980s. The picture that emerges is one of toleration and even de facto encouragement of loyalist paramilitaries.

During the worst year of the conflict, 1972, many within civil society carried out the onerous task of documenting what was happening nightly on the streets. In this context the Association for Legal Justice and Fathers Raymond Murray and Denis Faul stand out as a light in the darkness. Another individual, a member of the Central Citizens' Defence Committee, Jim O'Callaghan, was literally mapping all sectarian murders in the city of Belfast. Mr O'Callaghan used his influence to get a meeting in late 1972 with Secretary of State William Whitelaw, to voice his concerns at the level of assassinations. He brought along the map on which he had painstakingly plotted all the sectarian murders that had occurred that year. His daughter, Eimear, writing about the incident years later, described her father's account of the meeting – 'the Secretary of State closed his deep-set bloodhound eyes and drifted off into a doze, as the group – including my father – delivered their presentation'.[10] Was this a metaphor for British attitudes to loyalist violence?

The ambiguous and contradictory British attitude towards loyalist violence and threat of violence, as argued below, was not a new phenomenon. According to Max Caulfield, General John Maxwell, who was responsible for the execution of the leaders of the Easter Rising in 1916, 'blamed all the trouble on the Government's pusillanimity in allowing Carson to form the Ulster Volunteers, naming this as the primary cause of the Rebellion and the growing unrest which succeeded it'. Clearly no lessons were learned.

*Paul O'Connor*
Director
Pat Finucane Centre

# 1

# FROM CONFLICT ORIGINS TO INTERNMENT AND DIRECT RULE

'A series of positive actions by employees of the State actively furthered and facilitated Patrick Finucane's murder and ... in the aftermath of the murder, there was a relentless attempt to defeat the ends of justice.' The Government accept[s] these findings unequivocally.

*Former British Prime Minister David Cameron speaking in the House of Commons on 16 January 2015, accepting the conclusions of Sir Desmond de Silva's Report of the Patrick Finucane Review[1]*

The purpose of this book is to explore the tangled web of relationships between British government ministers, senior civil servants and senior police and military officers with loyalist paramilitaries in both the UDA and the UVF. By using the lens of official British and Irish declassified documents from the 1970s and early 1980s, it will also put into context the loyalist intimidation and sectarian assassination campaigns that occurred in Northern Ireland throughout this period.

That the British government would engage in a collusive relationship with loyalist paramilitaries in Northern Ireland is consistent with British counter-insurgency operations in other theatres of conflict since the Second World War.[2] Having introduced counter-insurgency methods in a number of colonial campaigns – Malaya, Muscat, Oman, Cyprus and Kenya – British Army brigadier Sir Frank Kitson was posted to Northern Ireland in 1970 as commander of 39 Brigade, Belfast.[3] He soon set about introducing these methods in his new posting by establishing plain-clothes soldiers in covert units, which evolved into the Military Reaction Force (MRF), and encouraging the use of 'proxy' or supporting forces – local friendly forces employed throughout the colonies by the British Army.[4]

Just as the use of 'Q_Patrols' of Turkish Cypriots was an important feature in the British victory in Cyprus, and tribes hostile to the Kikuyu in Kenya played a major role in the defeat of the Mau-Mau, so the loyalists of Northern Ireland were the natural allies of the British in their war against republicans, especially the Provisional Irish Republican Army (PIRA).[5] In fact, the loyalists of Northern Ireland had a stronger incentive to become involved than any colonial group. They were British citizens and wanted Northern Ireland to remain part of the United Kingdom, sharing a common identity and mutual self-interest.

While it would be simplistic to make direct comparisons between the colonies and Northern Ireland, the British Army did discuss among themselves precedents established in Cyprus, Aden and Hong Kong.[6] All army officers who held the top job (general officer commanding) in Northern Ireland during the 1970s had colonial experience. Many of the tactics used in the colonies were employed in Northern Ireland (but on a much smaller scale) as is exemplified in the Falls Curfew of 1970,[7] internment, in-depth interrogation, Bloody Sunday,[8] screening of the population,[9] undercover units and the use of 'friendly forces'.

The main 'friendly forces' were the UVF and the UDA. While a number of less important loyalist organisations were also established in the early 1970s – Vanguard, Red Hand Commando (RHC), Tara, Orange Volunteers (OV) and Down Orange Welfare (DOW) – the focus here will be on the two main organisations.

Numerous official documents establish that British government policy was to portray these loyalists as reactive and defensive, but also largely undisciplined and unstructured – only loosely bound by constraints or leadership control (although these documents also reveal that, in reality, the government knew very well that they were both structured and disciplined).[10] The benefit of portraying them in this way was that there would not be organisational accountability for their actions (unlike the disciplined and structured IRA). Once adopted, this policy position continued through the decades, giving cover to the UDA and, to a lesser extent, the UVF, in their murderous sectarian campaigns.

\*\*\*

An examination of the origins of the modern UVF leads directly to the opening shots of the conflict in Northern Ireland. From at least 1965 unionist unease was growing. Several factors, both political and economic, contributed to mounting unionist disquiet: the reforms of Prime Minister Terence O'Neill and his meetings with Irish Taoiseach Seán Lemass; the economic downturn, resulting in job losses in the shipyard and aircraft industry (both had mainly Protestant/unionist workforces) and the terminal decline of the linen industry; a decision to dedicate the new bridge over the River Lagan to Queen Elizabeth II rather than Edward Carson;[11] and constant rumours of a new IRA campaign.[12]

Several factors were stoking unionist fears about IRA intentions. In November 1965, during the election campaign, members of the Stormont Parliament announced that the IRA was planning to disrupt the election. Rumours were also circulating that the anniversary of the IRA's previous campaign – 12 December 1965 – would provide the impetus for the resumption of an armed campaign. The IRA's previous 'Border Campaign', which ended in 1962, began on 12 December 1956. When these predictions failed to materialise, speculation then began about the potential for IRA violence during the upcoming fiftieth anniversary of the Easter Rising in April 1966.

Rev. Ian Paisley was in the vanguard of those fuelling the flames. Although Easter Rising commemorations were to be confined to nationalist areas, Paisley led public objections to the government's decision to permit the events.[13] An RUC report on 'the Paisleyite Movement' was sent by RUC Inspector General A. H. Kennedy to the Ministry of Home Affairs on 20 June 1966. The inspector general wrote:

> While there is always the IRA in the background ready to seize any opportunity to disturb the peace, the fact is that an equal or even greater threat is posed at present by extremist Protestant groups, many of whom are members of loyalist organisations. These are the people whom it may be possible to reach at meetings of the Loyal Orange Order and other similar bodies and it may be that leaders of Protestant churches could also play their part before it is too late.[14]

The report advised that Paisley and his followers had decided to form 'a new extreme Protestant organisation' which would operate under a number of different names:

1. The Ulster Constitution Defence Committee
2. The Ulster Protestant Volunteer Force
3. The Ulster Volunteer Force
4. The Ulster Defence Corps
5. Ulster Protestant Action[15]

The report contained the following information on the UVF:

> The Ulster Volunteer Force is regarded as the militant wing of the
> organisation and operates under great secrecy. Small divisions are
> known to have been formed in Belfast, Counties Antrim, Armagh
> and Tyrone. There is little doubt that a good number of personnel
> in the Ulster Special Constabulary are active members; indeed it is
> feared that some have been recruited from other branches of the
> Crown Forces and government departments.[16]

Inspector General Kennedy observed that in the event of force
being used, the UVF would be entirely dependent on sympathisers
in the Ulster Special Constabulary and crown forces.[17]

When Prime Minister O'Neill banned the UVF on 28 June 1966,
after the killing of three people in sectarian attacks in May and June
of that year, he insinuated that there was a connection between the
UVF and Rev. Paisley. He referred to a statement made in the Ulster
Hall on 16 June, when Paisley purportedly read out resolutions from
the UVF that they were 'solidly behind Paisley'. The prime minister
also referred to a statement of thanks that Paisley had extended to
the UVF at a march on 17 April.[18]

UVF leader Gusty Spence, a former soldier in the Royal Ulster
Rifles who was convicted of one of the killings, later claimed that
the RUC and Stormont government in 1966 deliberately tried
to connect Paisley to the UVF to discredit him. However, he also
claimed that some members of the Ulster Unionist Party (UUP)
were 'key to the UVF'.[19] Although Paisley flatly denied that his Ulster
Constitution Defence Committee or his Ulster Protestant Action
had any links to the UVF, according to Margaret O'Callaghan and
Catherine O'Donnell, loyalist activist Noel Doherty was listed as

secretary of both the Ulster Constitution Defence Committee and the Belfast UVF, while William (Billy) Mitchell was said to be a member of both Ulster Protestant Action and the Belfast UVF.[20]

David Boulton notes that the modern UVF was formed in March 1966 and began a petrol-bombing campaign on Catholic premises in March and April, which accelerated in May.[21] After Spence and two others were convicted in October 1966 of the three killings, the UVF went quiet until March 1969 when it was responsible for causing explosions at power stations, reservoirs and water pipelines. These explosions were initially blamed on the IRA. Paisley's newspaper, the *Protestant Telegraph*, described the four bomb explosions at the electricity substation in Castlereagh, Belfast, as 'the first act of sabotage by the IRA since 1956 ... the sheer professionalism of the act indicates the work of the well-equipped IRA'.[22] A number of former B Specials were later charged with but acquitted of these bomb attacks, while one former member, Samuel Stephenson, was convicted.[23]

Questions remain as to who planned and financed these attacks. They had the desired effect, as far as Paisley and his supporters were concerned, as in the unionist uproar after the explosions Terence O'Neill was forced to resign.

In November 1970 enquiries from an *Irish Press* journalist as to whether the UVF was recruiting in a number of areas of Belfast, and whether arms were being manufactured in certain unionist-owned factories, were met with a flat denial from the British Army that the UVF even existed.[24] These denials were made despite the fact that the organisation had caused explosions at the homes of MPs Sheelagh Murnaghan, Ulster Liberal Party; Austin Currie, Social Democratic and Labour Party (SDLP) – for which the UVF had claimed responsibility; and Richard Ferguson and Ann Dickson, both Unionist Party, earlier in the year. Bombs had also been set off at Crumlin Road gaol in Belfast and the adjacent courthouse in February 1970, and at a Belfast Catholic students' hostel in March.[25]

In the same year, the British government showed its sensitivity to potential criticism regarding its selectivity in arms searches. An official in the Western European Section of the Foreign and Commonwealth Office (FCO) wrote to the Ministry of Defence (MoD) in November expressing concern about arms searches in nationalist areas. Statistics he had received showed that the number of searches in these areas was double the number in loyalist areas, relative to the size of the population.[26] Although he expressed the view that it would be wrong to try to 'cook the books', he wondered if there was some way of 'putting the Army's activities in a more favourable light'. The period chosen, he said, covered a time when 'Catholics were for obvious reasons' the target of a particularly large number of searches, suggesting the period be extended 'which might remove the imbalance', again stressing that he was not deliberately trying to give a false impression. There would be many people, he believed, who would like to prove that the army was discriminating against Catholics, so it had a 'perfect right' to present its statistics in such a way as not to do its detractors' work for them.[27]

These remarks show that, from a very early stage in the conflict, there was evidence that some officials were willing to massage the statistics to preserve the myth that the rule of law was being applied fairly and to maintain Britain's reputation.

\*\*\*

In September 1971 the UDA evolved from a number of loyalist vigilante groups or local 'defence associations', and it soon became the largest paramilitary group in Northern Ireland. It attracted many thousands of members – at its peak in 1972 it was said to have had a membership of 40,000–50,000 men. They openly engaged in military-style marches; the sight of thousands of UDA men – usually wearing sunglasses and masks, bush hats and combat jackets – marching through the centre of Belfast became common, particularly in 1972.

According to Paul Bew and Gordon Gillespie, the UDA provided certain benefits for working-class loyalists in boosting morale, but there was also a very sinister side to many of its activities. They claim that it used kangaroo courts to discipline its members, that racketeering emerged early in the organisation's history, and that, for some members, the organisation was merely a front for attacking Catholics.[28]

Martin Dillon claims that, before the formation of the UDA, William Craig held discussions with William McGrath (of Kincora infamy),[29] John McKeague,[30] Charles Harding Smith and Tommy Herron.[31] Craig, the former minister for home affairs in the Stormont government, had founded the Vanguard Unionist Progressive Party on 9 February 1972, as a result of a split in the UUP. During these talks the men were impressed by Craig's advice about combining street-defence groups.[32] *The Sunday Times* later described the UDA as the military wing of the Vanguard Party.[33]

The British government, which publicly denied the UDA's murderous campaign for two decades, was aware from an early stage of the nature of the organisation. In April 1972 the UDA's chairman, Charles Harding Smith, along with another member, John White, went to London to procure weapons for the organisation.[34] They were caught red-handed in a sting operation by MI5; however, the case collapsed when it came to trial in December 1972.[35] In May

1972 *The Sunday Times* reported that 'Woodvale District Commander is ex-British Army: the UDA has many former servicemen
and B-Specials as well as active members of the UDR.'[36] Woodvale was one of the defence associations from which the UDA had
evolved. Despite its involvement in extensive violence and intimidation, the UDA was permitted to remain a legal organisation for two
decades and was not proscribed until 1992.

***

In contrast to its tolerant attitude towards the two developing loyalist paramilitary organisations, from August 1970 the government
was considering the possible internment of IRA members. The
then UK Representative,[37] Tony Hewins, advised a Home Office
official that he had been approached by Christopher Herbert, the
director of intelligence, Northern Ireland Command, about contingency planning for the power of detention.[38] Hewins expressed
concern about the adequacy of RUC Special Branch dossiers on
potential internees. He suggested:

> [The British authorities] should be ready to take prompt action if
> and when a decision to use the power of detention is made and
> in making any approach to the police would be careful not to give
> the impression that the question was under active consideration by
> Ministers.[39]

Hewins also referred to the internment of persons the previous year.
It is not generally known that two men, Malachy McGurran and
Proinsias MacAirt, were arrested and detained under the Special
Powers Act on 15 August 1969 at MacAirt's home in the Lower

Falls area of Belfast.[40] They were still being held in December 1969.[41] In his memo, the UK representative complained that the RUC had had great difficulty in producing adequate dossiers on those interned in 1969.[42]

A draft reply to Hewins' memo suggested that the British government would be very reluctant to countenance such a development as it would be 'counter to the spirit behind the reform programme'. Since taking power in 1963, Terence O'Neill had begun a policy of rapprochement with the Irish Taoiseach, Seán Lemass, as well as introducing a five-point reform programme in response to the demands of the Northern Ireland Civil Rights Association – in housing allocation, voting rights and review of security. If the IRA or 'any other dissident organisation', however, 'began a powerful offensive designed to imperil order in Northern Ireland', the government might have to agree to the internment powers being invoked.[43]

At the beginning of September 1970, Ronnie A. Burroughs replaced Tony Hewins as UK Representative. On 9 September he reminded Robin North in the Home Office of a previous discussion when they had both agreed that they found the idea of internment 'distasteful' – but, however distasteful, it could not be stated that it would never be used.[44]

On 4 November an internal Home Office memo reported that all the intelligence assessments emanating from the 'Ireland Current Intelligence Group' for many weeks had made it clear that the IRA threat should be taken seriously, as a considerable amount of training had been taking place. It was believed that the trainees 'would be unlikely … to let the skills they have acquired go to waste'. The Home Office was of the opinion that 'the RUC were still violently opposed to detention on the practical grounds that it would make the security situation worse rather than better'.[45]

On the same date, Philip Leyshon, Home Office, wrote to C. Johnson, MoD, seeking his department's views on internment. He referred to increased IRA activity and suggested that, while detention should be a last resort, they should be prepared in case that scenario developed at short notice, perhaps in connection with 'murderous attacks on British troops'.[46]

On 4 December an announcement by the Taoiseach, Jack Lynch, added to the debate. He stated that the Irish government would be prepared to introduce internment 'in the face of a conspiracy of kidnapping, bank raids and murder'. A Home Office official speculated that this was a warning to Saor Éire – a militant republican group based in the Republic of Ireland.[47]

In a letter to Philip Woodfield, Home Office, on 8 December, Ronnie Burroughs was very optimistic about the security situation.[48] Burroughs was just back from leave and reported a great improvement in the 'law and order' situation since early October. This progress was marred only by explosions, the vast majority of which were IRA bombs, although two 'small recent bangs' had been attributed by the police to 'Protestant extremists'. All the bombs were 'pretty trifling affairs'. He repeated the Home Office view that the RUC believed internment would be counterproductive.[49]

On 9 December Home Office official D. R. E. Hopkins wrote to Burroughs reporting that, although Chief Constable Sir Graham Shillington was against internment, in view of Lynch's statement he had decided that contingency plans should be made. The lists of suspects had to be kept updated and, since the prisons were full, a holding centre for the internees would have to be found. Both Shillington and Burroughs favoured the *Maidstone*, a former submarine depot ship that was being used in 1970 to provide accommodation for British troops in Belfast harbour. According to

Hopkins, Burroughs believed, however, that Shillington wanted to avoid interning anyone.[50]

The home and defence secretaries were opposed to the use of the *Maidstone*. In an undated paper by the Northern Ireland Department of the Home Office, Rathlin Island was suggested as a possible location for internment camps, but was quickly dismissed as preparations on the island would be obvious and their purpose clear.[51]

In a memo of March 1971 to Woodfield, Burroughs noted that at some time between December 1970 and March 1971, the head of RUC Special Branch, David Johnston, had changed his mind about the use of internment. This may have been because a senior member of Special Branch, Cecil Patterson, had been killed by the IRA on 26 February.[52] While Burroughs noted that Johnston had regular meetings with Northern Ireland Prime Minister James Chichester-Clark, and would likely have conveyed his views to him, he had not detected any signs that the prime minister was considering internment, nor did he believe that the chief constable was in agreement with his head of Special Branch. He advised Woodfield that the general officer commanding (GOC) and his staff 'remained firmly of the view that internment is undesirable and would be ineffective'. He observed that the army virtually exercised a veto, since internment would require a massive military effort.[53]

On 16 March a proposal for consideration was sent by MI5 to Home Office official Robin North, which suggested that internment, if deemed necessary, might be confined 'within the boundaries of Greater Belfast'.[54] It was noted that the possible inclusion of the illegal UVF 'would be a sop for the minority community'.[55] Before it was put into effect in August 1971, however, a decision was taken not to include loyalists in the swoop.

In a briefing note, in preparation for a House of Commons debate on 6 April, the head of DS6, a section of the MoD, wrote that contingency planning for internment was 'in hand'. He noted that Chichester-Clark had discussed the subject with the British prime minister some weeks previously and that, subsequently, discussions had taken place between RUC Special Branch and British Army Headquarters Northern Ireland (HQNI) about potential detainees. A decision had been taken that the best long-term solution regarding a suitable site would be to construct a special camp at Long Kesh, which would be ready in about five months' time. He also noted that HQNI were 'continuing their studies into the way in which the rounding up of internees might be effected'. Arrangements were also in hand to train RUC Special Branch in 'interrogation techniques'. He advised that it would be for Stormont to authorise internment 'even if this were only done after consultation with Westminster'.[56]

In a paper on 'Detention and Internment' (undated, probably written in late July 1971) it was remarked that in the House of Commons debate on 6 April the home secretary had said internment was a 'hideous step' to have to take, 'but it was no more hideous than a campaign of murder'. The author advised that assessments at that time had been that the use of internment was counterproductive, but since then 'the campaign of violence and murder has escalated and four more soldiers have been killed'. It also reported that work had commenced on MoD land at Long Kesh on 1 June and that accommodation for 150 internees would probably be available by mid-September.[57] As 1971 saw the first deaths of soldiers – ten were killed in the period between 1 January and 9 August – it would appear that soldiers' deaths at the hands of the IRA were the real impetus for the introduction of internment.

In an internal FCO memo of 3 August, Kelvin White informed Sir Stewart Crawford, the deputy under-secretary, that the Defence Secretary Lord Carrington 'is determined that any decision to intern should be properly under-written by the politicians in Northern Ireland, who should not be allowed to shuffle off the responsibility for so unpopular a move onto the Army'.[58]

While Home Secretary Reginald Maudling favoured the inclusion of some loyalists, the UK representative at that time, Howard Smith, in a telegram on 8 August to Jack Howard-Drake, assistant secretary at the Home Office, informed him that the RUC Special Branch had drawn up a list containing only IRA members and a few members of People's Democracy (PD) – a legal, radical, left-wing organisation that opposed the Special Powers Act. The UVF, the only loyalist organisation in existence at that time, had been responsible for very few deaths (from 1966 up to 9 August 1971 it had killed nine people) but had caused non-fatal explosions both north and south of the border in 1969, 1970 and 1971. Yet the RUC Special Branch still argued that the threat from loyalists was potential rather than actual and could not be equated with that from the IRA.[59] There was also the practicality that the army was going to be 'stretched to the limit' pulling in republicans and 'what is desirable for public opinion in Britain and abroad is therefore in conflict with what is desirable in Northern Ireland'.[60] In the circumstances, Howard Smith recommended to the Home Office that 'the initial grab' should go ahead 'on the basis of the list that has been worked out'.[61]

Smith's telegram informed Howard-Drake that the list of those to be picked up comprised 'IRA Brady [PIRA] 283; IRA Goulding [Official IRA] 143; IRA General 29; PD 7; Anarchist: 1; Saor Éire: 1'.[62] He explained that there was nobody of particular prominence

– one local councillor, O'Kane; twelve teachers or lecturers including Michael Farrell and J. C. Gray (both PD), and D. O'Hagan of 'IRA Goulding' – an instructor at a teacher-training college in Belfast.[63]

In the first wave of raids, 342 people were arrested in the early hours of 9 August, all but two of them Catholics. The only two Protestants included – Ronnie Bunting and John McGuffin – held openly republican sympathies. The total number arrested in the raid fell well short of the British wish list – not everyone was at home when the army came calling.

Over the next four days twenty-four people were killed – twenty civilians, two IRA members and two British soldiers. Three other civilians shot at this time died before the end of the month. The British Army was responsible for twenty-four of these twenty-seven deaths, which included the eleven civilians killed by the Parachute Regiment in what has become known as the Ballymurphy Massacre.[64]

A military appreciation document, with which General Anthony Farrer-Hockley, the first commander of Land Forces Northern Ireland (CLF) agreed, was overly optimistic about the effect internment would have:[65]

The residue of IRA men left with arms would throw their bombs and shoot wildly. There would then ensue a lull while the IRA organised with [*sic*] the Republic; finally, IRA activity would begin again, but probably in the form of flying columns operating in the Border areas. There was a fair chance here of pitched battles, in which the Army would come off the best. Then activity would tail off.[66]

Two SDLP members, Gerry Fitt and Paddy Devlin, were quick to react to the introduction of internment, almost immediately lodging a complaint about its one-sided nature. At a press conference they stated that internment was a political decision (presumably rather than a military one) and claimed that there was evidence of active involvement by armed UVF men in eleven areas of Belfast, which had resulted in hundreds of nationalists leaving their homes.[67]

Two weeks after internment began, in an internal MoD memo, Brigadier J. M. H. Lewis, the senior army intelligence officer in Northern Ireland, stated:

> There is a difference between the Protestant extremist and the IRA. The Protestant is usually more vulnerable to the normal processes of law; he is often a true criminal; he is even more inefficient than the IRA; but above all witnesses against him will come forward. Therefore he often ends up in the criminal courts and is to that extent not good 'detainee material'.[68]

This memo suggests that a marker was being set to enable the continued future exclusion of loyalists from internment. This view is borne out by the figures and by the 'Arrest Policy for Protestants' explained below. It would be another eighteen months before any loyalist was interned. By December 1975 – when internment ended – 1,981 persons had been held in custody. Of this total, approximately thirty to thirty-eight were women. Only 107 (or 5.4 per cent) of the 1,981 were loyalists.[69]

It is clear from declassified documents that, around the time internment was implemented, a decision was taken to adopt as official policy the exclusion of loyalist paramilitaries from detention. This 'Arrest Policy for Protestants' was introduced, and in 'Directives' issued, the army based its instructions 'closely on guidance which we have received from the Northern Ireland Office'.[70] The various categories of persons who might or might not be detained were listed as follows:

(a)   Anyone against whom there is known to be evidence to justify the preferring of criminal charges;

(b)   Anyone against whom there is thought to be evidence which might, after questioning, justify the preferring of criminal charges;

(c)   Anyone known to be holding officer rank in the PIRA even though there is no evidence to justify criminal charges;[71]

(d)   PIRA volunteers who, on the strength of reliable intelligence, are known to be an exceptionally serious threat to security;

(e)   Anyone in the company of a person arrested 'red-handed' if the arresting soldier suspects him of having committed or being about to commit an act prejudicial to peace.[72]

In other words, a member of the IRA would be automatically detained, while loyalists were to be arrested only if there was a prospect of bringing criminal charges against them. Consequently, all citizens were not equal before the law.

In October 1971, soon after the introduction of internment, a decision was taken to allow 'vigilantes' to assist the security forces. MI6 officer Frank Steele, deputy to Howard Smith, the UK representative, and his eventual successor, informed the FCO of a decision to liaise with paramilitaries and to coordinate their activities.[73] He enclosed a list of instructions from the CLF to troops in 3, 8 and 39 Brigades, as well as to the UDR.[74] In relation to vigilantes willing to help the security forces, army units were instructed to:

> ... effect informal contact with unofficial forces in order that their activities and areas of operation can be co-ordinated and taken into account in the security plans for the area concerned. The aim will be to effect liaison normally at company or platoon level between the security forces and all unofficial bodies who are seen to be working in the public interest.[75]

Although the directive did not specifically refer to loyalist vigilantes, it is quite clear from other declassified documents that this is what was intended.[76]

In a follow-up telex message from the GOC at HQNI to the army under-secretary (AUS) at the MoD, there was a further discussion on the role of vigilantes. The GOC noted that Frank Steele was of the opinion that the problem must be left entirely 'to local military initiative' and expressed the view that those who wished to serve the community should preferably volunteer for either the UDR or the RUC Reserve (RUCR). However, 'in the present troubled conditions' the government recognised that unofficial unarmed bodies 'with a purely defensive purpose' had been formed in many areas. He went on to say:

> While it should be understood that these cannot be encouraged or given any official standing, nevertheless, the security forces are ready to accept help from any quarter provided the bodies concerned operate within the framework of the defensive arrangements controlled by the police and the Army. Accordingly, these unofficial forces are required to make contact with the nearest police station

or Army post in order that their activities can be co-ordinated and taken into account in the security plans for the area concerned.[77]

In December 1971 it was confirmed in a routine Situation Report (SitRep) that vigilante groups in loyalist housing areas such as the Shankill Road had already received a measure of *ad hoc* recognition from the security forces: they had been given police and army telephone numbers which they should ring if they had any information.[78] The author of the report cautioned against formalising their existence any further, contrary to the view of Brian Faulkner, Northern Ireland prime minister, who was anxious that this should happen.[79]

The idea of recruiting loyalists as an auxiliary force in Ireland had a historical precedent. In *The Tree of Liberty*, historian Kevin Whelan notes that Major General John Knox, who commanded the Dungannon District in 1797–8, wrote in 1797 regarding the threat posed by the United Irishmen: 'I proposed some time ago that the Orangemen might be armed and added to some of the loyal corps as supplementary yeomen.'[80]

In more recent times, at a Joint Security Committee meeting of the old Stormont Parliament on 28 June 1970, where attendees included the prime minister and other ministers, the GOC, the chief of staff, the chief constable and deputy chief constable of the RUC, the director of intelligence and the UK representative, such a proposal was mooted.[81] Then Prime Minister James Chichester-Clark raised the question of 'granting official status to vigilante activities'. It was agreed that any such organisation would have to be brought under some authority – possibly the RUCR, while the 'membership ceiling' of the reserve should be raised in order to accommodate it.[82] The available vigilantes at that time, before the formation of the UDA, would likely have been its predecessor, the defence associations, as well as the UVF. The proposal, however, appears not to have been put into effect.[83]

All the evidence from these official documents suggests that by the end of 1971 loyalist paramilitaries were in a favoured position, contrary to the rule of law. They were shielded from internment, with a brigadier arguing that they were more amenable to prosecution; a special arrest policy was formulated to ensure their continued exclusion from detention; and a decision was taken by the army and the British and Northern Ireland governments to adopt loyalists as an auxiliary force.

*** 

After Bloody Sunday, when Parachute Regiment soldiers shot thirteen men and boys dead during an anti-internment march on the streets of Derry on 30 January 1972 (a fourteenth died later from his injuries), the security situation deteriorated rapidly. On 30 March, as a direct result, the Stormont government was prorogued and direct rule was introduced. The likely necessity for the introduction of direct rule had been under discussion for many months before Bloody Sunday, but it had been judged that the time was not then right.[84]

Vanguard leader William Craig called a widely supported two-day strike in protest. Street demonstrations and UDA marches began soon afterwards. Large numbers of UDA members in paramilitary uniform – some of them masked, wearing dark glasses and carrying sticks or cudgels – took part. While it was illegal to wear a paramilitary uniform or carry an offensive weapon, the security forces made no attempt to arrest those taking part, because they claimed to fear that major riots would result.[85] In contrast, republicans who had worn uniforms at the funeral of IRA member James Saunders in February 1971 were arrested and charged.[86] The Irish government, in its European case against the United Kingdom, claimed that the UDA demonstrations were provocative.[87]

At a meeting of the chiefs of staff in June 1972, the very formal structure of the UDA was laid out as follows by Brigadier M. S. Bayley:[88]

*Inner Council*
*(15 members, Chairman Harding Smith, Deputy Chairman Ernest Willis)*

*Security Council – (10 members)*

*District Branch (i.e. Woodvale, Shankill, etc.)*

*Area Level (a number of streets)*

*Street Level (Street Commander of one street – approximately 40 men)*

*Section Level (Section Commander – approximately 10 men)*[89]

Brigadier Bayley informed the meeting that there was reliable evidence of the recent rapid development of the UDA, which had originated from loosely knit vigilante street groups. The army and Special Branch in Belfast, he said, had gathered intelligence on the UDA's structure. It was well developed in the Shankill, Woodvale, east Belfast and Rathcoole areas, but information on other areas was 'blurred with the growing Vanguard organisation' and was much sketchier. Bayley indicated that both Captain Austin Ardill

(Vanguard) and Billy Hull (Loyalist Association of Workers) were associated 'with the top echelon [*sic*] of the UDA'.[90]

BBC reporter and author Peter Taylor also observes that 'the UDA grew enormously in 1972 and was structured more formally along military lines'.[91] After the fall of the Stormont government, the UDA began organising actively and, in the following months, grew exponentially in numbers and confidence. Brigadier Bayley expressed no concern at the 'rapid development' of the UDA or of its formal structure when he discussed the organisation with the chiefs of staff at the June 1972 meeting. While official documents up to then gave the impression that the British believed the UDA to be undisciplined and unstructured, the evidence from Brigadier Bayley proves that they knew from the organisation's early days that this was a fiction. Although they publicly continued to claim that the UDA had no structures and no identifiable leadership, by mid-1972 British government officials and, indeed, the secretary of state were meeting with UDA leaders.

The British state, in viewing republicans as offensive and loyalists as defensive, showed complete disdain for the rule of law. The one-sided nature of internment and, particularly, the adoption of an official 'Arrest Policy for Protestants', based on religious affiliation alone, was a policy that was, most likely, unique in Europe.

# 2

# THE FIRST IRA CEASEFIRE AND THE REPERCUSSIONS OF ITS BREAKDOWN

It was arguable that Protestant areas could be almost entirely secured
by a combination of UDA, Orange Volunteers and RUC.

*Sir Harry Tuzo, general officer commanding Northern Ireland*[1]

By the summer of 1972, the worst year of the conflict, state and non-state participants, both republican and loyalist, were developing a complex set of relationships. In particular, the British military were actively pursuing tacit understandings with loyalists.

Between January and May 1972, the PIRA had killed more than ninety people, many of them British soldiers and members of the UDR. The Official IRA (OIRA) had killed fourteen more. According to Stephen Dorril, MI6 representative Frank Steele regarded internment as a disaster and believed that – since it was not proving possible to defeat the IRA militarily – they would, at some point, have to talk.[2] Realising that internment was a failure, the British authorities now found it necessary to try to persuade the IRA to end its campaign.

The British authorities held two meetings (on 20 June and 7 July 1972) with the PIRA. At the first, held at Ballyarnett on the outskirts of Derry city, Steele and Philip Woodfield met two IRA representatives. This meeting was merely a testing of the waters, where possible conditions for a truce were discussed. The British side agreed that if the IRA maintained a ceasefire for ten days, they would meet a larger IRA delegation.[3] The previous day, William Whitelaw had conceded Special Category Status to eight republican and forty loyalist prisoners.[4]

The IRA called a ceasefire from 26 June and, ten days later, on 7 July, a larger delegation met Secretary of State Whitelaw in Cheyne Walk, London – the home of Guinness millionaire Paul Channon, MP. At this second meeting, where the IRA delegation was led by Seán MacStiofáin, it was clear the positions of both sides were too far apart, and two days later the IRA truce broke down.[5] Even before the truce came into effect, the UDA had erected barricades in Woodvale, Belfast, ostensibly to protect loyalist areas against IRA attacks, but in reality as a bargaining chip with the British authorities, to force them to remove barricades in Republican 'no-go' areas. They also facilitated the escalation of its sectarian murder campaign against Catholics, as will be shown later in this chapter.

The incident that prompted the renewal of hostilities by the IRA occurred in Lenadoon, Belfast, on Sunday 9 July. The UDA threatened to burn houses that had been vacated by Protestants if Catholics (who had been forced out of their homes elsewhere) were permitted to move in. When Catholic families did try to move in, they were stopped by the British Army, which provoked a riot by local nationalists. Seamus Twomey, commander of the IRA's Belfast Brigade, declared the British Army had violated the truce and, shortly afterwards, his men opened fire on the troops. The IRA condemned the British for yielding to UDA pressure, while the British insisted they were preventing serious loyalist disturbances.

One of the more detailed descriptions of the Lenadoon incident was provided by *Private Eye*. It claimed that on 3 July sixteen refugee Catholic families were allocated houses in 'the mixed Suffolk area' of

Belfast.[6] The allocation was made by the Northern Ireland Central Housing Executive, and the families were told they could move in as soon as they received clearance certificates from the officer commanding British troops in the area.

*Private Eye* claimed that five of the families received certificates on 6 July but, on arriving, were met by a UDA barricade. The hooded man on the barricade told them they could not move in and a British Army officer explained that there was nothing he could do about it.[7] The following day, according to the same source, 1,000 Catholics from Andersonstown accompanied the families arriving in the Suffolk area, waving their clearance certificates, but, once again, the UDA barricade barred the way and the army 'abdicated responsibility'. Exactly the same thing happened on 8 July.[8]

On the following day, Sunday, when a repeat confrontation took place, the army responded by 'ramming the truck, which contained the families' furniture, with an armoured car'. The author of the *Private Eye* article regarded this as proof 'that the promised British response to the IRA truce had not been forthcoming and the pressure from the extremist UDA had pushed Mr Whitelaw and his advisers into an increasingly anti-Catholic position'.[9]

After the breakdown of the truce, eleven people were killed on 9 July, six of them by the British Army, including two youths, aged sixteen and fourteen, a girl of thirteen and a Catholic priest, in what became known as the Springhill Massacre. Again, soldiers of the Parachute Regiment were responsible for the majority of these deaths. The IRA killed five people on the same day – a sixth died two days later.[10] Three of the six – one of whom was a Catholic sergeant in the British Army Territorial Volunteer Reserve (TAVR) – were found in a car in the Grosvenor Road area of Belfast. They had been shot in the head. Two of the young men died almost immediately and a third two days later. An attempt had been made to set fire to the car.

On the same day as the truce ended, GOC Harry Tuzo presented to Whitelaw a plan that must have been several days in preparation.[11] This plan envisaged an all-out military offensive against the IRA.[12] Tuzo commented that, if IRA hostilities resumed, they might expect an onslaught, including a major car-bomb offensive, attacks on commercial interests and on security-force personnel, indiscriminate attacks on Protestant communities, the establishment of new 'no-go' areas, intimidation of Catholic communities and the assassination of prominent citizens. He was worried that 'the major threat from the UDA is that their militant action would lead to widespread inter-sectarian conflict and eventually civil war', but opined that 'strenuous military action against the IRA should prevent the latter'.[13] However, he stressed that the army should 'acquiesce in unarmed UDA patrolling and barricading of Protestant areas. Indeed, it was arguable that Protestant areas could be almost entirely secured by a combination of UDA, Orange Volunteers and RUC.'[14] He also recommended that 'it might even be necessary to turn a blind eye to UDA arms when confined to their own areas'.[15]

Tuzo anticipated that the IRA would be neutralised in a matter of weeks – using maximum force for the shortest possible time, offensive rather than defensive: 'Vigilantes, whether UDA or not, should be encouraged in Protestant areas to reduce the load on the security forces. The RUC might be given responsibility for discrete liaison with the organisation.'[16] In conclusion, Tuzo observed that this course of action could have the full backing of the Protestant community 'particularly if their co-operation was encouraged'. Rather sinisterly, he recommended that in order to improve selectivity in offensive operations, the MRF should be expanded and either reinforced or replaced by Special Air Service (SAS) personnel.[17]

It is likely that Tuzo was suggesting extra resources for the MRF so that its targeting of republicans might be more effective. There are interesting comments in Tuzo's paper, which suggest that the army may have been intending to break the ceasefire: 'Much will depend on the circumstances leading to the resumption of hostilities, but *the blame must be laid fair and square on the IRA* [emphasis added]' and, perhaps more tellingly, 'If the IRA abandons the ceasefire, and there is a good chance that they may at any time from now ...'[18] Of course, responsibility for the breakdown was disputed.

As noted above, Tuzo decided it might be necessary to 'turn a blind eye to UDA arms when confined to their own areas'. When the consequences of such a proposal from the most senior British Army officer in Northern Ireland are considered, its illegality and immorality are striking. Tuzo appeared to be unconcerned about the origins of the UDA's arms, whether they were legally held weapons or had been imported or obtained illegally. He must have been aware that weapons were being 'stolen' from the UDR. Moreover, it would have been impossible to ensure that UDA arms were 'confined to their own areas'.

It is important to note that, according to *Lost Lives*, by 9 July 1972 the UDA had killed twenty-three people (one in 1970; four in 1971 and eighteen up to that point in 1972).[19] The four killed at the beginning of July 1972 had been stopped at barricades, abducted and shot. Almost all of the murders were sectarian. The UDA did not claim responsibility for these, or any other, murders. It appears that the only exception to this policy was on two occasions where the UDA claimed responsibility for bombings in the Republic of Ireland.[20]

SECRET

doubt that they have made the most of their opportunity to recruit, reorganise, retrain and re-equip.

4.   Past experience shows that the level of violence, having increased steadily up to the moment of ceasefire, is likely to surpass anything that we have known so far in the opening stages of a new campaign.   The IRA will be encouraged to make the maximum effort to topple the establishment; later on, when counter-measures begin to bite, a sense of desperation may lead to even more indiscriminate measures than before.   New weapons will be used and more sophisticated bombs.   There will be a serious threat from the AP round, heavier weapons such as rocket launchers, remote controlled explosive devices. *and perhaps mortars;*   The IRA are capable of considerable firepower, operating in groups of gunmen with modern weapons and almost unlimited ammunition.   Road movement in IRA areas will require armoured protection.

5.   Traditional IRA tactics are unlikely to change, but may be expanded.   They will hope to carry out:-

   a.   A major car bomb offensive as a curtain raiser to their new campaign.

   b.   Attacks on the Security Forces personnel and installations possibly extending to service and RUC families.

   c.   Attacks on commercial interests and public utilities; especially power.

   d.   Indiscriminate attacks on Protestant communities.

   e.   The establishment of new No Go areas.

   f.   Intimidation of Catholic communities; more severe than before, to redress loss of Catholic support.

   g.   Assassination of prominent citizens.

6.   The traditional centres of IRA violence are unlikely to change either i.e. Belfast, Londonderry, the mid Ulster towns and the border, but increased IRA strength and confidence will result in

attacks on other centres of population hitherto almost untouched, as was demonstrated just before the truce. In short the intensity of the IRA campaign will reach a new level demanding a response from the Security Forces greater than anything we have achieved so far.

7. No differentiation is made between the Official and Provisional wings. The latter are more likely to resume hostilities first, but the former can hardly afford not to follow suit.

## The UDA Threat

8. The major threat from the UDA is that their militant action will lead to widespread intersectarian conflict and eventually civil war, although strenuous military action against the IRA should prevent the latter. Nevertheless, assuming that civil war is averted and an anti IRA campaign begun in earnest, the UDA could be a constant source of irritation and worry to the Security Forces. Their strength is now approximately 25,000 of which about 12,000 are in Belfast. Having tasted power, they will no doubt attempt to influence both the political and military situation. They will demand to assist the Security Forces in their task; they will barricade their own areas and generally provoke trouble on the interfaces. They may indulge in indiscriminate shooting into Catholic areas. All this will increase Catholic support for the IRA and lend credence to their claim that they are defending the minority. It will be even more necessary to acquiesce in unarmed UDA patrolling and barricading of Protestant areas. Although no interference with Security Forces action could be tolerated, it would be as well to make the most of the situation and obtain some security benefit from UDA control of their own areas. Indeed it is arguable that Protestant areas could almost be entirely secured by a combination of UDA, Orange Volunteers and RUC. It may even be necessary to turn a blind eye to UDA arms when confined to their own areas.

9. A further threat well within UDA capability is effective strike action to bring essential services to a halt although this is unlikely once vigorous Army action is in train. Electricity is particularly vulnerable in this respect. Military contingency plans exist to

3

Although Tuzo's plan was not implemented, the killing rate of the UDA increased exponentially and, between 9 July and 31 December 1972, it killed a further fifty-three people.[21] Tuzo's plan is redolent of British strategy invoked in colonial situations, but cooler heads appear to have prevailed – probably from a realisation that such a strategy could not be tolerated in a part of the United Kingdom. John Newsinger observes:

> If south Armagh were a province in Malaya many of its Catholic inhabitants would have had their homes burned down and have been either forcibly resettled in heavily policed 'new villages' or deported across the border. Obviously such draconian measures were not politically possible in the context of contemporary Britain and of the European Community.[22]

This dilemma was confirmed by former Tory minister Michael Mates during an interview for the RTÉ programme *Collusion*, broadcast on 15 June 2015. He told the interviewer that the problem did not exist in Malaya or Kenya, where there would not have been the same 'sensitivities'. He explained that this was a unique aspect of the Northern Ireland conflict compared with other post-colonial situations – that it was occurring in a part of the United Kingdom and, politically, it would be highly undesirable for the British authorities to concede they were fighting a 'war' in their own country.

British policies were often accompanied by propaganda from the Information Policy Unit (IPU).[23] The erection of UDA barricades led the IPU to complain:

> Protestant violence gave us our first specific dilemma. There remained

the need to condemn utterly all violent action in Northern Ireland.
Nevertheless, it was the Protestants who had been pushed nearer
the brink by direct rule and we did not wish to give them reason or
excuse to go over it. Condemnation at this time was fairly muted and
efforts were concentrated on behind-the-scenes briefing of the media
that they would point out to Protestant extremists the folly of their
ways without the rebuke appearing to come from the NIO. This was
fairly successful and the Secretary of State was helped by his informal
contacts with the Press Corps in Belfast.[24]

In contrast, the IPU was eager to publicise the tarring and feather-
ing of a young woman by the IRA. The unit welcomed this action
as 'our first opportunity to indulge in "black" propaganda and we
ensured that pictorial evidence of the outrage was readily available
to the media at home and overseas'.[25]

Rather esoterically, an IPU report described July 1972 as 'The
month when our insurance policies matured. Because we had not
been overjoyed about the truce, we were able to appear that we were
not taken aback when it ended.'[26] The meaning of this statement can
only be speculated upon. It suggests that elements on the British
side might have welcomed the ending of the truce, and saw this as
an opportunity to adopt the all-out offensive envisaged by Tuzo.

Meanwhile, weeks before the IRA truce commenced – amid
rumours of a ceasefire and fears of concessions to the IRA, and in
response to republican 'no-go' areas in Derry and Belfast – David
Fogel, leader of B Company UDA, had ordered the erection of its
first barricades and roadblocks at the end of May, making Woodvale
a 'no-go' area for republicans. Ian Wood quotes from an interview
with Fogel in a *Sunday Times* article:

> After that [the erection of the UDA barricades], there was no stopping
> us. In June, three of us drove up to Stormont to see Willie Whitelaw.
>
> Whitelaw wrote in his memoirs: 'I met the UDA leaders in mid-
> June. They arrived looking quite absurd in hoods and sunglasses.'[27]

Absurd or not, Whitelaw did not baulk at meeting paramilitaries
disguised in this way. In fact, journalists Ed Moloney and Bob
Mitchell claim that the secretary of state met the UDA three times
during June – twice when they arrived wearing hoods and dark
glasses and, on a third occasion, when he met their entire Inner
Council.[28] The official 'Diary of Meetings' shows that he met two
UDA leaders on 13 June and held a further meeting with the
organisation on 28 June.[29]

On 20 June, at a Joint Security meeting in Stormont Castle
attended by the secretary of state for Northern Ireland, the secretary
of state for defence, the GOC, the RUC deputy chief constable
and officials, all agreed that it was essential to take a course which
would 'satisfy the UDA that some positive action was being taken
to deal with the problem of the enclaves [no-go areas]'. Otherwise
the chances were that its barricades, some of which seemed to have
come down since May, would go up again, more determinedly than
before and with 'greater provocation by hooligan elements', leading
to serious sectarian violence and 'large-scale shooting incidents'.[30]

On 30 June, in an apparently provocative move, the UDA decided
to expand its remaining barricades southwards to include the mixed
Catholic–Protestant area around March Street/Ainsworth Avenue
on the tinderbox peace line in west Belfast.[31] In a SitRep of 3–4
July, it was noted that this was unacceptable to the security forces as
it could provoke a Catholic reaction, but the UDA announced that
it intended to go ahead irrespective of the security forces' wishes:

Discussion took place throughout the afternoon and at 1900 hours the UDA, drawn from all Protestant parts of the city, began to assemble. Their strength was estimated at 1,200–2,000 and they were armed with batons, clubs and some shields. Security force reinforcements were brought in and APCs [armoured personnel carriers] were deployed in March Street. Discussions continued throughout the evening between senior Security Force officers and UDA. Agreement was reached at 2300 hours after CLF [General Sir Robert Ford (deputy to Tuzo), who, six months earlier, had had overall responsibility for the Parachute Regiment in Derry on Bloody Sunday] had intervened.[32]

The official 'Diary of Historical Events' for 1972 noted on 3 July: 'Army agree that soldiers should set up road-blocks and that UDA should be allowed to patrol the streets behind them.'[33]

Following this incredible state of affairs – in effect joint patrolling by the British Army and a loyalist paramilitary group – the following day a meeting note described the UDA as having made a 'disciplined withdrawal' after the confrontation. An upsurge of loyalist intimidation, which had caused some Catholics to flee their homes, was noted without comment. It was also remarked that the UDA 'may have gained in confidence' as a result.[34]

An army operational summary for the week ending 5 July reported that the most significant event was the setting up by the UDA of three 'permanent' 'no-go' areas in the Shankill Road area. In Derry, five republican barricades within Creggan and the Bogside had been removed 'but the UDA maintained that their "no-go" areas would remain until all barricades were down in Derry and the area properly policed by the RUC'.[35] This policy of appeasement towards the UDA in the summer of 1972 led directly to the sectarian killing of Catholics, who were abducted at these barricades, taken away and shot.

On 10 July a security meeting in Stormont Castle discussed the breakdown of the ceasefire the previous day. It was attended by Secretary of State Whitelaw, Permanent Under-Secretary (PUS) Sir William Nield, the GOC, the deputy chief constable, Frank Steele and several senior officials. The ending of the ceasefire was discussed and 'it had to be recorded that the Army were fired at many times before they replied'.[36] It was also noted: 'If the Army did not attack the IRA the probability was that the UDA would.' It was decided that Whitelaw would return to London immediately to make a statement in the House of Commons in which he would confirm he had held talks with the IRA on 7 July and would 'put the blame for the ending of the "truce" fairly and squarely on the Provisionals who must now take the consequences, and announce the Government's intention to carry on the war with the IRA with the utmost vigour'.[37] It was acknowledged that 'more troops and material would be needed for the operations visualised' and that 'the Army should not be inhibited in its campaign by the threat of court proceedings and should therefore be suitably indemnified' – probably recognition of the growing number of civilian casualties as a result of British Army actions.[38] The GOC announced that he would meet UDA leaders that afternoon and impress upon them that, while their efforts as vigilantes in their own areas were acceptable, their position in any riot or shooting situation would not be tolerated.[39]

The conclusions of the 10 July meeting strongly suggest that serious consideration was being given to implementing General Tuzo's plan in full, although there was a retreat from that position by 20 July.

The contents of a letter sent by Sir William Nield to Sir Burke Trend, cabinet secretary, also on 10 July, undermines the official British narrative of the UDA as a loose, undisciplined, unstructured force. Nield made it clear that he was well aware of the very formal structure of the UDA:

> These groups are now well-disciplined, centrally co-ordinated … The UDA never believed in the conciliation policy [towards the IRA] nor in the ceasefire, and now that the ceasefire is over they are demanding action to bring IRA terrorism to an end and to open up and police properly the Catholic 'no-go' areas. They say they will extend their own 'no-go' areas until this is done … There is also plenty of evidence to suggest that they also intend to use their undoubted force to press for a restoration of a Northern Ireland Parliament and perhaps to go for a unilateral declaration of independence by Northern Ireland if they do not get the terms they want from Westminster. In short, they are challenging the authority of the Government …
>
> If a force of this size is not satisfied with HMG's [Her Majesty's Government's] reaction to the IRA's breach of the ceasefire there is no reason to think that they will not put into effect their threats to extend their own 'no-go' areas and they may go in for increasing intimidation of the Catholic population and assassinations of those individuals whom they believe to be IRA terrorists. In so far therefore that HMG appears to the UDA to be continuing to try to placate the Catholic minority and also not to be acting with what the UDA regard as satisfactory severity against the IRA terrorists, the UDA may decide to push their luck further, to extend their organisation of intimidation and propaganda, to be seen to be defending the Protestant population against the IRA and to decide increasingly to

oppose the security forces, if the latter seek to defend the Catholic population against intimidation.

As I see it the Secretary of State's anxiety is that he is not opposed by one violent and subversive force, but by two, the IRA and the UDA. And moreover, that between these forces, the Army can neither ally with the one or the other, because both are challenging the authority of the Government; nor can they take on both at once with anything like this present strength, quite apart from the considerable sympathy for the UDA which 2.5 years of bombings has aroused in the Army's auxiliary security forces, i.e. the UDR and the RUC.[40]

While accepting that the army faced two 'subversive forces' and could not openly 'ally' with loyalism, Nield indicated it could not fight a war on two fronts. This assessment differs sharply from the official British position at the European Commission of Human Rights (ECHR), where one of the planks upon which it was relying in the Ireland v UK case, in its attempt to justify its decision not to intern loyalists, was that the UDA, unlike the IRA, was not challenging the government's authority.[41] The problem with Nield's assessment of the situation is that the UDA was already carrying out sectarian assassinations of Catholic civilians.

Other revealing remarks were made around this time, reflecting some British political sympathy towards loyalists in general and the UDA in particular. For example, at a meeting of MPs in London at which Ulster Unionist MPs were present, there were expressions of dismay at the secretary of state's meeting with the IRA and remarks about appeasement.[42] Sir Frederick Corfield, a Tory MP and former army officer and lawyer, said he understood why loyalists were anxious and 'sympathised with those who go to the UDA'. At a similar meeting on 19 July, Tory MP Sir Julian Critchley said London 'must restore the morale of the loyalists ...'[43]

On 13 July the Irish ambassador in London wrote to the assistant secretary of the Department of Foreign Affairs detailing a meeting he had had with the junior minister at the Foreign Office, Anthony Royle, MP.[44] He quoted Royle as stating that 'In the new situation, with the UDA ready to explode, all that seemed possible in the next month or so, was a total effort to prevent a holocaust.'[45]

In the record of a meeting on 20 July on future policy in Northern Ireland – between the prime minister, the secretary of state for defence, the secretary of state for Northern Ireland and the chief of the general staff (CGS) – it was observed that Harold Wilson, leader of the opposition, was in favour of developing 'high level contacts with the UDA and the secretary of state already had this possibility in mind'.[46] After conflicting indications, a final decision was taken by those at the meeting not to proceed with Tuzo's recommendations of an all-out offensive, as it was feared that this would seriously alienate Catholic opinion.[47] It was decided instead to maintain the policy of responding to IRA attacks, although the meeting was warned that pressure was developing within the army for more aggressive action against republicans, and that soldiers disliked having to operate 'in direct opposition to the Protestants'.[48]

Clearly, it was an affront to the army's authority that the Derry 'no-go' areas continued to exist. But, despite the increasing pressure, there were no immediate plans to clear the republican 'no-go' areas. However, 'if no other way of making progress could be found it would probably be necessary in due course to mount a military operation to clear the no-go areas'.[49]

Far from being merely an organisation of street protest at this time, the UDA was carrying out numerous – mostly sectarian –

murders. In July alone, the organisation killed at least twenty-one people – seventeen Catholics, three Protestants and one Englishman (the perpetrators believed the latter four men to be Catholics). Yet on 10 July, as already noted, the GOC met with UDA leaders to impress upon them that their 'efforts as vigilantes in their own areas were acceptable'.[50]

On the following day, UDA members committed a shocking sectarian double crime of rape and murder in north Belfast. Fourteen-year-old David McClenaghan, a special-needs child, was killed while his mother, Sarah, was raped.[51] The child had fetched his mother's missal and rosary beads when asked by the killers to produce his prayer book. The gunmen were convicted in 1973. Sarah McClenaghan described how one of them was wearing a balaclava and 'had UDA written in ink on his hands'.[52] McKittrick *et al.* also claim in *Lost Lives* that the man who killed David 'had UDA associations'.[53]

The barricades erected by loyalist paramilitaries facilitated their killing campaign. During the first weekend of July 1972, four young men, having been stopped at barricades, were abducted and killed. On 1 July Daniel Hayes and a young Englishman, Paul Jobling, who was working as a volunteer in a camp for children in deprived areas, were killed. The following day Gerald McCrea and his friend and business partner James Howell suffered the same fate.[54] According to McKittrick *et al.*, 'In a number of cases it emerged that UDA vigilantes had stopped people at such barricades, questioned them and sometimes beat them. In several such instances, people were killed, usually when they were discovered to be Catholic.'[55]

The prediction made by GOC Tuzo of a major car-bomb offensive by the IRA if hostilities resumed came to pass on Bloody Friday, 21 July: twenty-six bombs exploded in Belfast within an hour, killing nine people and injuring more than 130. The bombings were horrific attacks, and attempts to blame the authorities for not acting on warnings were not credible given the number of bombs that exploded almost simultaneously. The day's bloodshed led to an influx of youths into loyalist organisations, just as Bloody Sunday six months earlier had boosted the IRA's ranks.

As well as being horrific attacks, the bombings were also a huge miscalculation by the IRA. As had been noted in the security meeting of 20 July, pressure was building within the army for more aggressive action against republicans, but 'they feared the alienation of Catholic opinion'.[56] Bloody Friday presented the British Army with the justification it had been seeking to go in and dismantle the barricades in republican 'no-go' areas, and it wasted no time in doing so. A paper was prepared by the CGS urging the quick exploitation of the new situation in which, he believed, firm action by the army against the IRA would now be more acceptable to a wide range of opinion. The IPU issued its first major 'propaganda broadsheet' in the wake of Bloody Friday.[57]

On the night following Bloody Friday, at least three Catholics, including a young couple in their twenties, Patrick O'Neill and Rose McCartney, were stopped at a UDA barricade, taken away and murdered. The third person abducted from a barricade and killed on that night was Francis Arthurs.

A case that chillingly illustrates this tactic is that of James McGerty and Frank Corr. On 26 July both men, in separate cars, were stopped at the same UDA barricade, abducted and killed. Their bodies were recovered the following day from Mr Corr's car, which had been set on fire. In February 1979 two men were arrested for these killings. One of them, Denis David Bryson, said he had been a member of the UDA at the time but had since left the organisation.

He admitted he had been operating barricades where Catholics stopped by him were taken away and shot. He specifically referred to James McGerty and Frank Corr. The second man convicted, Albert Bole McKibben, was arrested some days after Bryson. He admitted his part in the killings, but made no admissions as to UDA membership; however, intelligence suggested he was a member.

Bryson provided a chilling account:

> I was doing duty at the barricades – my job was to stop cars and check licences. I remember stopping a grey Austin Cambridge car. I asked the man for his licence and he handed it over. I looked at it and the name on it was a Catholic name [Frank Corr], so I called a fellow over to us … This fellow took the licence off [sic] me and looked at it and told the man I was holding to move over into the passenger seat. The car was driven down Caledon Street and into Mayo Street and stopped on the right-hand side …
>
> About an hour and a half later I stopped a Morris 1100 … I asked him for his licence and he … got it from the dash pocket. When I looked at it, it looked like half a Protestant and half Catholic name [James McGerty]. I called the same fellow I had called over before. He took the licence and told me it was alright … The car was drove [sic] down the street to the same place and I saw the man get out and go inside the same house …[58]

Bryson had been involved in the killing of Frederick Maguire two days earlier and was later (in October 1972) responsible for the death of William Clarke – both cases of mistaken identity. They were Protestants but were believed to be Catholics. This is hardly surprising when it is noted from the above account that people were selected for killing on the mere off chance that they might be Catholic.[59]

What is striking about the above-mentioned cases is the fact that UDA barricades were in place over an extended period of time, yet no action was taken by the British Army.

In a memo to the prime minister on 26 July, Cabinet Secretary Sir Burke Trend warned, 'the Army wish to avoid any major confrontation with the UDA, in the hope that they would remove their barricades if they believe that firm action is to be taken against the Bogside and the Creggan'. He went on to say that it would be desirable to reoccupy UDA strongholds for PR purposes 'in order to make it clear beyond doubt that we are not operating as allies of the UDA against Roman Catholic enclaves alone'.[60]

The decision to proceed with the removal of 'republican' barricades was taken by ministers on 27 July, following which the chief of staff sent instructions to the army on how to conduct the operation. The instructions were headed 'Operation Motorman'.[61] The logistics having been worked out, it was decided to proceed into the 'no-go' areas in the early hours of 31 July, 'a date and time preferred by the Secretary of State'.[62]

Motorman, which began at 4 a.m. that day, has been described as the largest British military operation since Suez in 1956.[63] Twelve thousand soldiers with bulldozers and tanks entered the 'no-go' areas. In Derry, two teenagers were killed in disputed circumstances.[64]

In the immediate aftermath of Motorman, Trend wrote to the prime minister lauding the success of the operation, claiming the IRA 'had gone to ground' and adding that 'the UDA are also quiet and have accepted the Army's help in the removal of their barricades'.[65] The IPU described Motorman as 'an unqualified success both in military and human terms'.[66]

Not everyone agreed. At a meeting on 7 August between the NIO and the SDLP at Laneside, SDLP leader Gerry Fitt complained that Operation Motorman had convinced the minority community that harsh military tactics would be adopted against it alone.[67] On the one hand, he said, there had been tanks in Creggan and the Bogside, and on the other, friendship between the army and the UDA, and the voluntary removal of its barricades.[68]

This British partisanship towards loyalists, and the UDA in particular, is clearly illustrated in an internal army memo of 31 July 1972 regarding membership of the UDR, from J. F. Howe, civil adviser at HQNI, to the GOC:

> The UDA is not an illegal organisation and membership of the UDA is not an offence under the military laws; it is also a large organisation not all of whose members can be regarded as dangerous extremists. One important (but unspoken) function of the UDR is to channel into a constructive and disciplined direction Protestant energies which might otherwise become disruptive. For these reasons it is felt that it would be counter-productive to discharge a UDR member on the grounds that he was a member of the UDA.[69]

Howe advised that, if a member's UDA activities conflicted with his UDR duties, then he would be discharged.[70] The prohibited activities would include connivance with the UDA in providing military information or the theft of army weapons. (At this point UDR weapons were already going missing with monotonous regularity – six self-loading rifles (SLRs) had been lost in July alone, and in all cases the UDA was suspected of being the culprit.)[71]

Howe continued:

> I am sure that this moderate line towards UDA supporters is the right one in view of the role of the UDA as a safety valve. In my

opinion it would be politically unwise to dismiss a member of the UDA from the UDR unless he had committed a military offence; the dismissal of a member of the UDR on lesser grounds could well lead to wide-spread morale problems particularly in certain areas ... it might be very damaging politically if Ministers were to make a public statement which implied that the UDA was an outlawed organisation.[72]

In August specific instructions were issued by the NIO regarding 'UDA Road Checks'[73] – not that they should be removed peremptorily as illegal obstructions to free movement, but that the UDA might consider claiming their patrols 'were on the look-out for terrorists and they might, therefore, want to invoke S.2 (3) of the Criminal Justice Act (NI 1967)':

Where an arrestable offence has been committed, any person may arrest without warrant anyone who is, or whom he, with reasonable cause, suspects to be guilty of the offence. Thus if a car were seen to be driving at speed from the scene of an explosion, a member of the UDA might be justified in stopping it.[74]

Presumably, that is, unless the UDA had caused the explosion.

A member of the UDA did not, according to the memo, 'have the power to search a vehicle, though presumably he may carry out a search if the person in charge of the vehicle authorises him to do so.'[75] The reference here to 'the person in charge of the vehicle' authorising its search by masked paramilitaries carrying batons speaks volumes about the extent to which British officials were prepared to go to minimise and obscure the impact of loyalist paramilitary violence in the summer of 1972.

From: J.F. Howe, Civil Adviser to General Officer Commanding

Asst Sec. ................

## HEADQUARTERS NORTHERN IRELAND
Lisburn  Co Antrim

Principal ......................

AAG ......................

Army Network Lisburn Military } ext   426
Post Office Lisburn 5111

HEO ......................

DAAG 1 ......................

DAAG 2 ......................

Lt Col J.L. Pownall, OBE,
AG Secretariat,
Ministry of Defence,
Main Building,
Whitehall,
London,SW1.

|  |  |
|---|---|
| Your reference |  |
| Our reference | 1347/72 |
| Date | 31st July 1972 |

EO ......................

UDR to General ......................

Chief Clerk ..................

Dear John,

UDR - MEMBERSHIP OF UDA

120

Thank you for your letter of 17th July about UDR involvement in the UDA.

It is inevitable that a part of the Protestant element of a part-time Regiment in Ulster will sympathise with the aims of the UDA; and it is suspected that there are cases where this sympathy is carried to the extent of active membership.  There are however no proven facts as yet on which to base an estimate of the scale of the problem.  The following are the firmer reports that have been received, and they are being investigated:

a.   In a television interview in Belfast on 15th July, a masked man wearing a beret claimed that he was a UDR officer.

b.   A UDR part-timer from a City battalion has furnished a list of nine other UDR men, including one officer, whom he says are active members of the UDA.

c.   Two series of weapons losses are thought to be almost certainly in part the work of Protestant organisations. These are the losses of 9 SLRs since the beginning of the year in 8 UDR (East Tyrone), and 12 SLRs in the last few weeks in the Portadown area (2 UDR).

The losses of two pieces of radio equipment in West Tyrone in March are not necessarily attributable to Protestant organisations.

The areas where HQ UDR believe that this involvement is most likely to exist are Portadown and Lurgan (2 UDR), the Bann Valley (5 UDR), Ardboe and Aughnacloy (8 UDR), Carrickfergus (9 UDR), and West Belfast (10 UDR).

The UDR has to draw a line somewhere between hard-line Protestants who can safely be contained in the UDR, and those who cannot.  The UDA is not an illegal organisation, and membership of the UDA is not an offence under the military laws; it is also a large organisation not all of whose members can be regarded as dangerous extremists.  One important (but unspoken) function of the UDR is to channel into a constructive and disciplined direction Protestant energies which might otherwise become disruptive.  For these reasons it is felt that it would be counter-productive to discharge a UDR member solely on the grounds that he was a member of the UDA.

- 3 AUG 1972
293/4
MINISTRY OF DEFENCE

STAFF-IN-CONFIDENCE
CONFIDENTIAL

/Similarly..

*NAUK (no reference), Memo to Lt Col J. L. Pownall from J. F. Howe, civil adviser, HQNI, 31 July 1972, p. 1*

Similarly, it is not formally laid down that where an applicant to join the UDR is found to be a member of the UDA, his application must automatically be rejected.  But the screening process for UDR applicants has recently been tightened up so that due weight is given to extreme Protestant sympathies and although each application is considered on its merits a person who was known to be a member of the UDA would be most unlikely to be admitted.

Commander UDR has recently written to Battalion Commanders instructing them on the line to take with members of the force who are found to be involved in the UDA.  I attach a copy.  Officers are expected to resign if they take an active part in UDA activities, and other ranks are to be warned that such behaviour is inconsistent with their position in the force.  If a soldier's involvement in the UDA constitutes a military offence, the UDR takes a hard line and dismisses the man under Regulation 0490 Serial 7.  Such circumstances are:

a.  where a soldier has failed to meet an UDR commitment because he was taking part in UDA activities.

b.  where a soldier wears UDR uniform while taking part in UDA activities.

c.  where a man carries an Army Department firearm while taking part in UDA activities.

d.  Connivance with the UDA in providing military information or in the theft of Army weapons, or encouraging other soldiers to commit such acts.

I am sure that this moderate line towards UDA supporters is the right one in view of the role of the UDA as a safety valve.  In my opinion it would be politically unwise to dismiss a member of the UDA from the UDR unless he had committed a military offence; the dismissal of a member of the UDR on lesser grounds could well lead to wide-spread morale problems particularly in certain areas.

I recognise the reasons why Ministers might wish to be able to say unequivocally, in reply to Parliamentary Questions, that membership of the UDA is not compatible with membership of the UDR and that we have no evidence that any UDR member is actively associated with the UDA.  But I fear it would be wrong to offer categorical assurances on either point, and indeed it might be very damaging politically if Ministers were to make a public statement which implied that the UDA was an outlawed organisation.  I suggest that the line to take is that the UDR is a non-sectarian force and that its members represent a wide range of political viewpoints; but that if a member's conduct, arising out of his membership of the UDA or any other organisation, constitutes a military offence or calls his future loyalties in question, action is taken.  Any reported involvement of UDR members in extremist activities is a matter of concern to the military authorities and we would be grateful for details of cases so that they may be investigated.

Yours ever,

John.

*NAUK (no reference), Memo to Lt Col J. L. Pownall from J. F. Howe, civil adviser, HQNI, 31 July 1972, p. 2*

This instruction regarding 'UDA Road Checks' may well have been a quid pro quo for the dismantling of UDA barricades.

UDA paramilitary activity continued unabated. In a SitRep of 20–21 August, it was noted that a car with three beer kegs containing a total of eighty pounds of explosives had partially exploded on the Upper Newtownards Road next to a Catholic church. The device was described as 'a typical Protestant bomb'.[76] This suggests knowledge that loyalists were engaged in a bombing campaign. The same document reported that security forces had uncovered 337 rounds, four magazines and ten 'Schermuly' rockets at Dundonald, east Belfast, in a garage owned by a man reported to be a member of the UDA. There followed a confrontation between security forces and sixty UDA men outside Dundonald RUC station. The UDA, having thwarted the security forces, promised to deliver the garage owner to them the following morning.

The 20–21 August SitRep also reported that Ivan Cooper, SDLP MP, had alleged that the UDA had beaten up Catholics and set up roadblocks in the Maghera area. One block, operated by masked and baton-armed UDA men, had been located at Desertmartin; another roadblock operated by masked men carrying batons and shields was at Kellen, near Castlederg. This was removed on RUC instructions.[77]

What these events indicate is, as a government briefing paper noted, that the UDA was attempting 'to direct Government policy by establishing "no-go" areas' and that the government was prepared to let them away with it.[78]

# 3

# ARMING THE LOYALISTS

If we were so stupid, how were our boys able to enter and take over a UDR camp and clear it out of weapons?

*Andy Tyrie, commander of the UDA for fifteen years*[1]

The possession of weapons is crucial in any conflict. The most practical way for loyalists to arm themselves was through weapon 'thefts' from the UDR. These thefts, by both the UDA and the UVF, occurred throughout the conflict. In the early 1970s there were several raids on armouries as well as instances of individual weapons being stolen.

There were many thefts of single weapons throughout 1972 and 1973 for which the UDA and/or the UVF were believed to be responsible. In most of these instances, collusion was 'strongly suspected'.[2] In a letter dated 25 September 1972, J. F. Howe reported to the NIO that nine SLRs were missing in County Tyrone and that east Tyrone was an area where, he believed, certain UDR members might be sympathetic to the UDA.[3]

An armoury raid was carried out on 14 October 1972, when four SLRs were stolen from the UDR's 10th Battalion headquarters in Belfast. As a result of information received, these weapons and three others, as well as 762 rounds of ammunition, were recovered in a garage on 29 December. The garage owner, David Payne, was arrested and charged with possession. He was 'reliably suspected' of being second-in-charge of C Company, Shankill UDA.[4]

Two of the most notorious armoury raids occurred on 23 October 1972 in Lurgan and exactly one year later, on 23 October 1973, in Portadown, with the UVF claiming responsibility for both. In the first of these, on the TAVR Centre in Lurgan – which shared its armoury with the UDR's 11th Battalion – eighty-three SLRs were stolen, as well as twenty-one sub-machine guns (SMGs), ammunition, cartridges, flares, flak jackets and magazines. A few hours after the raid, sixty-one SLRs and one SMG were recovered, along with some of the ammunition, in an abandoned Land Rover eight kilometres south of Lurgan. According to his report on the raid, Colonel Dalzell-Payne believed the raiders had stolen more than they could handle and had decided to dump the surplus.[5]

The second of these raids was carried out on E Company UDR armoury, Portadown, and yielded four SLRs, two SMGs, five pistols, assorted ammunition, flak jackets, phone radios and Bardic (signalling) lamps.[6] According to the military, collusion by the UDR was strongly suspected in both these cases, as noted in an official minute.[7]

In a document entitled 'Subversion in the UDR', dated August 1973 and prepared by 'Int. and Sy' (British Army Military Intelligence and Psychological Operations) staff at HQNI for the Joint Intelligence Committee and, ultimately, for the prime minister,[8] it is noted that 'joint membership of the UDA and the UDR became widespread and, at the same time, the rate of UDR weapons losses greatly increased'.[9] The author cites the intriguing example of a member of the UDR's 1st Battalion – the deputy chairman of a district council – who had the following 'traces' (suspected links to paramilitary organisations):

> Officer Commanding Ballymena UDA; had obtained ammunition
> for the UDA; was suspected of illegal arms dealings and of selling

them to UDA and of acquiring an SLR and SMG in Scotland and selling them to the UDA. He was, however, described as 'a model soldier' by his UDR Commander.[10]

Incredibly, this man told *The Irish News* in 2006 that he was later permitted to join the RUC.[11]

A Historical Enquiries Team (HET) report states that between October 1970 and March 1973, 222 weapons – including thirty-two handguns – belonging to the UDR were misplaced, lost or stolen from the homes of soldiers, UDR armouries, duty posts, or while in transit. In the main, the stolen weapons were obtained during well-coordinated raids on armouries.[12] Many years later, former UDA commander Andy Tyrie, referring to a series of raids on armouries between 1972 and 1987, made the farcical comment that opened this chapter. The reality was that the UDA was able to enter armouries and steal weapons simply because UDR members based in the armouries were colluding with them and not because the UDA had any clever plan.

These thefts had obvious and deadly consequences, of which the British Army and government at the highest levels must have been aware. The 'Subversion in the UDR' document also contained an example of how just one stolen weapon – an SMG – had been used. It was involved in eleven incidents: one murder, seven attempted murders, one kidnapping and two discoveries of bullet cases.[13]

\*\*\*

Relationships between government officials and paramilitary organisations can wax and wane over time. It would be oversimplistic to see these associations as linear throughout the conflict. Relations between the army and the UDA reached a low point on 16 October 1972 when John Clarke, aged twenty-six, and a fifteen-year-old youth, William Warnock, both UDA members, were knocked down and killed by a British Army armoured personnel carrier while at a barricade in east Belfast during street disturbances.

A high-level meeting at Stormont Castle was quickly convened at the request of Roy Bradford, Ulster Unionist MP for Belfast Victoria, in an apparent attempt to repair the damaged relationship. On the following day, the UDA met with the parliamentary under-secretary, Lord David Howell of Guildford. Bradford, acting as intermediary, was accompanied by UDA leaders Tommy Herron, Jim Anderson and Edward Jones. Even GOC Tuzo was present. Bradford said he was appalled by the events of the previous night and had contacted members of the UDA to try to re-establish contact between them and the authorities.[14]

Herron complained bitterly that the army had provoked the UDA. The UDA leadership had responded by withdrawing control over its members and, as a result, he said, the security forces were no longer able to maintain law and order.[15] General Tuzo replied that he could not accept the UDA claim that relations had broken down because the army had been provocative. The army could hardly be to blame, said Tuzo, since it was not in its interest to be engaged in east Belfast when it would be better employed dealing with the IRA. Ideally, Tuzo went on, he would be prepared to withdraw from east Belfast entirely, were it not for the need to protect isolated Catholic communities that saw themselves as being under continual threat of violence from their Protestant neighbours.[16] Herron responded by saying that when the Green Jackets regiment had arrived in (Protestant) east Belfast from (Catholic) Andersonstown, it had behaved in a fashion more appropriate to the area from where it had come. He was apparently suggesting it was perfectly acceptable for the soldiers to behave in an aggressive manner towards the Catholic population, but not towards Protestants.

At the same meeting, MI6 officer Frank Steele said it was difficult to see why the previous satisfactory relations between the UDA and the security forces, particularly the army, had broken down. He warned the delegation that Protestant violence would alienate the British public and the important thing was to cool the situation.[17]

Herron remarked that it would be unprofitable for the two forces to confront one another as enemies; the UDA and the army should be seen to be getting on and talking. He insisted, however, that when complaints were made against the army, they must be acted upon and the results made public. Lord Howell suggested it would be useful if the UDA and the army were to have discussions at a local level, and the GOC agreed to arrange this in order to reduce tensions.[18]

The details of this high-level meeting between the British representatives and the UDA reinforces the authorities' view of the organisation as a safety valve for loyalists rather than one involved in widespread assassinations and bombings.

Shortly after this meeting, on 7 November 1972, new security legislation was introduced: this raised concerns among NIO officials that it might affect the 'Arrest Policy for Protestants'. The Detention of Terrorists (NI) Order was introduced, revoking the specific sections of the Special Powers Act 1922 that, until then, had been used to effect internment. The new legislation was important because it was used to convince the European Commission that a more liberal form of detention had been implemented.[19] The new order allowed the secretary of state for Northern Ireland to make an 'interim custody order' (ICO), which permitted detention for twenty-eight days. However, although this appeared to be more liberal, the chief constable could, during the twenty-eight-day period, refer the case to a commissioner, requesting the issuance of a 'detention order' permitting indefinite detention.

Before issuing such an order, the commissioner had to offer the detainee an oral hearing, where the nature of the case to be answered could be heard. The detainee could be represented by a lawyer. The commissioner had to be satisfied not only that the detainee was involved in terrorism, but that detention was necessary for the protection of the public. Law professor Brice Dickson argues that these new safeguards might have seemed satisfactory, but that they actually fell far short of what the European Convention requires for such deprivation of liberty to be lawful.[20]

Officials were only too well aware of the problem the Detention of Terrorists (NI) Order posed in relation to the 'Arrest Policy for Protestants'. Under the Special Powers Act a person could be detained indefinitely without trial. But, as was noted earlier, there was in place a special, covert 'Arrest Policy for Protestants', guided by the NIO, whereby Protestants – unlike Catholics – were to be arrested only on criminal charges and were not to be interned. An MoD official wrote at the time:

> Arrest policy is of course in political terms a critical issue, at the heart of our military profile ... I must advise strongly that any important change which we wish to incorporate should be agreed by Ministers ... The problem is to decide whether, and if so in what form, our arrest policy should be adjusted in respect of Protestants.[21]

What is extraordinary about this note is that ministers were discussing this arrest policy on the basis of religion.

The British had been careful not to publicise the 'Arrest Policy for

Protestants'. In October 1972, before a meeting with Taoiseach Jack Lynch, British Prime Minister Edward Heath was briefed to tell Mr Lynch that 'the police draw no distinction between Catholics and Protestants in the investigation of security offences and the prosecution of such offences'.[22] Heath went to the meeting, armed with statistics on Protestant arrests, and arms and explosives finds – and with advice which amounted to being 'economical with the truth'.[23]

The view that a political decision had been taken to introduce new internment legislation in order to assist the British with the Irish government case is borne out by a reference in the UK's 'counter-memorial' to the European Commission's findings, in which British officials quoted from the commission's report on the new legislation as follows:

> In regard to the problems of detention without trial they [UK] have revoked the Special Powers Act which had been in force since 1922 and had given rise to much criticism. They have introduced legislation in its place which, while maintaining detention by means of extra-judicial procedures, has given the individual concerned greater protection by fixing clear time-limits and introducing a right of appeal against detention orders and systems for reviewing them.[24]

Clearly, the introduction of this new legislation was a factor in the commission's finding that there was no discrimination in how internment orders were implemented.

The MoD felt that it would be a big step to take to extend its policy to arrest Protestants 'who are not chargeable'.[25] It was aware that 'there *are* Protestant terrorists who fall into this category, and also within the terms of the Detention of Terrorists (NI) Order'. However, it insisted it was 'very difficult to lay down precise criteria for arrestable Protestant terrorists because we don't know enough about their Orbat to talk about "Officers" as in the case of the Provos'.[26] The officials also argued:

> This is not the moment to start arresting Protestants for detention; there has been something of a decrease in large-scale organised Protestant terrorism, and detention of Protestants (and particularly the arrest of leaders such as Herron) might provoke a backlash which it would be difficult to contain.[27]

This is not an analysis, one imagines, with which the hundreds of bereaved families of victims of UDA and UVF violence would concur.

The discussions continued throughout November and into December. On 8 December A. W. Stephens, head of Defence Secretariat 10 of the MoD (DS10), wrote to the deputy under-secretary (army) regarding the 'arrest policy for Protestants'.[28] He suggested that the difficulty facing anyone trying to draft an arrest policy for loyalist extremists 'stems from the position of the UDA'. He wrote:

> As you know, this body covers a wide spectrum of opinion and activity extending from, at one end, deep involvement in UVF-type thuggery to, at the other end, comparatively harmless vigilante activity and political activism. Our present policy is specifically aimed at isolating the most extreme elements within the UDA from the remainder ...[29]

With his memo, Stephens enclosed a paper prepared by the civil adviser, which reported:

Ministers have judged that the time is not at the moment right for an extension of the arrest policy in respect of Protestants. The object of this note is, however, to suggest a form of words which can be incorporated in the AP [arrest policy] instructions when the time comes for such an extension. A category defined along the following lines: 'Protestant terrorists who are known on the strength of reliable intelligence to be an extremely serious threat to security, and for whom, in the absence of evidence which could form the basis of a criminal charge, a strong case could be made for an ICO.'[30]

The British prime minister was due to meet with his Irish counterpart, Taoiseach Jack Lynch, on 24 November 1972. In an NIO briefing for the prime minister before the meeting, it was noted that an instruction on security-force policy towards the UDA had been laid down by HQNI dated 6 November. The instruction was confidential and was not passed in writing below battalion level. It was noted that the RUC had similar instructions. The main points were:

> Operations against the UDA should be directed against their criminal extremist elements whilst making every endeavour to maintain good relations with law-abiding citizens in the organisation;
>
> Contact should be maintained at Company Commander level with the UDA;
>
> Unarmed, locally resident vigilante-type patrols should be tolerated provided they did not break the law;
>
> Marauding patrols or barriers on roads should not be tolerated, nor should the harassment of drivers or other members of the public. Persons should be required to discard offensive weapons, including clubs. Masks should be strongly discouraged.[31]

The instructions would apply equally to 'operations against the UDA and CESA [Catholic Ex-Servicemen's Association]'.[32] They were not to be disclosed to the Taoiseach, but, if he were to ask for 'evidence of action by the security forces against the UDA', the prime minister was advised to tell him that a member of the UDA council had been charged with illegal possession of a pistol and ammunition; that the former chairman of the UDA council, Charles Harding Smith, was one of those charged in London in the arms-conspiracy case; and that a UDA inner-council member had been charged with attempted murder. Mr Lynch was also to be told that 'the security forces act impartially against extremists on both sides. When members of the UDA act illegally, it is not always possible to distinguish their action from those of other Protestant extremists (Tartan Gangs, UVF).'[33]

The same month, an official briefing paper on the UDA stressed that it was not always possible to know whether an apprehended person was affiliated to a particular organisation, but 'it was believed' that more than fifty members of the UDA and some twenty members of the UVF had been, or would soon be, brought before the courts.[34] The (unnamed) author went on to suggest, however, that not all members of the UDA 'behave in an openly aggressive or anti-social manner'. He said there was a great deal of cooperation with the security forces and in many instances the UDA leaders had helped the police and army 'to cool matters down'.[35] He gave an example of a recent disturbance at Lenadoon where a number of Catholics had been attacked by Tartan gangs. He said the local UDA leaders had assisted greatly in restraining their followers 'who resented the squatting of Catholic families in houses out of which Protestants had been forced by intimidation and IRA activity' and concluded by insisting that the army believed the local UDA was not involved in the attack.[36]

At a meeting with the Taoiseach in October, Canon Pádraig Murphy of Ballymurphy, Belfast, and two members (businessman Tom Conaty and solicitor Seamus O'Hare) of the Northern Ireland Advisory Commission (NIAC) had complained of UDA intimidation of small Catholic enclaves.[37] They said 'the UDA looked good on parade and the British Army was not taking them on' – in other words that UDA members were permitted to parade in uniform. They explained to the Taoiseach that the army had warned that it would take serious action on paramilitary uniforms in Catholic areas, but, when asked to act against the uniform-wearing UDA in the Shankill area, it dissembled, claiming there was no law on the matter but that it would act against people wearing uniforms 'in a provocative way'.[38] As in other matters, it seemed that British Army reaction to the same offences in the UDA and IRA was not equal.

On 5 December 1972, in a debate on the future of Northern Ireland in the House of Lords, Lord Windlesham, NIO, responded to a parliamentary question from the Earl of Longford on the legal status of the UDA. He told the House that the UDA was not an illegal organisation.[39] As its name suggested, he said, the Ulster Defence Association was originally formed to defend Protestant areas against IRA terrorist attacks. If it had confined its activities to that role, there would be less concern about it than there now was. While Windlesham conceded that there was some evidence that 'certain members' of the UDA had been involved in intimidation of Catholic families, others in armed robberies and firearms offences, and others in shooting attacks on the security forces, he offered assurances that wherever and whenever there was evidence that UDA members had committed a criminal offence, action had been taken, and would continue to be taken, against them, not simply for being members of the UDA, but for whatever criminal offence they were accused of having committed. A glaring omission from Windlesham's contribution was his failure to acknowledge the UDA's responsibility for sectarian killings.[40]

Echoing the briefing note of 23 November, he explained that when members of the UDA acted illegally it was not always possible to distinguish their actions from those of other Protestant extremists, such as the Tartan gangs and the Ulster Volunteer Force.[41]

Windlesham said the UVF was another matter altogether. This organisation, like the IRA, was a proscribed one. The UVF did not normally parade or operate openly. It did not disclose its membership or leadership. It had not recently claimed responsibility for any incidents. The police, however, suspected that it might have been involved in some of the sectarian killings in Belfast, and a prominent UVF leader, Gusty Spence, had recently been rearrested by the security forces and was continuing to serve his sentence for murder.[42] These comments are disingenuous, as illegal organisations – such as the UVF and the IRA – could not operate openly or disclose their membership or leadership. If they did so, their leaders and members would be liable to be arrested and charged.

Lord Kilbracken enquired as to why the UDA was not proscribed, while the UVF was. Windlesham blatantly deflected the question by suggesting that Kilbracken should 'get together with Lord O'Neill of the Maine' after the debate. He remarked that when Lord O'Neill was prime minister of Northern Ireland, he had proscribed the UVF.[43]

The above-mentioned information was also contained in a briefing for the meeting with the Taoiseach dated 23 November 1972. It suggested that if Mr Lynch asked about the recent Lenadoon incident, when the houses of five Catholic families were burned, the prime minister could say that the army had no firm evidence that the UDA was involved. He should simply say that 'it was a well-organised attack by a gang of extremists'.[44]

Throughout this whole period, while the British authorities were downplaying UDA involvement in sectarian killings and other crimes, the UDA was responsible for the deaths of seventy-one people, all civilians. With the exception of two of its own members, the vast majority of the killings were sectarian.[45]

\*\*\*

At the end of January 1973 a *Daily Telegraph* article quoted Tommy Herron boasting of having recently imported 300 AK-47 Kalashnikov automatic rifles through the Republic of Ireland. He bragged that they had come in from mainland Europe and were 'now scattered throughout Ulster, guarded in secret caches by quartermasters'. He claimed that the UDA had some legally held arms, but it had 'a great number of weapons which have come in illegally'. He commented that the UDA was not afraid to admit this openly. The article suggested that this disclosure would be embarrassing for Mr Whitelaw, who was already in a difficult position over the UDA's admission that it was cooperating with the proscribed UVF. The article noted that 'the UDA – the Protestant secret army – was allowed to hold parades and marches in a bid to release some of the Protestant frustration in the North but the UDA was now clearly challenging Mr Whitelaw to act'.[46]

The following day, 31 January 1973, Herron announced that the UDA could no longer stop assassinations by 'Protestant extremists': 'We have tried to stop the murders but the renewed bombing onslaught by the republican rebels is a provocation to them. They cannot keep turning the other cheek and it is futile for us to try to stop them.'[47] As the newspaper article reporting Herron's announcement suggested, he seemed to be challenging the secretary of state. In hindsight, it would also appear that Herron was trying to distance himself from the imminent bloodletting.

In late January and early February 1973 the UDA went on a killing rampage that led to the first internment of loyalists. At least seven people were killed by the organisation between 29 January and 3 February. This is not to downplay concurrent republican violence, but it is necessary to chart why a small number of loyalists were eventually interned.

On 29 January the UDA killed a fifteen-year-old boy and a young man of twenty-three. Two days later, a fourteen-year-old boy and a motor mechanic aged seventeen met the same fate. On 1 February the UDA unit run by Albert Walker Baker and Edward (Ned) McCreery was responsible for throwing a grenade into a bus carrying building workers to the site of a new Catholic primary school. This attack resulted in the death of a fifty-year-old man, Patrick Heenan. The grenade used was standard British Army issue, which raises the obvious question of how the gang got its hands on it.[48] The UDA killed a CESA member on 2 February and a café owner on 3 February.[49] The grenade attack on the bus led, finally, after eighteen months' resistance by the British government, to the internment of the first loyalists on 5 February 1973.

Two UDA members were detained, which led to widespread violence two days later.[50] Loyalists, led by Bill Craig of Vanguard, staged a one-day general strike, which resulted in all industry and most businesses being brought to a standstill. Power and public transport were affected, while many people were prevented from going to work. In a twenty-four-hour period, five people were shot dead and seven wounded by gunfire. One of those killed was a fireman who was trying to quench a fire in Sandy Row. The police said that the fireman was shot deliberately to prevent the fire being put out.[51] It emerged in court eleven years later that the UDA had been responsible for his death.[52]

The official weekly intelligence report of 9 February 1973 observed that the arrest of 'two UDA/UVF members' for the attack on the bus was the direct cause of Protestant violence.[53] The report noted that Protestant resentment and frustration at continued IRA activity contributed to the violence. The strike and the protest marches were described by Bill Craig as 'a show of strength'. Once again, loyalist violence was portrayed as being reactive to IRA violence.

The two arrests were followed on 9 February by the arrest of seven other Belfast men 'with UVF or similar connections, including the Red Hand Commando leader, John McKeague',[54] against whom it was stated a charge would be brought.[55]

At a meeting of the NIAC on 5 February 1973 chaired by the secretary of state, there was discussion on the advisability of detaining UDA leaders at that time. It was suggested that recent statements by the UDA vice-chairman appeared to imply that the organisation was able to regulate the number of sectarian killings. The statements also admitted that it was importing illegal arms.[56] The recent demonstration by 'loyalist extremists' outside RUC headquarters was cited as one example of the UDA behaving as though it was 'beyond the law'.[57]

It was suggested that the secretary of state should make regulations under the Special Powers Act to revoke gun licences held by prominent UDA leaders, prosecute UDA men when they organised parades or usurped the functions of the police, and order the security forces to return fire when they were fired on by Protestant snipers. While some NIAC members claimed that there would be no purpose in proscribing the UDA, since its members would simply re-form in alternative organisations, others believed that the security forces should act equally and impartially 'against extremists in both sections of the community'.[58]

The secretary of state was against proscribing the UDA and agreed with the viewpoint that there were other organisations to which its members could simply transfer. He explained that troops had not returned fire during the recent riots in east Belfast because they had been unable to identify their targets clearly. Where this could be done, he said, the troops would have no hesitation in returning fire.[59]

At that time the IPU noted that sectarian murders and pressure for action against the UDA were mounting. The report's author suggested:

> ... the question of taking action against the UDA was probably the hardest put to us since 'Why do you allow IRA military funerals to go unchecked?' The answer – woolly but sufficient – was the same in both cases – that all factors had to be taken into consideration when making this kind of judgment and the Secretary of State had decided against it for the time being.[60]

Incredibly, it seems the IPU felt that the secretary of state was justified in making that decision because of the 'extreme violence' and murders that had followed the serving of two ICOs.[61] This demolishes the British government's oft-vaunted declaration that it did not give in to terrorism.

Paul Rose, Labour MP for Manchester Blackley, questioned the secretary of state in the House of Commons on 8 February about the status of the UDA.[62] Mr Rose asked if the prime minister would now take action against the UDA 'following its sanction of sectarian murder in NI'. Rose suggested the UDA was 'the mirror image of the IRA' and believed 'an even-handed policy against both will have fruitful results'. He was fobbed off with platitudes.[63]

Coinciding with the upsurge in UDA violence, the Irish embassy in London sent a memo to the FCO raising concerns about the UDA on 1 February 1973. An FCO official, Stewart Crawford, wrote to P. J. Woodfield, NIO, informing him that he had received the memo, which was about current problems presented by UDA statements, sectarian assassinations and so on, from Charles Whelan of the Irish embassy. Whelan said that John Peck (British ambassador in Dublin) was also being called in and given a similar text. When interviewed on the RTÉ documentary *Collusion*, broadcast in June 2015, Seán Donlon, former secretary-general of the Irish Department of Foreign Affairs, made it very clear that the Irish government was aware that Britain was conspiring with loyalist paramilitaries from the very beginning of the conflict.

The memo was treated with derision by FCO officials. The attitude of Kelvin White, head of the Republic of Ireland Department (RID) in the Foreign Office in a memo to Kenneth Thom, counsellor at the British embassy, Dublin, concerning the Irish embassy's memo is very revealing.[64] White was responsible for the British government's relations with the Irish government and was the direct link within the FCO for the Irish ambassador in London. Instead of dealing with Dublin's concerns, he agreed with a previous comment made by Thom that the memo from the Irish embassy was inspired by the 'Dáil coming to the boil' (a general election was due in the Republic of Ireland later that month). He suggested that it might be the first shot in the 'election battle'. He

CONFIDENTIAL

Foreign and Commonwealth Office
London S.W.1                     2

7 February 1973

K C Thom Esq
DUBLIN

Dear Kenneth,

In your telegram No 60 you gave the text of the Memorandum
which, at about the same time, Whelan had been giving to
Stewart Crawford here.

2.   At the time you commented, and correctly in our view, that
the Memorandum was doubtless inspired by the "Dail coming to the
boil".   I suppose, in retrospect, it may have been the first
shot in the Election battle.   Be that as it may, we do not
propose to make any formal reply.   We assume it was an Irish
PR exercise, and we assume also that you are content with the
service you are getting from Northern Ireland on such matters
as the arrests and now the internment - the latter very helpful
politically speaking - of Protestants.   Statistics of weapon
searches, etc, may also be helpful.   I expect there will be
many more occasions in the Election period when we will face
some public accusations of the sort contained in the Memorandum,
and we shall have to play each one as it occurs.   At the
moment our inclination is to refuse to be drawn in to such
debate, but to make it plain that we are remaining silent since
we consider such accusations to be electoral gimmicks.   Since
this will apply to the highest in the land, it may not always
be well received.   But it seems preferable to continuing
arguments.

3.   I hope you will let us know if there is anything more you
need in the way of ammunition to counter Irish assertions.

4.   Meanwhile, I enclose what is I believe called a jeu d'esprit

5.   I am sending copies of this letter to Frank Steele in
Belfast, Cliff Hill at Stormong and to Bill Smith in the Northern
Ireland Office.

Yours ever,

Kelvin

W K K White
Republic of Ireland Department

*NAUK, FCO87/227, Letter to Kenneth Thom, British Embassy, Dublin, from
Kelvin White*

did not propose to make any formal reply and would assume it was 'an Irish PR exercise'. The British, he said, would refuse to be drawn into debate by making it plain they were remaining silent. Such accusations should be considered electoral gimmicks, he continued, before adding that the embassy should let him know if there was anything more it needed in the way of ammunition to counter Irish assertions. He enclosed an altered version of the memo from the Irish embassy, replacing 'IRA' in every instance where 'UDA' was mentioned and adding that 'the IRA are allowed to operate from sanctuary within the Republic of Ireland'. He described this as a *jeu d'esprit*.[65] He copied his memo to several officials, including Frank Steele, showing the contempt with which the British government treated its Irish counterpart and highlighting the unequal relationship between them.[66]

Despite the FCO's peremptory dismissal of the issue, the Irish government's concerns about the UDA were clearly valid. Loyalists had the capacity to mount deadly attacks across the border into the Republic of Ireland from an early stage of the conflict. Seven people were killed in loyalist attacks between 1 December 1972 and 20 January 1973 – busmen George Bradshaw and Tommy Duffy in Dublin by a car bomb on 1 December; teenagers Geraldine O'Reilly and Paddy Stanley, in Belturbet, County Cavan, by a car bomb on 28 December; Oliver Boyce and Bríd Porter, an engaged couple, near Burnfoot, County Donegal, by stabbing and shooting in the early hours of New Year's Day; and Tommy Douglas, another busman, in Dublin by a car bomb on 20 January. It is likely that the UVF carried out the Dublin and Belturbet attacks, while the UDA carried out the killings in County Donegal.[67]

On St Patrick's Day 1973 a car bomb exploded in the car park of Kirk's public house, Cloughfin, near Lifford, County Donegal, where

350 people were attending a cabaret event. The bomb exploded prematurely, killing Lindsay Mooney, a nineteen-year-old member of the Derry UDA. Fifteen people were injured in the explosion. Had the bombing operation gone according to plan, there is little doubt that serious loss of life would have resulted.[68]

On 28 April 1973, not long after the Irish-memo incident, thousands of masked UDA men gathered for an hour-long protest on the streets of Belfast, as well as in towns and villages throughout Northern Ireland. This massive show of strength was a protest against Irish attempts to extradite a UDA man, Robert Taylor, to face charges in Dublin in connection with the killing of the engaged couple in County Donegal on New Year's Day 1973. Tommy Herron threatened 'to bring the country to a standstill' unless the extradition order was withdrawn; the *Newsletter* reported that more than thirty roads were completely blocked by protesters, with police and troops staying in the background.[69] In spite of this, Taylor was extradited to the Republic on 14 June, the House of Lords having refused to grant him leave to appeal against the extradition order.[70] When his case came to trial in the Special Criminal Court in Dublin, he was acquitted.

\*\*\*

On 9 June 1973 representatives of the *Sunday World* newspaper were summoned to UDA headquarters, where a document was issued, signed by Andy Tyrie and Jean Moore.[71] Martin Dillon claims that this document, which he describes as the 'birth certificate' of the UFF, was written for the organisation by a lawyer with deep connections to loyalism. According to Dillon, this lawyer 'was involved in the cabal which formed the UVF in 1966'.

Dillon believes his information to be correct because the UDA leadership, he observed, would not have had the skill to craft such a statement.[72] The document was not issued as a UFF text but as a policy document of a new UDA leadership – a disingenuous move because, just hours later, the UFF emerged.

Later that day a bomb was thrown into a Catholic bar in Belfast. A barman bravely picked it up to throw outside. His hand was blown off, but he saved the lives of many customers. Fifteen minutes later, the so-called UFF rang the *Belfast Telegraph* and made its first claim of responsibility for a terrorist attack. Some hours later, it abducted a Catholic, thirty-five-year-old Daniel O'Neill, and shot him through the head.[73]

Just a month later, General Sir Frank King, HQNI, wrote to Sir Michael Carver, MoD, claiming:

> The UFF number about 30, of whom we have so far arrested a third. We know the names of the others but to date have too little on them to support ICO action. I have no doubt that their depredations will continue and will collect publicity but they are currently a nuisance rather than a threat.[74]

At an IPU meeting on 13 June 1973, there was a general discussion on the problems posed by the contemporary actions of the UDA. It was agreed at the meeting that 'the Baker story needed to be carefully watched'.[75] This is a reference to Albert Walker Baker, who, in late May, had walked into Warminster police station in England and admitted his role in four sectarian killings in Belfast the previous year as a member of the UDA. He was convicted and sentenced to life imprisonment in October 1973. As was noted earlier, the Baker/McCreery gang had been responsible for the attack on the bus on 1 February, which had led to the internment of the first loyalists. It is suspected that this gang carried out many more killings than the four to which Baker admitted; persistent claims have also been made that Baker was working as a British military intelligence agent within the UDA. One of his four convictions was for the murder of the bus driver, Patrick Heenan.[76]

The emergence of the UFF was discussed at another IPU meeting on 19 June 1973. Significantly, it was agreed that the UFF should not be treated as being separate from the UDA. It was observed that a pattern had emerged: when a particularly horrifying incident occurred it was claimed to be the work of the splinter group.[77]

At its 27 June meeting, the IPU committee discussed the murder of SDLP Stormont Senator Paddy Wilson and a friend, Ms Irene Andrews. It was noted that Liam Hourican of RTÉ was alleging that the security forces had recently been prevented from arresting UDA leaders by orders from Stormont Castle. The committee suggested this was an attempt to split the security forces from the government.[78]

In a memo to the CGS, following his visit to Northern Ireland on 24–25 July 1973, an official complained: 'The RUC still tended to operate against the Protestants as criminals rather than terrorists, despite the fact that, with less IRA activity, Protestant bombs receive far more than their fair share of publicity.' He noted that ICOs were ready to go against twenty-four of the hardest Protestant extremists, so that if the Paisley/Craig attempts to prevent the Northern Ireland Assembly – elections for which had been held in June that year – from working succeeded, and this was followed by Protestants taking to the streets, the secretary of state could intern the hardest of the extremists, one by one, on information prepared well in advance.[79]

On 21 August the IPU decided it would be counterproductive to 'knock' the UDA at that stage. However, a careful watch would be kept on the situation.[80]

Ian Wood claims that John White, one of the founders of the UFF, told him what lay behind the UFF's emergence:

> The feeling was that the UDA had got too big and that we needed to re-organise the real activists into small, streamlined units who could hit the IRA where it hurt most, by attacks on the communities who were not just making excuses for them but actually supporting them. It was simple and it was brutal, there's no point in denying that.[81]

Wood states that, a month after the formation of the UFF, reporters from the *Belfast Telegraph* and *The Daily Telegraph* were granted an exclusive interview with two men who described themselves as representing the UFF brigade staff. The murders of Senator Wilson and Irene Andrews were raised. The journalists were told by one of the men, in racist language redolent of Nazi propaganda, that 'Wilson and Andrews was a ritual killing. It was a godsend to get rid of vermin like that.'[82]

In a note on 'Protestant extremist organisations' in late 1973, the UFF is described as follows:

> First came to notice in June 1973 but is considered to be the 'flag of convenience' used to cover militant acts by UDA Commanders or Heavy Squads and originally, but probably less so now, UVF/YCV [Young Citizen Volunteers] groups. UFF is thought to have no chain of command or any leaders.[83]

Interestingly, RHC is described as coming under the control of the

UVF 'probably as a result of discussions between [John] McKeague and [Gusty] Spence in the Maze'.[84]

It seems clear from the note cited that even in official circles it was accepted that the UFF was never anything more than a cover name for the UDA, which enabled the organisation to continue its campaign of sectarian murder without fear of proscription.

\*\*\*

In late October 1973 levels of loyalist violence began to rise again, in advance of talks at Sunningdale to negotiate the establishment of a new Northern Ireland Assembly, which would be elected by proportional representation. A Council of Ireland would have a consultative role. Just as the increase in violence in February had led to the internment of the first loyalists, this upsurge resulted in the proscription of the UFF and the RHC. This, however, was for propaganda purposes, as the UFF was simply a cover name for the UDA, and the RHC was under the control of the UVF.

On 22 October a Protestant man was killed when a UDA bomb exploded in the doorway of a bar on the Newtownards Road as he was passing by. Six days later, the UVF's soon-to-be-notorious Robin Jackson carried out what was probably his first murder in Banbridge, County Down, when he shot dead a former work colleague, Patrick Campbell.[85]

On 1 November – the day Jamie Flanagan, the first Catholic to hold the post, replaced Sir Graham Shillington as chief constable of the RUC – four bombs were detonated in Belfast. These bombs wrecked the Republican Clubs' Headquarters and caused serious structural damage to the Beehive Bar and Royal Victoria Hospital, all on the Falls Road. They also caused blast damage to the Four-in-

Hand pub on the Lisburn Road. The bomb that exploded outside the Avenue Bar in Union Street killed a pensioner. There were three shootings on the same day: in a sectarian attack, a young Catholic husband and father, Daniel Carson – working in the Shankill area – was shot dead as he left his place of employment; a man was shot and injured on Cavehill Road; and men in a Morris Oxford opened fire on the occupants of another car, wounding the driver. Some of these were UDA attacks, others UVF.

Three more people were killed by loyalists on 7, 8 and 9 November. Then, on 12 November, the UFF claimed seven bomb attacks in Belfast. As a result, the UFF and the RHC were both proscribed on 12 November 1973. This was noted by an IPU meeting the following day, where it was remarked that proscription of the UDA was being kept under review.[86]

A US state paper (a telegram from the Belfast US consul to the secretary of state in Washington) provided information on the proscription of these two organisations. The consul described them as the 'smallest but most vicious loyalist paramilitary organisations'. He wrote that the UFF had claimed responsibility for seven bombings of Catholic-owned property on 12 November, without prior warning – one of the bombs severely damaged the SDLP's former headquarters. However, the document's American author seems to have had a good grasp of which loyalist paramilitary organisations were in fact responsible for the violence:

> Perhaps for tactical security reasons, Whitelaw did not proscribe the UDA despite SDLP urging. Although proscription does arm HMG with new legal weapons to fight loyalist terrorism, it seems likely to have little immediate effect on the level of loyalist violence, in which the UDA and UVF are thought to play far more important roles.[87]

The proscription order was issued after consultation with the GOC, General Frank King, who had succeeded Tuzo the previous February, and the chief constable of the RUC, Jamie Flanagan. The SDLP met with Whitelaw to urge the proscription of the UDA, but Whitelaw resisted its demands, declaring that such a move 'would drive it underground, decrease intelligence-gathering about its activities and risk confrontations between the security forces and large sections of [the] Protestant population in areas where [the] UDA remains strong'.[88]

The sheer reluctance during this whole period to deal effectively with weapon thefts and raids on UDR armouries meant that loyalists were well armed throughout the conflict. As was observed in August's 'Subversion in the UDR' document, coterminous with the joint membership of the UDR and the UDA was a large increase in UDR weapons losses. Yet, nothing was done to call a halt to this practice. Moreover, having in place a religion-based arrest policy was a complete abrogation of the rule of law.

# 4

# IRELAND V UNITED KINGDOM (EUROPEAN COMMISSION OF HUMAN RIGHTS)

> [The UDA] neither claimed nor did in fact use violence in the forms of bombs, explosives or guns to achieve what they wanted.
>
> *Philip Woodfield at hearings before the ECHR in London*[1]

The European Convention on Human Rights had been adopted post-Second World War by various European states as a mechanism to achieve greater international unity through a collective promise to respect certain fundamental rights and freedoms, thus preventing a recurrence of the atrocities that had taken place in the early to mid twentieth century. The European Commission (ECHR) and the European Court of Human Rights (ECtHR) provided a legal mechanism for the enforcement of the convention rights by individual citizens against a state or by one state against another (inter-state applications).

In December 1971 Ireland brought a case against the United Kingdom to the ECHR, alleging a number of breaches of the European Convention. At this stage the European human-rights judicial system was still in its infancy.[2] Although the ECHR no longer exists, in 1971 it held an important role in the European human-rights system.[3] The commission would consider the admissibility of applications to the ECtHR. If the commission determined that an application was admissible, it would consider the *prima facie* case, determine the facts and seek to assist the parties in reaching a friendly settlement. If a friendly settlement could not be achieved, the commission would then issue a report outlining the established facts, along with an opinion on whether a violation of a particular convention right had occurred. At this stage the commission, or either party to the proceedings, could refer the case or specific elements of it to the ECtHR for a full hearing.[4]

In its December 1971 application to the ECHR, the Irish government stated that the United Kingdom had violated a number of the convention rights in Northern Ireland. The violations alleged by the Irish government included a breach of the duty to respect human rights (Article 1), a breach of the right to life (Article 2) and a breach of the prohibition on torture and inhuman and degrading treatment (Article 3).[5]

The Irish government also claimed that Article 5 (right to liberty) and Article 6 (right to a fair trial) were breached by the UK government in respect of its internment policy. They argued that the internments amounted to extrajudicial detention and that this was not justifiable by claiming that a state of emergency applied that would allow derogation under Article 15.[6] The Irish government further argued that the actions of the British government in searching homes and arresting, detaining and interning persons was carried out with discrimination on the grounds of political opinion, and thus breached Article 14.[7] The Irish government argued that these powers were exercised on the basis that the person held certain unspecified political opinions, and not on grounds connected with the actual activities of the person concerned.[8]

The commission and, subsequently, the ECtHR, rejected this argument and held that 'no discrimination contrary to Articles 14 and 5 taken together is established'. Likewise they judged that there was no discrimination in respect of Article 6.[9]

Thirteen witnesses gave evidence on behalf of the United Kingdom. Ten of those were members of the security forces who were identified only by code, all of whom had responsibilities in Northern Ireland during the relevant period. The last three witnesses who gave evidence in London on 20 February 1975 on behalf of the British government were General Harold Craufurd Tuzo – director of operations and GOC Northern Ireland from March 1971 to February 1973; Sir Robert Edward Graham Shillington – chief constable of the RUC from November 1970 to October 1973; and Philip John Woodfield – deputy under-secretary of state for Northern Ireland.

Utilising ECHR evidential rules, the British government elected for these witnesses to be heard in the absence of counsel for both governments. As a result, the Irish government was precluded from cross-examining the British government's witnesses and challenging their evidence. The Irish representatives were insistent that the British government should make the relevant ministers available to give testimony to the commission. The Irish demand was strongly resisted by the British and was eventually rejected by the commission.[10]

The focus of the commissioners' questioning of the last three witnesses centred on the allegation of discrimination in the policy of internment. Although the allegation was that the policies of internment and detention were discriminatory on the basis of political opinion, much of the evidence considered the policies of detention and internment in terms of 'Catholics' and 'Protestants'. This use of language is not explicitly referred to in the Report of the Commission but the ECtHR in its 1978 judgement refers to the 'Protestant, Unionist or Loyalist' and 'Catholic, Republican or Nationalist' communities.

Tuzo was questioned as to whether there were two concurrent terrorist campaigns, to which he replied:

> They were not concurrent, if there were two at all they were consecutive, not concurrent. The UDA was not a terrorist organisation, it was a frightening, if you like, very militant manifestation of a point of view and I think you could say a misguided and utterly horrifying manifestation. But that is what it was, not a terrorist campaign. I would not describe it as terrorist at all, but this does not preclude at all, of course, the campaign of murders and things later on, but that cannot necessarily be levelled at the UDA.[11]

He stressed to the commission that there was no need to detain Protestants because the RUC was strong in their areas and its members were able to arrest these people on ordinary criminal charges. He also said that the UVF had ceased to be an operational terrorist force in 1971. He claimed that there were cases in which a pub might be owned by a Catholic but was frequented by Protestants and, in these cases, it would be just as likely that 'these incidents', that is, bombings, could have been committed by the IRA, just as much as by Protestants:

> Any serious bombings were done by the IRA. One or two incidents of pipe bombs, which are minor things for frightening rather than causing serious injury, they might have been caused by Protestant hooligans. I would stress they appeared to be the impromptu Protestant hooligans rather than an organised effort by somebody like the UVF.[12]

When Shillington gave evidence, the commission reminded him

that, in his written statement, he had claimed it was apparent that Protestant terrorists were much more freelance than those of the IRA, meaning that if an individual was involved in bombing or shooting, it did not necessarily follow that the Protestant organisation to which the individual belonged had any responsibility or knowledge – that is, individuals could act without overall direction. Thus, Shillington was promoting the idea that loyalists acted without leadership or structure. Shillington verbally confirmed his written statement: 'The behind-the-scenes organiser was not so apparent in Protestant activities because they were more freelance. It was more individuals acting without an overall direction.'[13]

Commissioner Frowein asked Shillington whether, before the first Protestant was interned in February 1973, they had any cases between August 1971 to February 1973 where the question of interning Protestants was considered, or special cases where it was recommended to intern a Protestant.

Shillington's response was:

> No, I think it would be right to say that the picture we had was that the extremist Protestant organisations which had been dormant according to our intelligence assessment since 1969, only began to re-emerge after Direct Rule which was in March 1972 – from March to April onwards. It was, first of all, bodies like the UDA who were not in our reckoning terrorists but more concerned in street demonstrations and that type of thing, but we began to see again the emergence of the UVF, sectarian murders starting. I think it would be right to say, mid-1972, and the latter part of 1972, in the greater number of cases we were able to prefer ordinary criminal charges against those people.[14]

Although taking a somewhat contradictory position, senior civil servant Philip Woodfield was prepared to jump through hoops to defend the UDA:

> The UDA were well-organised and a well-structured body, as was evidenced by the discipline they were able to enforce ... If they said there would be a massive demonstration ... they were able to organise it and it took place, but as far as the UDA as an organisation was concerned, although they adopted threatening postures and uttered threatening words, they neither claimed nor did in fact use violence in the forms of bombs or explosives or guns in order to achieve what they wanted. They relied in the main upon hoping to pressurise the authorities by showing that they had large numbers of people at their disposal, and hoped they would get their objective. There were also, of course, a number of smaller organisations of fluctuating membership ... and fluctuating activity, which did employ violence, again, rather of the kind like the sectarian murders that I referred to earlier. They were of the same character but sometimes organised by these small groups, very horrible episodes, such as going to a hut where men were working, repairing the road, and murdering those who were found to be Catholics there – that sort of thing. Those were by small organisations, not structured like the IRA, and I think it is very likely, in fact, certain, that membership of some of these small organisations coincided with membership of the UDA.[15]

When asked if the UDA and smaller organisations worked together, he replied, 'No, I think it is more a question that a handful of people in the UDA, who belonged to the UDA, also belonged to these violent organisations – UVF, UFF, the RHC and so forth.'[16]

When asked if any major operation against these small organisations had been considered, Woodfield replied:

> The difficulty is that their structure and organisation are unknown … it is very doubtful whether they have got a structure in the sense that the IRA has, that they are really groups of criminals who give themselves a rather grandiose title.[17]

He went on to stress that the UDA's activities were not of that nature: 'The UDA declare themselves, they state who they are, there is no evidence that they engaged systematically in campaigns of terrorism.'[18]

The NIO prepared a memorandum for the commission to accompany the hearings. Officials originally hoped that William Whitelaw would 'father' this memorandum, but he clearly declined, so it was presented by the NIO, which was the officials' second choice.[19] The IRA was answerable, the memo said, for all explosions where responsibility could be attributed to any organisation in the period August 1971–March 1972. Specifically, there was no evidence that the Protestant UVF cells had been engaged since the spring of 1969 in illegal and clandestine activities.

Dealing with post-direct rule the memo stated:

> Although there were demonstrations on the part of Protestant organisations such as Ulster Vanguard, the reaction did not for the most part take the form of violence. It is likely that the deaths of some Catholics – at most a dozen and probably less – during the first six months of 1972 were at the hands of Protestant groups. Protestant organisations were not involved in a terrorist campaign, and unlike the PIRA, were not at war with society as a whole.[20]

This commentary was as inaccurate as it was self-serving. It is a matter of record that the UVF had carried out several non-fatal bomb attacks during 1970. In 1971 they killed twenty-two people, fifteen of them in the horrific McGurk's Bar explosion on 4 December.[21] Other loyalist bombings that year included a fatal attack on the Fiddler's House pub in Durham Street at the bottom of the Falls Road, which left a Protestant woman dead, and a UVF bomb planted in a Catholic-owned public house on 17 December, which killed a sixteen-year-old Catholic apprentice barman.[22] In 1972 loyalists killed twenty-five people in the first six months and five more in the first three days of July.

A deliberate decision was taken by the RUC, the British Army and politicians to present the McGurk's bomb in December 1971 as an IRA 'own goal', despite reliable evidence, both eyewitness and forensic, to the contrary in the immediate aftermath.[23] This was reinforced by the dissemination of blatant disinformation including an untruthful claim made by the chief constable that two of those killed were known IRA members.[24] It is an entirely credible proposition that the disinformation campaign that emerged in the aftermath of the McGurk's Bar bombing was intended to justify the failure to intern loyalists.

On 13 November 1974 a meeting took place between senior officials of the NIO, the FCO, the MoD, Mr de Winton of the attorney-general's office and Mr Hall and Mr Wilkinson of the treasury solicitor's office. Mr de Winton sought an answer to a question from the counsel representing Britain in the European case as to why 'only Roman Catholics were interned before 1972 [*sic*].'[25] Mr Hall replied that in the view of the security forces there was 'no serious Protestant threat in that period of a kind which led to death and serious injuries'. He admitted, though, that he was worried about the situation during the latter part of 1972, when this argument 'probably did not apply'.[26] This deception was accepted by the ECHR, as is shown in its report published on 25 January 1976:

> There appears to have been relatively little serious violence by Protestants, apart from rioting, between August 1971 and the end of the year. Nevertheless, a minor bombing campaign, in particular of public houses, continued throughout 1971. The 'Schedule' produced by the applicant Government [Ireland] lists a total of eight bombings attributed to Protestants during that period. One of those referred to was an explosion at a Catholic public house on 4 December 1971, in which 15 people were killed. Responsibility for this explosion was claimed by a group calling themselves the 'Empire Loyalists'. No such group had been heard of, however, and the police subsequently received information to the effect that the explosion had been caused by an IRA bomb which had exploded prematurely whilst in transit to its intended target which was a hotel nearby.[27]

As the Irish government was not in a position to contradict British statistical evidence, the commission accepted the figures provided by the respondent (British) government. It is stated that in the period 1 April 1972 to 5 February 1973:

> The most serious aspect of loyalist activity was the perpetration of a large number of assassinations, these being mainly sectarian assassinations of Catholics. Protestants were believed to have been responsible for 67 [sectarian] assassinations between 1 April 1972 and the end of the year and a further four in January 1973.[28]

- 188 -

that internment had been introduced to placate extreme
Unionists and that in many cases people were being interned
simply because they were opposed to Unionism (1).

It is now generally accepted that in many cases in
August 1971 persons were arrested, and in some cases also
detained, on the basis of inadequate and inaccurate information.
(2).

Arrests continued to be made during the rest of the year,
partly of persons who had been on the original list, and partly
of persons who became subject to suspicion thereafter. It
appears that a total of 770 detention orders were made during the
year under Regulation 11 (2) and 525 internment orders were made
although a considerably larger number of people were arrested.
Thus it seems that some 980 people had been arrested by 10 November
The numbers actually held under detention or internment orders ros
steadily to over 500 in December 1971 (3).

e)   The situation from 9 August 1971 until 30 March 1972

The introduction of internment provoked a violent reaction
from the Catholic community and the IRA. Serious rioting broke
out in Belfast and elsewhere and there was a considerable
increase in shootings and bombings. In the immediate aftermath
barricades were erected in Catholic areas and gun battles took
place between the army and the IRA when the army attempted
to clear them. The extent of the reaction surprised the
authorities (4). In the course of sectarian rioting thousands
of people were forced to leave their homes. Many houses were
burned, frequently by the occupants who set fire to them on
leaving to prevent them from being occupied by members of
the opposite community. In the Ardoyne district of Belfast
some 200 homes were thus burned by Protestants leaving them and
a number by Catholics (5). There was also some shooting
between the rival factions in the course of sectarian rioting (6)

Throughout the period from August to December 1971 the
numbers of deaths and explosions recorded by the police for
each month were higher than in any previous month of the
year. A total of 146 people were killed and 729 explosions
were caused. Of the 146 persons killed, 47 were members of
the security forces and 99 were civilians. Explosions caused

./.

---

(1)   See e.g. VR 7 pp. 29-30 & 77.
(2)   See e.g. The Diplock Report p. 15 para. 32.
(3)   VR 10 I p. 122 & Annex p. 15; VR 10 II p. 797; VR 7 p. 34
      and Statistics of Monthly Holdings prepared by the applicant
      Government.
(4)   See e.g. VR 10 I pp. 40-47; VR 11 pp. vi-vii.
(5)   VR 10 I pp. 180 and 216-217.
(6)   VR 10 I p. 379.

- 189 -

a considerable number of deaths.  Thus in September 1971
7 civilians were killed in explosions and in the period from
October to December 1971 41 persons were so killed, 7 of them
being members of the security forces and 34 being civilians (1).

The introduction of internment and the riots which
followed it led to a rise in support for the IRA within the
Catholic community and further alienation of the Catholic
community from the authorities and security forces (2).  On
the Protestant side the serious violence at this time led to
the formation of further local defence associations or
vigilant groups in Protestant areas.  These eventually
amalgamated to become the Ulster Defence Association.  The
precise date when this occurred is not clear but it appears
to have been in about September 1971, although this
organisation did not become openly active until about the
spring of 1972 (3).  The police apparently looked on the
various associations primarily as defensive organisations
which patrolled their areas.  They were aware that there was a
dangerous element within them but apparently did not have
sufficient intelligence to identify the violent element in
1971 (4).

There appears to have been relatively little serious
violence by Protestants, apart from rioting, between August
1971 and the end of the year.  Nevertheless a minor bombing
campaign, in particular of public houses, continued throughout
1971.  The "Schedule" produced by the applicant Government
lists a total of eight bombings attributed to Protestants
during that period.  One of those referred to was an
explosion at a Catholic public house on 4 December 1971, in
which 15 people were killed.  Responsibility for this
explosion was claimed by a group calling themselves the
"Empire Loyalists".  No such group had been heard of, however,
and the police subsequently received information to the
effect that the explosion had been caused by an IRA bomb
which had exploded prematurely whilst in transit to its
intended target which was a hotel nearby (5).  One death
only, between August and the end of the year, was attributed
by the police to Loyalists.  This was an assassination of
a Protestant in September 1971 (6).

Intimidation appears to have become more serious after
the disturbances following the introduction of internment.
Much intimidation appears to have taken place on both sides

./.

(1)  VR 10 I pp. 180-181.
(2)  See e.g. VR 7 p. 31.
(3)  VR 10 I pp. 180-181; VR 9 p. 14; VR 7 pp. 147-148.
(4)  VR 10 I pp. 377-378.
(5)  Schedule of Loyalist Acts of Terrorism; VR 10 I pp.
     368-369.
(6)  VR 10 I p. 181, Annex p. 6; VR 10 I , Annex p. 89.

Yet again, the British were being very economical with the truth. The reality was that loyalists had carried out 101 sectarian killings during the period April–December 1972. The figure of four for January 1973 is correct. At least sixty-three of these persons were killed by the UDA.[29]

The British memorandum to the ECHR disclosed information that between July 1972 and March 1973, some 120 murders fell into the category of 'sectarian', with two-thirds of the victims being Catholics. In an attempt to change the focus, however, the memo observed that sectarian assassinations attributable to Protestant organisations were considerably fewer than the total figure of deaths attributable to the IRA. It did concede that sectarian assassinations by Protestant groups were a serious and disturbing development. It claimed, however, that the relentless campaign of the IRA had produced a willingness in some Protestant circles to use 'other kinds of violence to serve their political purposes'. The information contained in the memo was further qualified:

> On the whole, however, the main manifestation of Protestant anxiety was not violence. Goaded by the IRA's persistent violence, and in some degree encouraged by the oratory of some of their [own] political leaders, and undoubtedly fearful about what constitutional change in NI might bring, there arose a willingness in the Protestant community to use their strength of numbers to demonstrate their resentment ... it is not surprising that in all these circumstances, there was widespread support in the Protestant community for organisations such as the Loyalist Association of Workers and the UDA which sought concessions by organising massive demonstrations or using their numbers to block roads or interrupt civil life. Although careful consideration was given to proscribing the UDA, it appeared

on balance that no good purpose would be served by doing so, not least because most of its members were not involved in violence and proscription would almost certainly have encouraged a substantial number of UDA members to follow the militant extremists. It was for the same reason that the Catholic Ex-Servicemen's Association was also not proscribed.[30]

CESA was an unarmed organisation, and there is no publicly available evidence that it was associated with violence, so this comment is duplicitous. Indeed, it had been previously agreed internally that CESA would be included in parallel with the UDA in such circumstances solely for 'presentational reasons'.[31]

The so-called UFF is referred to in the NIO memo to the ECHR as 'a new terrorist organisation which was proscribed in November 1973'.[32] The British knew this to be a fiction. In actual fact, the commission's report, published in January 1976, referred to the applicant government [Ireland] submitting that:

> when the Commission came to consider the role of the UDA generally, it was the significance of N1's [one of the British security force witnesses] evidence in this respect that, when claims to murdering Catholics were made by the organisation called the UFF, it turned out that no such organisation existed and that in fact the murders were committed by members of the UDA itself.[33]

It was also noted that witness N1 had admitted that 'by the middle of 1972 the police would have had lists of the terrorists in the UDA and he had envisaged no difficulties in identifying the terrorists from that time if their internment had been decided upon'.[34] The European Commission and, subsequently, the European Court, however, were persuaded by British arguments that the practice of interning only Catholics was not discriminatory. In the judgement of the European Court, there were two dissenting judges. The Irish judge, Philip O'Donoghue, was one of them. The other was the Austrian judge, Franz Matscher. The majority judgement of the commission, with which the court agreed, stated:

> It is clear from the evidence given by members of the security forces and others that there was a tendency to look on loyalist terrorists as 'criminals' or 'hooligans' and on the IRA as the organised 'terrorist' enemy. Although it is clear that acts of serious terrorism were committed by both sides from political motives, the security forces were in many ways justified in this belief. Extreme loyalists were highly organised in bodies such as the UDA and those bodies undoubtedly included terrorist elements, but the UDA was not itself engaged at the time or since in carrying out a campaign of terrorism comparable to that of the IRA. Such evidence as there is suggests that the loyalist organisations such as the UVF and UFF which were themselves engaged in serious terrorism were at the time more amorphous than the IRA. The risk of a severe outbreak of Protestant violence was a very real one.[35]

The majority judgement of the European Court also concluded that it was easier to institute criminal proceedings against loyalists than against their republican counterparts. It found that 'although Loyalist terrorists were not extra judicially deprived of their liberty, they do not seem to have been able to act with impunity'. Arrests often led to convictions, above all in sectarian assassinations.[36]

In May 1975, in a draft letter and paper to the secretary of state's private secretary, Frank Cooper, NIO official Bill Webster advised that, out of 346 sectarian murders, there had been charges in fifty-six cases. Only eighteen of these cases had, at that point, resulted in convictions for murder, while there had been seven convictions for manslaughter. Of the nineteen people convicted of murder, fifteen were Protestants and four were Catholics; of those convicted of manslaughter, five were Protestants and two were Catholics.[37] This hardly suggests that the authorities were successful in prosecuting loyalists for sectarian killings.

The separate opinion of Judge Franz Matscher concluded that, although from the quantitative point of view a larger number of serious outrages were attributable to republican terrorists than to loyalist terrorists, this did nothing to alter the fact that 'two brands of terrorism were simultaneously rife in Northern Ireland'. Judge Matscher was unconvinced by British attempts to justify such a difference and pointed out that the British government was very unforthcoming during the inquiry so that 'an unfettered assessment of the evidence does not operate in their favour'. He continued, 'Examination of the material before the Court' showed that there was 'hesitation over taking equally energetic action against the Loyalist terrorists … because of fear of the political repercussions of such a step.'[38]

The separate opinion of the Irish judge, Philip O'Donoghue, suggested that there was a disregard of the massive build-up of organised Protestant paramilitary bodies and their threat to peace, bearing in mind the terror inflicted on Catholics in 1968–9.[39] He was adamant in his conclusion that:

> It is just not accurate to say the Loyalist terrorist groups were more amorphous than the IRA and were 'criminals' or 'hooligans'. This might have been a convenient way for the security forces to so regard

the massive para-military strength of the UDA, the UVF and the Vanguard movement.[40]

O'Donoghue referred to the authorities' apprehension, acknowledged by the court, regarding Protestant paramilitary strength and their reluctance to contemplate the detention of loyalists. They were right to be apprehensive, he said, because loyalists had proved capable of organising a politically motivated strike and had destroyed the short-lived power-sharing Executive in May 1974.[41]

The court noted: 'At the beginning of February 1973, a British soldier was shot dead in a Protestant part of Belfast. Shortly afterwards, on 5 February 1973, two interim custody orders were made in respect of Loyalists.'[42] The implication is that loyalists had killed a soldier and, as a result, two loyalists were interned. There is no such death listed in *Lost Lives*. The Irish government claimed, correctly, that the impetus for the decision to intern the first loyalists came about because of a public outcry at a sectarian attack on a bus, which killed a Catholic man. The court noted that the decision had been taken only after discussions between the secretary of state for Northern Ireland, the GOC and high-ranking civil servants, who had recognised it would lead to security repercussions. The court accepted that the risk of a severe outbreak of Protestant violence in response was clearly a very real one.[43]

British representatives, including Tuzo, Shillington and Woodfield, had provided misleading information to an international commission. They lied about the extent of sectarian bombings being perpetrated by loyalists, specifically but not exclusively with regard to McGurk's Bar; they lied about the UFF being a separate organisation from the UDA (although it appears that one honest security-force member admitted that it wasn't); they lied about the so-called unstructured, undisciplined, amorphous nature of the main loyalist organisations, when they were well aware of their formal structures; they lied about loyalists being 'more amenable to the normal criminal system'; they lied about 'members of organisations' being involved in terrorist acts but not the organisations themselves; and they lied about 'Protestant organisations' being dormant between 1969 and the introduction of direct rule. Most importantly, they lied about the UDA's involvement in sectarian killings.

There is some evidence of British concern regarding their submission to the European Commission in relation to discrimination in internment. In a letter from a Home Office official to legal counsellor Paul Fifoot in January 1973, the writer demonstrates his anxiety, commenting:

> We may have been able to say at the admissibility hearing that hitherto most of the violence had come from the Republican side but this becomes less and less possible as time goes on. It is perhaps on this aspect (particularly in relation to internment) that we may be particularly vulnerable.[44]

Again, apprehension surfaced regarding discrimination when the Irish government made the decision to refer the case to the European Court in 1976. During the preparation of their counter-memorial, Anthony Lester, QC, wrote to the Foreign Office's legal advisers requesting that the section on Article 14 be checked 'with particular care':

> because it is one of our more vulnerable areas and also because the presentation of our case before the Commission was not entirely

consistent or coherent. I was tempted … to admit that there had been some lack of consistency in the presentation of the case and to explain it away. However, on reflection I think it preferable to leave this to an oral reply.[45]

British evidence to the ECHR, which was intended to justify the British government's failure to intern loyalists before February 1973, also serves to illustrate British policy and attitude towards loyalists. British submissions tended to describe some loyalist attacks as criminal rather than terrorist; they claimed that most UDA members were not involved in violence; they minimised loyalist bomb attacks by suggesting their bombs were 'minor things for frightening rather than causing serious injury'; they claimed that loyalists were more freelance – individuals acting without direction; and argued that the UDA was not a terrorist organisation. All the evidence from the official documents shows that British submissions, in particular their downplaying of responsibility for sectarian murders, presented a misleading account to the commission. Above all, it casts serious doubt on the conclusions of the ECHR in respect of this aspect of the Irish complaint.

# 5

# LOYALISTS TORPEDO THE NORTHERN IRELAND POWER-SHARING EXECUTIVE

We want to make it quite clear that we are appalled by these explosions. It is indiscriminate and definitely against our policy. At the present time the UVF have made a firm declaration that we will not engage in any physical activities including bombings and shootings.

*The untruthful denial by the UVF of involvement in the Dublin/Monaghan bombings*[1]

The year 1974 was another crucial time in the conflict. It began very promisingly. An agreement had been signed at Sunningdale in Berkshire, England, on 9 December 1973, which resulted in the establishment of a new Northern Ireland power-sharing Executive in January. The Ulster Unionist Council, however, voted to reject the agreement and the position of Brian Faulkner, leader of the UUP, became untenable. He resigned and formed a new party – the Unionist Party of Northern Ireland. To add to Faulkner's woes British Prime Minister Edward Heath called a snap election on 7 February. The only pro-agreement candidate elected was Gerry Fitt, leader of the SDLP. All the other eleven new MPs were anti-agreement. The election was won by the British Labour Party, and Harold Wilson replaced Heath as prime minister. Merlyn Rees was appointed as the new secretary of state for Northern Ireland and took office in March. One of his first tasks was to de-proscribe (legalise) Sinn Féin and the UVF.[2]

A paper – described as a 'think-piece' by NIO official J. F. Halliday and compiled just before the general election of February 1974 – suggested that the outgoing British government was considering the de-proscription of Sinn Féin.[3] The de-proscription of a loyalist organisation was also being considered for the sake of 'balance'.[4] The paper examined the pros and cons of negotiating with Sinn Féin and the UVF on the issue. Halliday worried that the negotiators might not be able to deliver 'their side of the bargain', in which case 'HMG would be embarrassed and might have to consider re-proscription'.[5]

If they proceeded with the UVF's planned de-proscription, it would appear that the British were prepared to turn a blind eye to its violent activities. The paper states:

> It has been thought in the past … that legalising Sinn Féin would be too much for moderate unionists to swallow and, therefore, damaging to Mr Faulkner. The situation has changed, however, in that the UVF is no longer the only 'Protestant' proscribed organisation and is claiming to observe a 'cease-fire'. It is therefore possible for the legalising of Sinn Féin to be balanced by the legalising of the UVF, without there ceasing to be any 'Protestant' organisations on the proscribed list to counter-balance the continued proscription of the IRA, etc.[6]

It is stated repeatedly that the UVF '*claims* to be observing a cease-fire'.[7] Clearly, the NIO was aware that the organisation was not, in fact, observing a ceasefire.

When the new Labour government under Harold Wilson took office in March 1974 it decided to continue with the process of de-proscribing the two illegal organisations. In a paper prepared on 21 March, an official advised that the attorney-general had directed the director of public prosecutions (DPP) for Northern Ireland to bring no further proceedings against members of these organisations and that any current proceedings in relation to the UVF and Sinn Féin should be dropped.[8]

The possibility of proscribing the UDA was also discussed in this paper. The official explained that the secretary of state was not satisfied this would be justified, and that the UDA, 'in origin at least', engaged more in parading in uniform and patrolling Protestant districts than in terrorism. The document continued, using the by now familiar mantra, 'Some of its members no doubt are concerned in terrorism, but it is less easy to be sure that the organisation as such is so concerned.'[9] It concluded that the necessity of taking into account the effect on security of proscribing the UDA meant such a move could lead to more violence rather than less. The paper also warned that the chief constable might need to 'exercise his discretion' by ascribing damage or injury to other proscribed Protestant organisations if the UVF were to engage 'in sporadic acts of violence' after it had been de-proscribed.[10]

It is bizarre that the chief constable would be advised to consider ascribing responsibility for bombing and shooting attacks to an organisation that he knew was not the guilty party. The official rationale for such advice was that it would have been very embarrassing for the authorities if an organisation they had recently de-proscribed was shown to be responsible for a terrorist act. Also, compensation for injuries to persons was limited to two years' average earnings, unless the injury was caused by a person acting on behalf of a proscribed organisation, in which case there was no limit. There would probably be an outcry if victims of an attack were unable to claim the proper compensation. Damage to property was payable only where the damage could be attributed to an unlawful association proscribed under the Northern Ireland (Emergency Provisions) Act. This ambiguity could also be used, however, to give cover to the UVF if it carried out bombings and shootings, allowing the British authorities to avoid censure for de-proscribing an organisation that was clearly involved in violence.

The process of de-proscribing the UVF and Sinn Féin began on 4 April 1974 when Merlyn Rees announced his plans during a debate in the House of Commons. As has been noted, the imperative to de-proscribe Sinn Féin and the UVF had begun with the previous government. Rees announced that 'on both extreme wings there are people who, although at one time committed to violence, would now like to find a way back [*sic*] to political activity'.[11] (Loyalists could not be said to be finding a way *back* to political activity as they had not previously engaged in it.) He expressed the view that it was 'right to encourage this as much as possible'. He referred to the previous administration's de-proscribing of the Republican Clubs the preceding year and stated that he intended to move in the same direction by bringing forward the necessary order to take the UVF and Sinn Féin off the list.[12] He stressed that this would be 'no protection for men of violence and … no person can expect to be allowed to claim to be acting politically at one moment and then, given what appears a favourable opportunity, to turn to violence and subversion', remarking there was 'a balance to strike between political and military action' and that the time was right 'to try to make further political progress'.[13]

The attitude of the British government towards de-proscription reflected changing, and often contradictory, views, which is perhaps unsurprising given that the discussion was being fuelled from such diverse sources as the FCO and the Security Services through to HQNI, civil servants and politicians. There is nothing fundamentally wrong with Rees' argument that de-proscription might, in certain circumstances, encourage those involved in violence to engage in democratic politics. This initiative, however, was based on the flawed premise that Sinn Féin could be compared with the UVF. Sinn Féin, as a registered political party, *was* in fact on a par with the Republican Clubs, which had been de-proscribed the previous year. Both the Official and the Provisional IRA, of course, continued to be proscribed.

The net effect of de-proscription of the UVF in May 1974 was that the two largest loyalist paramilitary organisations involved in violence – the UDA and UVF – were legal and legitimate, and, crucially, the official view was that neither was involved in violence. The only loyalist organisations that remained illegal – the UFF and the RHC – were in fact fronts for the UDA and the UVF respectively. This reinforced the view in the Catholic community that the British government was in a state of denial about the nature and extent of loyalist violence, and that the rule of law simply did not apply.

Immediately after Rees' statement, the attorney-general directed the DPP for Northern Ireland not to bring criminal proceedings in relation to the two organisations being de-proscribed, and to drop any proceedings that had already started.[14] It was much less likely that proceedings were under way in respect of Sinn Féin members. People were not being charged with membership of Sinn Féin but, rather, with membership of the illegal IRA.

In a briefing of 10 May by J. F. Halliday for an upcoming meeting with UVF spokesman and Independent Unionist Councillor Hugh Smyth[15] and UVF leaders (Smyth had sought advice on the holding of public meetings), Halliday advised that Smyth could be told of the decision not to bring criminal proceedings.[16] It did not constitute any change in the law, but rather meant that, until parliament's view had been made known, there would be no prose-cutions. He advised that the possibility that the order would not be approved could not be ruled out, and until it was approved it was impossible to guarantee absolutely that prosecutions would not be resumed at some future date.

Halliday explained:

> the security forces might have to attend [any public meeting], as they attend lawful meetings to prevent disorder and respond appro-priately to any criminal activity. If they saw someone there who was wanted for some serious offence, or as a suspected terrorist, they might want to arrest him (although they would consider the overall situation before attempting to make an arrest). A member of the security forces who did exercise his powers of arrest in relation to proscribed organisations would be acting perfectly lawfully and the possibility that one might make such an arrest cannot be ruled out. It is extremely unlikely, however, that any charges would be brought. If the UVF did plan any public meetings it would be helpful if they notified the RUC to prevent any misunderstandings.[17]

On 14 May, in the House of Commons, the Labour under-secretary of state, Stan Orme, moved an amendment to the Northern Ireland (Emergency Provisions) Act 1973, which de-proscribed Sinn Féin and the UVF. He, like Merlyn Rees, stressed that the proposals were intended to encourage people in Northern Ireland 'to take peaceful political action'.[18] The amendment was passed by the House of Lords the following day. During the debate, Lord Donaldson of Kings-bridge stated that there was every reason to give extra opportunity for the UVF to 'express their enthusiasm' through politics rather than through violence.[19]

In a memo from an NIO official to Lord Donaldson dated 14 May, the day before he took the de-proscription order through the House of Lords, he was informed that the purpose of de-proscription was twofold – to encourage political activity by extremist groups and to continue to protect the public against the effects of violence by these groups. It was admitted that on the republican side the pattern was reasonably clear, with Sinn Féin representing the political wing of the PIRA and similarly with the Republican Clubs and the OIRA. However, on the loyalist side, the NIO official conceded that the pattern was more confused. The official remarked that both the UDA and UVF 'engage in political activities either directly or through front organisations. On the other hand, semi-autonomous or "heavy duty" groups were also responsible for bombings and shootings under the general umbrella of both. It is difficult to identify these groups …'[20] Yet again, there is the reference to 'semi-autonomous' groups, suggesting these were acting without direction or leadership. On the republican side, the Official and Provisional IRAs were the only republican paramilitary organisations in existence at that time, as the Irish Republican Socialist Party (IRSP) and INLA were not formed until December 1974.

***

The Ulster Workers' Council (UWC) was established in late 1973 to oppose the Sunningdale Agreement. It comprised unionist politicians opposed to power-sharing with nationalists – Ian Paisley, Democratic Unionist Party (DUP); Harry West, United Ulster Unionist Party; Bill Craig, Ulster Vanguard – loyalist para-militaries (UDA, UVF, OV, DOW),[21] Ulster Special Constabulary

Association (USCA),[22] Ulster Army Council (UAC)[23] and key workers from the Harland and Wolff shipyard and the power stations. The organisation held a meeting with the secretary of state at Stormont Castle on 8 April 1974 to demand new Assembly elections in May in the wake of the success of anti-Sunningdale MPs in the British general election (eleven of the twelve members elected were against power-sharing). Rees refused categorically.[24] The UWC decided to call a strike to demand fresh elections, to overthrow the power-sharing Executive and to scupper the Council of Ireland. The strike began on Wednesday 15 May. The story of the first few days was one of massive intimidation, as workers were threatened by loyalist paramilitaries. The UVF played a major role in this.[25]

On the same day, Stan Orme and James Allan of the NIO met with UVF leaders at Laneside to discuss the de-proscription of their organisation.[26] The delegation included Hugh Smyth, Ken Gibson, Tommy West and Stanley Grey.[27]

At the meeting, Orme sympathised with the UVF leaders' anxiety about the delay in proceeding to de-proscription, but he hoped the deputation would be reassured by the steps now being taken. Gibson said there were two points concerning them: the loyalists who were detained and their desire to see an election in Northern Ireland to enable the UVF to campaign politically. Orme told the delegation he was anxious to see the UVF develop close political links with all other political parties in the UK. He did not believe there was any credence in the argument that claimed there was common ground between the UVF and the IRA. This lack of common ground was demonstrated, he said, by the recent discovery of IRA plans for taking over parts of Belfast.[28] This is a mischievous reference to IRA documents seized in the raid on a house in

CONFIDENTIAL

NOTE OF A MEETING BETWEEN THE MINISTER OF STATE AND A DEPUTATION
LED BY MR HUGH SMYTH, HELD AT STORMONT CASTLE ON WEDNESDAY 15 MAY 1974

Present:   Minister of State
           Mr Hugh Smyth
           Mr Stanley Gray
           Mr Tommy West
           Mr Ken Gibson
           Mr James Allan
           Mr Finlayson

**S. OF S. HAS SEEN**

Mr Orme said that he had taken the de-proscription order through the
House of Commons the previous night. Lord Donaldson would be dealing
with the order in the Lords that day and once it was through the
Secretary of State would sign an order de-proscribing Sinn Fein and
the UVF. Seven days later this would take effect. He understood
the anxiety which Mr Smyth and his colleagues had felt about the
delay in proceeding to de-proscription and Mr Carson had spoken to
him of this. However, he hoped that the deputation would be reassured
by the steps which had now been taken. Mr Gibson said that there
were two points concerning them, the first was the men detained and
their position, and the second was that they would like to see elections
in Northern Ireland to enable the UVF to campaign politically.

Mr Orme said on the detention issue the whole matter was under urgent
consideration by the Government. The deputation would be aware of the
consultations which he had had with Mr Gibson and others about the
question of resettlement and they would be pleased to know that plans
for this were going ahead at some speed. However the decision to
release detainees would be the Secretary of State's and the Secretary
of State's alone and it was not possible for him to give any indication
of when releases would take place. The cases which the UVF had raised
with him before had all been examined by both him and the Secretary
of State and the points which the UVF had put about having certain
detainees released because of their political abilities had been noted.

CONFIDENTIAL

/2 ....

*NAUK, CJ4/1919, first page of notes from a meeting between Minister of State
Stan Orme and UVF leaders, 15 May 1974*

Myrtlefield Park, Belfast on 10 May. Orme's intervention suggests the British government wanted to discourage dialogue between republicans and loyalists. Earlier in the year, senior UVF members had held a meeting with IRA leaders Daithí O'Connell and Brian Keenan at a fishing lodge by Lough Sheelin, near Mountnugent, County Cavan – what was discussed is not known, but it may have been both parties' opposition to internment.[29]

Orme remarked that, although he 'knew the UVF were not involved', the current wave of sectarian assassinations put London under great pressure from Catholic sources to take firm action in Protestant areas. He hoped the UVF would be able to use its influence in the Protestant community to try to stop these assassinations and to point out that they would not achieve anything.[30]

The truth was that by 15 May 1974, the UVF had killed twenty-four people since the beginning of the year, eight in May alone.[31] On 2 May UVF members had bombed the Rose and Crown Bar on the Ormeau Road, Belfast, killing five people. A few days later UVF gunmen had killed James and Gertrude Devlin near their home outside Dungannon, County Tyrone.[32] The previous month a UVF leader, Joseph Neill of Portadown, had been killed, apparently by his own bomb. It is inconceivable that the NIO was unaware of UVF involvement in these deaths.

At a separate meeting with UVF spokesman Hugh Smyth, around 15 May, Orme was warned:

> Until the [de-proscription] order comes into effect the UVF continues to be proscribed. The position in law is that if members of the UVF held a public meeting before the de-proscription order came into effect the people taking part would be liable to be arrested on suspicion of the offences which continued in force (whether the

security forces would think it tactically right to make any arrests is another matter).[33]

On the morning of 17 May, James Allan received 'a personal telephone call' from UVF leader Ken Gibson, who said, in relation to the UWC strike against power-sharing, that his people were trying to 'cool it' and they were aware the British would not give in to the strike demands. Allan assured Gibson that he would be available to talk to him at any time 'over the next few days'.[34]

Later that day members of the UVF crossed the Irish border and bombed Dublin and Monaghan, killing thirty-four civilians. The organisation then vigorously denied responsibility. However, the British authorities were well aware of who the culprits were. Colin Wallace, senior information officer in the IPU at HQNI, claimed to have had the names of the ringleaders and others 'within 24–36 hours' – all UVF members, some of them agents of RUC Special Branch and British Military Intelligence.[35] It was later learned that the perpetrators were part of the notorious 'Glenanne Gang'.[36] The UDA's and UWC's press officer, Sammy Smyth, told the media: 'I am very happy about the bombings in Dublin. There is a war with the Free State and now we are laughing at them.'[37]

The UVF statement on the Dublin and Monaghan bombings issued on the day after the attacks, was shameless in its duplicity:

We want to make it quite clear that we are appalled by these explosions. It is indiscriminate and definitely against our policy. At the present time the UVF have made a firm declaration that we will not engage in any physical activities including bombings and shootings. We, at the moment, are engaged in the political field of Northern Ireland and we believe that the political solution to

Northern Ireland can only be found democratically by the people of Northern Ireland within Northern Ireland. Therefore, we are not concerned with the policy of Eire, or, indeed, the dictates of Westminster politicians.[38]

At 10 p.m. on the night of the bombings, the RUC had informed garda headquarters of a telephone call received by the editor of the *Irish News* from a man calling himself 'Captain Craig, Red Hand Brigade', purporting to claim responsibility. A similar call was received by the Belfast office of *The Irish Times*.[39] The Young Militants of the UDA had also claimed responsibility. RUC Sergeant John Weir identified the Red Hand Brigade as one of the pseudonyms used by the group of UVF, RUC and UDR officers operating from James Mitchell's farm at Glenanne, the staging post for many killings, including the bombings.[40]

Following a query to the RUC from Garda Chief Superintendent Larry Wren on 20 June 1974 regarding the 'Young Militants', a rather obscure reply was sent by RUC Assistant Chief Constable (ACC) Johnston on 23 July. Its intention may have been to obfuscate rather than elucidate:

I have had our SB [Special Branch] in all Divisions go diligently into this alleged organisation. In one case only a single source speculated that it could be a cover name for a group of militants within UDA ... As to the claims about the Dublin and Monaghan car bombings, we have no intelligence which would support a connection with this 'organisation'. What we have had, is some low to medium grade pieces, mostly Army, indicative of UFF West Belfast involvement. We have been going into this carefully, nevertheless, and have been able to eliminate most of it. ... We had one character mentioned by you subsequently I think by the name of Marchant. He was our guest for a number of hours (and CID) but with negative result.[41]

Marchant – a member of the UVF – had been interned in May 1974, and was still being detained in February 1975. It is not unreasonable to suggest that had the RUC attributed responsibility to the real culprits, the newly legalised UVF, this would have caused major difficulties for the British government. When interviewed on the RTÉ documentary *Collusion*, broadcast in June 2015, Seán Donlon, former secretary-general of the Irish Department of Foreign Affairs, told the interviewer that the Irish government distrusted any information that originated with the British security forces, which made it all the more questionable that the Irish government, in September 1974, agreed to set up formal structures enabling An Garda Síochána to cooperate fully with its counterparts in Northern Ireland, the RUC, through joint coordinating committees.

Despite the bombings, the secretary of state permitted the de-proscription legislation to come into effect on 23 May, which legalised the UVF. It is difficult to imagine that the de-proscription of the IRA would have been considered in the wake of Bloody Friday or, indeed, at any other time. No consideration appears to have been given to such a move, even at the time of the IRA truce. Though the policy began as a suggestion that Sinn Féin should be de-proscribed, the subsequent official documents and the fact that it went ahead despite the Dublin and Monaghan bombings point far more towards the UVF as the desired de-proscribed organisation.

Around midnight on 22–23 May, another meeting with the UVF took place at Laneside. This meeting, which included Gibson, concerned the UWC strike. Gibson assured James Allan that 'the UVF would continue to lower the temperature and certainly did not advocate violence'.[42]

On 27 May several UVF leaders, including Gibson, met with Allan and MI6's Michael Oatley.[43] They claimed to be having great difficulty in urging moderation on their colleagues in the UWC. They also expressed concern that UVF leaders might be arrested, which could 'undermine their position'.[44] In his notes of the meeting, Allan cautions, 'I believe we should think very carefully before action is taken vis-à-vis UVF politicals – and I should be grateful to have the opportunity to comment on possible arrest lists.'[45] This disturbing statement suggests that any investigation into the Dublin and Monaghan bombings was doomed from the start, if Allan was going to have a veto, or at least an influence, over who might or might not be arrested around that time. The decision that prosecutions would not be proceeded with was made in secret, and no public announcement regarding non-prosecution or amnesty was made.

The UWC succeeded in bringing down the power-sharing Executive on 28 May. Ironically, despite British government pronouncements on the IRA threat to the state, it was loyalists who caused the apparatus of government to fail. A key unanswered question over the decades has been why firmer action was not taken against loyalists during the UWC strike. An examination of the contemporary papers yields some telling answers.

On 23 May a meeting had been held at Stormont Castle to review the security situation. Among those in attendance were the secretary of state; the GOC; the chief constable; Frank Cooper, NIO; Denis Payne, the top MI5 officer in Northern Ireland; James Allan; and other senior NIO officials.[46] The GOC advised that the army 'should maintain its low profile'. He warned that 'any attempt to force the issue [the UWC strike] would provoke an ugly situation'. The chief constable agreed with the GOC's analysis and added that 'a policy of confrontation would only provoke a greater reaction'. He said there had been shots fired at the police 'which indicated the preparedness of the loyalists to use force'.[47]

Merlyn Rees warned that any announcement of possible security talks with the republic would be seen 'as stemming from the Dublin car bombs'. Even though loyalists had blocked all the main arterial roads into Belfast – including the roads leading to Stormont, which made it necessary for the secretary of state and Brian Faulkner to be flown in by helicopter – both the GOC and the chief constable expressed extreme reluctance to remove the barricades. Denis Payne warned of possible sabotage of electricity equipment in the power stations. Despite army and RUC concerns about annoying the loyalists, however, the secretary of state insisted that the GOC and chief constable make contingency plans to keep the arterial roads open. They reluctantly agreed.[48]

An internal memo in the Taoiseach's department stated that the SDLP attributed the unwillingness of the British to confront the loyalist strikers to a difference of opinion between Rees and the secretary of state for defence, Roy Mason; the latter took the line that troops could not be fully committed to confronting loyalists in circumstances in which they might also have to cope with a massive 'do or die' effort by the Provos.[49] This is clearly a reference to the bogus, or deliberately misinterpreted, Myrtlefield Park documents (for more information on these, see later in this chapter).

Also on 23 May, the British ambassador in Dublin sent a telegram to the FCO, expressing concern that British and Irish media criticism of the perceived lack of response by the RUC and army to the thuggery of the UWC strikers could influence the Irish government. Media reports, he complained, gave the impression of inactivity on the part of the security forces. There was no appreciation by the southern media, he went on, of the difficulties faced by the army or the constant judgement that had to be exercised to avoid a serious escalation in violence. The media's calls for tough action 'are those of the most ill-informed of armchair critics':

> My particular concern is that if they [Irish government] continue to believe that the Army is in effect standing idly by, their attitude towards security co-operation generally may become less forthcoming. In the wake of last week's car bombs the auguries for co-operation were good … But I fear that the position could quickly become eroded if we allow misleading impressions about the Army's role in the face of the strike and our alleged reluctance to tackle hardline Protestants, because they are Protestants, to go uncorrected.[50]

The UVF's final May meeting with government officials was held on 29 May, the day after the Executive fell. At this meeting the loyalists adopted a very conciliatory tone – they contemplated launching a new political party, expressed an interest in dialogue with the IRA, called for the repatriation of political prisoners from Britain, including the Price sisters, and claimed to have been in favour of calling off the strike.[51]

It is interesting to note that there is no reference to the Dublin and Monaghan bombings included in the minutes of any of these meetings between the UVF and senior British officials during the latter half of May 1974. Either the bombings were not mentioned at all, or, if they were, such a reference was deliberately omitted from the record. Either way, it is shocking that the greatest death toll in any single day in the conflict was not reflected in the decision to continue meeting those responsible, nor in questions or criticism of them during the meetings.

In an official memo of a meeting on 30 May – sent to the secretary of state, Lord Donaldson, Denis Payne and others – A. Huckle, private secretary, noted that the chief constable reported that there had been twenty arrests (seven PIRA and thirteen 'Protestants') for terrorist offences but 'the general level of violence had been very low.'[52]

Although the chief constable was clearly aware of the Dublin and Monaghan bombings, with the loss of thirty-four lives and the wounding of more than 250 people, he was content to refer to a low level of violence. It seemed to be of little concern to him if violence, although originating in Northern Ireland, occurred outside his jurisdiction. Huckle reported that the secretary of state suggested that 'the present calm was a good time to have an overall look at policy towards Protestant paramilitary organisations, both from the security and political point of view' and requested the GOC to prepare a discussion paper.

With the end of the strike, Rees accepted advice from both the GOC and chief constable that a proposed parade and rally at Stormont on the following Saturday afternoon, 1 June, should be authorised, and flags should be hoisted from Parliament buildings. The parade and rally were organised to celebrate the downfall of the Executive and the victory of the strikers.[53] It might strike people as rather odd that the top army and police officers, as well as a British government minister with responsibility for Northern Ireland affairs, were prepared to acquiesce in celebrating the defeat of their regional government by a loyalist strike, particularly when one considers that this had been the first serious attempt since 1922 to allow any nationalist participation in government in Northern Ireland.

***

On the eve of the UWC strike, events had taken place in an unremarkable house in south Belfast that had benefited the loyalist paramilitaries by shifting the focus away from their violence and putting it firmly back on the IRA. In the upmarket Malone Road area, the IRA had leased the ground floor of 64 Myrtlefield Park, which they were using as a depot and a headquarters meeting place for the Belfast IRA. A large number of arms were stored there, while Cordtex, detonators and timers were stowed in the adjoining garage.[54] The seizure of these arms and the sensational publicising of documents discovered during the RUC raid on the house illustrate, again, the role of propaganda in the conflict.

The seizure of the documents came about as follows. Brendan Hughes, officer commanding the IRA's Belfast Brigade, had been 'on the run' since he escaped from internment in Long Kesh in December 1973. By May 1974 he had adopted the disguise of a toy salesman, leaving home each morning as if going to work. He had toys in his car and a mock roster of shops on which he purportedly intended calling.

On Friday 10 May, just days before the de-proscription of the UVF and Sinn Féin, and exactly one week before the Dublin and Monaghan bombings, while Brendan Hughes and another IRA member were present, the RUC raided the apartment at 64 Myrtlefield Park, backed up by the army (the premises had been under surveillance for some time as a result of information provided by an informant). Hughes and his colleague were arrested. As well as the weapons and other *matériel*, plans for the protection of Catholic areas were seized. An RUC press statement described these documents as 'the most important seizure ever in Ulster'.

Shortly afterwards, Colin Wallace and his colleagues in the IPU at HQNI were told that IRA plans to burn loyalist areas of Belfast to the ground had been found in the house, but they were not shown any of the original supporting documents.[55] They were given copies of maps found during the raid and were asked to prepare visual materials, projections and transparencies for a press conference at Stormont Castle. Wallace says that the IPU controlled all the army's printing facilities and visual aids for briefings, so there was nothing unusual in that request.[56]

What Wallace did find surprising, however, was the lack of supporting documents. When he and his colleagues were preparing the maps for the press conference, he found that they were actually copies of those found in Long Kesh a year earlier. He had been aware, at that stage, that the maps represented a contingency plan for the defence of nationalist areas, should an August 1969-type situation recur in the future.[57]

Three days later, the British prime minister, Harold Wilson, employing singularly sensational rhetoric, announced the discovery to the House of Commons. He described the documents as evidence of an offensive plan by the IRA 'to foment inter-sectarian hatred and a degree of chaos'. He anticipated that the IRA would 'launch a propaganda counter-offensive' and stressed that the publication of the documents should be as complete as possible.[58]

Hearings by the ECHR in Ireland v UK had commenced in Stavanger, Norway, on 2 May; James Wellbeloved, Labour MP for Erith and Crayford, asked the prime minister if he was considering making the documents available to the commission. Harold Wilson agreed that this was being considered.[59]

The IPU reported that the prime minister's statement was 'a major propaganda defeat for the IRA'. The author of the report noted that the IPU had undertaken assiduous background briefing of lobby correspondents and 'succeeded in dispelling any scepticism that they might have had about the reality of the "scorched earth" policy'.[60]

However, a number of newspapers did express scepticism. *The Guardian* stated that the documents released to the press were 'somewhat ambiguous and scrappy and the IRA may well be able to claim its plans were defensive rather than offensive'.[61] Even *The Daily Telegraph* agreed that the documents 'did not substantiate all the claims made against the Provisionals'.[62]

*The Irish Times* speculated that the British reaction could be 'put down to anxiety to win Dublin's co-operation on security', but dismissed it as unlikely as 'the Republic's Ministers have said they would do everything constitutionally possible to co-operate with the forces in Northern Ireland'. Alternatively, the British government could 'use the evidence to support its case before the ECHR'.[63]

*The Irish Press*, it appeared, hit the nail on the head when it reported: 'There must be some suspicion when intelligence like this, normally treated as top secret security information, is used in a high-powered propaganda campaign.'[64]

The documents were presented to the Taoiseach Liam Cosgrave on 13 May, in rather dramatic circumstances, at the end of a meeting between Merlyn Rees and Dr Garret FitzGerald.[65]

The IPU prepared a propagandist broadsheet as it had done after the IRA bombings on Bloody Friday and at Claudy. A handwritten annotation on a draft of the pamphlet noted: 'Agreed version but suggested that, if possible, an additional comment should be inserted to answer suggestion that this is to deal with a Doomsday and not a current situation.'[66] This note reinforces the suspicion that the claims made about the documents did not stand up to scrutiny.

The British were indeed anxious to present the documents to the ECHR, and correspondence was quickly in train between the NIO and the attorney-general. However, Paul Fifoot, a legal counsellor at the FCO, poured cold water over the plan. He pointed out that the documents failed to support the claims made by the prime minister in the House of Commons. It seems he, too, understood the documents to represent a contingency plan in the event of a civil-war situation.[67] Interestingly, Mr Fifoot was the leading counsel for the British government at the Stavanger hearings.

The prime minister's House of Commons statement was tele-graphed to British embassies abroad for propaganda purposes.[68] The man who drafted the text for distribution to embassies around the world was Gary Hicks, political correspondent. Hicks has been de-scribed as 'a former political reporter who later "spun" for global cor-porations and the UK government, travelling worldwide with prime ministers from Harold Wilson to Margaret Thatcher'.[69]

A letter from Dennis Trevelyan, a senior NIO official, to Lord Tom Bridges, 10 Downing Street, regarding the recovered documents is very revealing. He advised Lord Bridges that the NIO was considering whether to provide a 'covering note' when making copies of the papers for both Houses of Parliament. He explained that 'this would be a *gloss* on the paper explaining the significance of the papers and the maps'.[70]

Author and journalist Robert Fisk has suggested that it was these documents that led to the bombing of Dublin and Monaghan.[71] He wrote that, having made enquiries in Portadown during the

UWC strike, he was told that the UVF there had paid considerable attention to a House of Commons statement by Prime Minister Harold Wilson:

> [A] map had been produced by the jubilant security forces in Belfast which showed the position of the IRA car bombs in Protestant streets. This, so the theory went, was how the IRA intended to provoke a civil war: by the wholesale slaughter of innocent men and women. In Portadown details of this plan had been studied with care and, so it was being put about in UVF circles, the IRA's tactics had been industriously employed by the loyalists south of the border.[72]

This account was written soon after the bombings occurred. Now that so much more information has emerged, it seems highly unlikely that such an ambitious project could have been planned and put into operation within three to four days. It would probably have been many months in preparation. Fisk was correct, however, in stating that the operation originated with the mid-Ulster UVF in Portadown.

From a British government standpoint, the Myrtlefield documents, despite their obvious shortcomings, served a number of useful purposes. Above all, they deflected the focus away from loyalist paramilitaries who were preparing for an all-out strike against the Stormont Executive and threatening serious violence. Some of them were also preparing to bomb Dublin and Monaghan.

A briefing for a meeting of the Cabinet Official Committee on Northern Ireland a year later, on 7 July 1975, noted ruefully that 'insufficient attention' was paid at the time to the advance intelligence received on the organisation and intentions of the UWC, and that 'the strike co-ordinating committee did not flinch from contemplating more drastic action, including the destruction of power stations and industrial plant and armed attacks on Catholic enclaves'.[73] Instead, because of the Myrtlefield documents, at a time of extreme crisis provoked by loyalists, all attention shifted to the IRA. The documents might also have been considered useful at the time for increasing pressure on the Irish government to set a date for formal discussions on cross-border security (for which the British had been pressing for some time).

Although these documents were not presented to the ECHR, they were used globally for propaganda purposes. They served to increase fear and paranoia among loyalist paramilitaries and ensured the continuation of their campaign. Also, as was noted above, at his 15 May meeting with UVF leaders, Stan Orme used them to discourage dialogue between the UVF and the IRA.

***

A significant meeting was held on 7 August 1974 between Secretary of State Merlyn Rees, Permanent Under-Secretary Stan Orme, Frank Cooper,[74] James Allan, and other senior NIO officials, and members of the various loyalist organisations who had come together at the end of 1973 to form the UWC.[75] These included the UDA's Glen Barr, Sammy Smyth and Andy Tyrie; the UVF's Ken Gibson and Andy McCann (McCann was also RHC – a proscribed organisation at that time); Colonel Edward Brush and Bill Hannigan of DOW; several members of the UWC; George Green, head of the USCA and former B Special, with other members of his organisation, and members of the Ulster Service Corps.[76]

The loyalists had sought the meeting to discuss their new policy document, which focused on the demand for the formation of a

'Third Force'. They envisaged total control of security by 'Ulstermen' – a three-tier structure including the RUC and RUCR, the UDR comprising two full-time battalions and part-timers, and a Home Guard, 'all officered by Ulstermen'.[77] The Home Guard would be similar to the former B Specials.

The campaign for a third force had been launched during speeches on 12 July, most notably by John Taylor, MP.[78] Sammy Smyth told the secretary of state at the August meeting that 'loyalists had been forced to take up arms at Westminster's failure to combat terrorism effectively'.[79] This is the man who, three months earlier, had proclaimed that he was laughing at the bombs exploding in Dublin and Monaghan.

On 2 September, within a month of the meeting, perhaps not coincidentally, Merlyn Rees announced the expansion of the RUC, the RUCR and the UDR. The RUC was to be expanded from 4,500 to 6,000 members, while the RUCR was to be doubled from 2,000 to 4,000. New local 'police centres' were to be established which would be run by the reservists working in their home areas. These would be trained in the use of firearms.[80]

The Irish government and the SDLP, which had not been consulted, were not at all happy with the proposals, but unionists and loyalists were said to have given them 'a guarded welcome'.[81] No figure was provided for the proposed increase in the UDR, but recruitment was to be stepped up. Two full-time battalions of the UDR, as demanded by the loyalist leadership at the August meeting, were formed less than eighteen months later, in January 1976. In response to a query regarding UDR full-time battalions in December 1975, NIO official T. C. Barker replied as follows:

I will now turn to the possibility of creating a full time element within the UDR. This was not mooted during the initial debate in House of Commons on the formation of the UDR in 1969. It was, however, raised in the House on a number of occasions between 1971 and 1973, and the whole question was argued in detail in a paper produced by the Ministry of Defence in 1974. This study was undertaken as a result of suggestions made by UWC representatives during their meeting with the Secretary of State in August 1974, i.e. that 2 full-time UDR Battalions be established.[82]

It is notable that the mutual interests of the British government and loyalist paramilitaries appeared to converge on the issue of locally recruited security forces at this time, particularly regarding the UDR, a regiment that, as the government knew, was heavily infiltrated by loyalist paramilitaries.

Unionists and loyalists secured most of what they had sought, with the exception of a Home Guard. Another demand of theirs, that the standard of educational qualifications for entry into the RUCR should be lowered, was granted.

*The Irish Times* reported late in September 1974 that several loyalist paramilitary organisations had launched a concerted campaign to encourage their members to join the expanded RUCR. It was noted that when Merlyn Rees had announced his plans earlier in the month he had made it clear that the only applicants who would meet with 'a blanket refusal' were suspected members of proscribed organisations.[83] If that was the case, members of the UVF and UDA would be eligible for consideration, as both organisations were legal at the time.

On 19 December NIO officials held a further meeting with members of the UWC strike coordinating committee, at which the UWC committee complained that the RUC was not recruiting enough people into the RUCR and that there was discrimination against loyalists, former B Specials and former detainees.[84]

Three major points emerge from the events outlined in this chapter. The first is that the British government was never prepared to take on unionists or loyalists, as was clearly demonstrated during the UWC strike. Secondly, loyalists were learning that violence and intimidation paid off. Extraordinarily, all loyalist organisations were now legal – the RHC and the UFF being mere fig leaves for the UVF and the UDA respectively. And finally, it is clear that propaganda continued to play a very important role in Britain's war with the IRA.

# 6

# THE NEW IRA CEASEFIRE AND
# THE LOYALIST BACKLASH

> Waves of sectarian assassinations seem to start from the Protestant
> side … once unleashed, the Protestant backlash continues for a fair
> time until the immediate frustration has ceased.
>
> *Frank Cooper, permanent under-secretary*[1]

The new year of 1975 began with an IRA ceasefire and a welcome
respite from the relentless death toll. There were no killings in that
first week of January, something that hadn't occurred since 1971.
Weeks earlier, in the small village of Feakle, County Clare, a group
of eight Protestant clergymen sat down with leading members of
the IRA and Sinn Féin, in an attempt to find a solution to the
conflict. The Irish government, whose policy was that there should
be no negotiation with the IRA, made a huge miscalculation in
sending in a large force of garda and army on the very first day to
raid the hotel where the talks, which were to continue over several
days, were being held. That the talks were being held at all was quite
remarkable in view of the fact that the IRA had carried out bombings
in Birmingham, killing twenty-one people, just weeks earlier.

Notwithstanding the disruption of the Feakle process, the ceasefire, which had broken down on 17 January, was renewed on 9 February after a direct meeting between members of Sinn Féin and NIO
officials James Allan and Michael Oatley.[2] These meetings continued over many months.[3] Seven 'Incident Centres' were established

in nationalist areas across Northern Ireland to monitor the ceasefire
and the response of the security forces. The centres were staffed by
members of Sinn Féin, who liaised with government officials at the
NIO.[4]

Peter Taylor claims that loyalists, not surprisingly, were bitterly
opposed to the Incident Centres, regarding them as a capitulation to
the IRA.[5] Immediately after the truce came back into effect, loyalists
killed five Catholics in a series of gun and bomb attacks – three in
Belfast and two in a pub near Pomeroy, County Tyrone.[6] This trend
continued throughout 1975, resulting in the greatest number of
deaths caused by loyalists in any year of the conflict.

Besides meeting with Sinn Féin in January, NIO officials at
Laneside also began a series of encounters with the UDA, as well
as less numerous meetings with the UVF. One of the purposes of
these gatherings was to soothe loyalist sensitivities regarding fears
of a deal with the IRA, particularly on the possibility of a British
withdrawal. At one of the early meetings, on 20 January, the UDA
expressed concern at possible underhand dealings by the government with republicans and sought the release of detained loyalists.[7]
David Payne and Andy Tyrie insisted that it would be impossible
to give absolute assurances that no member of the UDA would, in
all situations, be involved in retaliating against the IRA. (Payne had
been arrested and charged in December 1972 for the possession of
weapons, including stolen UDR weapons, and a large quantity of
ammunition. He was also one of the chief suspects in the murders
of Senator Paddy Wilson and Irene Andrews.)

James Allan said he had repeated *ad nauseam* that 'the rump of
loyalists were very bad men' and that some distinction should be
made between those picked up before and after 'the recent rash of
sectarian murders'.[8] Twenty-one killings, almost all of them sectarian,

had been carried out by loyalists since the beginning of November 1974.[9] On the day before that early meeting – Sunday 19 January – Frank Cooper of the NIO met with the Loyalist Coordinating Committee (LCC), which included Glen Barr of the UDA, Ken Gibson of the UVF and John McKeague of the UVF–RHC.[10] The LCC, too, expressed concern about 'negotiations' with the IRA.

Donal O'Sullivan, the Irish ambassador to Britain, reported to Seán Donlon, assistant secretary (later secretary-general), Department of Foreign Affairs, on the loyalist meeting with Frank Cooper. The ambassador had, presumably, been briefed on the meeting by the deputy secretary at the NIO, Douglas Janes, who had replaced Philip Woodfield. O'Sullivan advised Donlon that the loyalists had made it clear to Cooper that a return to violence by them could be expected 'if unreasonable concessions were made to the IRA or if there were to be any question of negotiations'. Janes had told O'Sullivan that the situation with the loyalists 'was very delicate indeed'.[11]

On 6 February, in a one-to-one meeting between UDA leader Andy Tyrie and James Allan, Tyrie expressed concern about the UDA's name 'being besmirched' by the murder of Ann Ogilby, a young woman who had been brutally beaten to death by loyalist women in a Sandy Row UDA club in July 1974.[12] Reporting on the meeting afterwards, Allan wrote that 'Libyan matters were still worrying the UDA … and could someone advise them on Libya's long term aims'. This was a reference to a visit by UDA leaders to Libya the previous November. Libya's Colonel Gaddafi had invited them to talks, believing the UWC strike had been an anti-imperialist uprising against Britain. UDA leaders were being castigated by their own people, however, for making the visit.[13]

At separate meetings with British officials on 11 February, both the UVF and the UDA denied responsibility for recent sectarian murders.[14] Allan wrote to a colleague that Tyrie and Payne 'apparently genuinely said that they were horrified by the recent murders'.[15] The truth was that both organisations were responsible – the UVF had killed three people the previous day and the UDA was responsible for the deaths of three more (two of them eighteen-year-old students), between 29 January and 9 February.[16] Given the level of security-force infiltration of both organisations, it would be absurd to suggest that the authorities were not aware of this. It also needs to be highlighted that the UDA and the UVF were, by and large, the only loyalist organisations engaged in violence. It is difficult to accept that Allan would have believed Tyrie's and Payne's denials.

At a meeting between the NIO and the UDA on 13 February, Allan returned to the issue of responsibility for the recent spate of sectarian murders. Once again, Payne was present, and both he and Tyrie assured Allan that the UDA had certainly not authorised them and had no idea who was responsible.[17]

Payne raised the continued detention of John White, whose case was due to be reviewed shortly. He said White was being kept in detention only because the secretary of state had told the SDLP that he had in prison the person responsible for the murders of Senator Paddy Wilson and Irene Andrews. The minute-taker noted that Payne 'hovered in a rather crazy way by Mr Allan declaring that even he, Davy, had been accused of this murder'.[18] Payne, along with John White, was suspected by the authorities, at the highest level, of being responsible for these killings. In a July 1973 letter, GOC Sir Frank King, HQNI, reported to Sir Michael Carver, MoD, that White and Payne had been captured the previous weekend. He described them as leading members of the UFF and claimed they 'were almost certainly responsible for the murders of Senator Paddy Wilson and the girl [sic] Andrews'.[19]

Despite this high level of suspicion, Allan does not appear to have had any misgivings about meeting with Payne.

On 27 February, at a meeting in Stormont Castle that lasted two-and-a-half hours, the leadership of the UDA (Tyrie, Barr, Payne, Sammy McCormick, Hugh McVeigh and John Orchin) expressed concern about the setting up of the Sinn Féin Incident Centres in response to the IRA ceasefire. The meeting had been arranged following a discussion the previous evening between James Allan and a UDA delegation which threatened that their organisation would declare certain areas to be 'no-go' to police. They had heard reports that Sinn Féin was using the Incident Centres as a basis for unofficial policing activities in republican areas. They also resented a government proposal to restrict the availability of firearms and wanted assurances that RUC policing would be enforced in republican areas. PUS Frank Cooper replied that such assurances could certainly be given and there could be 'only one police force in the province'.[20]

Cooper advised the UDA delegation that they would hear from the chief constable himself about what the police intended doing. At the conclusion of the meeting, the UDA delegation was advised to 'go forthwith' to discuss their policing concerns with police and army representatives at RUC headquarters, and it was agreed that the NIO would issue a strong statement dissociating Sinn Féin Incident Centres from party claims about policing and the control of republican areas. When the delegation arrived at RUC headquarters, the chief constable was not available, but the UDA leaders agreed to meet with Senior Deputy Chief Constable Kenneth Newman (later to get the top job).[21]

Following that meeting, the UDA began policing 'their own areas' in March 1975. RUC headquarters kept the permanent under-secretary informed of UDA activities on a daily basis. The 'low profile of the UDA' was emphasised in each day's report. There were details of patrolling in many areas – in Donegall Street and Tennent Street in Belfast, among others.[22] On one occasion, in Glengormley, Newtownabbey, police were operating a vehicle checkpoint (VCP) on the Ballyclare Road when six UDA men in uniform approached. According to the police, one of the UDA men held the rank of lieutenant.[23] They were joined by another four, and all ten stood 'supervising the police VCP'. In Larne, it was reported that some of the patrolling UDA men wore masks, while in Lisburn they sported red berets.[24]

Clearly, the security forces were unperturbed by the UDA's actions, despite the uniforms, masks and berets, and the incongruity of UDA members 'supervising a police VCP' apparently did not disconcert them. It is possible that the policy of permitting the UDA to police 'their own areas' was a sop to the organisation because of its concerns around the Sinn Féin Incident Centres. Their good working relations continued despite British authorities' knowledge of the UDA's involvement in sectarian killings.

On 10 March a clandestine meeting was held between Allan and Tyrie. Allan's notes on the meeting record that Tyrie was accompanied only by his bodyguard, because he wanted a private chat. Allan remarked:

> Since action on a number of matters he raised could be useful in keeping the UDA on the right track, I am addressing this minute to you [permanent under-secretary] and copying to those who might be able to steer the machine in the right direction.[25]

One wonders what 'the right direction' might be.

Allan held a further covert meeting with Tyrie and his bodyguard on 21 March. Tyrie expressed concern for his personal safety and hoped the NIO would assist him in procuring a firearms certificate. If not, Tyrie threatened, he might 'have to make provision outside the law'. Allan's response was that he would prefer not to know about that idea.[26]

With regard to the upcoming election, Tyrie said the UDA required a research assistant and the leadership was extremely keen to employ David Burnside, even though the Vanguard Party had the first option on his services; Burnside would require £3,500 and the UDA hadn't got that sort of money.[27] Tyrie enquired if the British government could help in some way. Allan reported that he pressed Tyrie very hard about UDA involvement in sectarian violence. Tyrie replied that 'other organisations' took the lead on this, but he could not entirely rule out the possibility that people connected with the UDA had also been involved in one or two instances.[28]

In a follow-up memo dated 24 March 1975 (the recipient's name has been redacted) Allan reported on Tyrie's concerns for his personal security and request for help in procuring a firearms certificate.[29] Allan said he had suggested it was 'just possible' that his bodyguard might be able to obtain one, if he was not a member of an extremist organisation. Tyrie had assured him that the man in question was not on the brigade staff of the UDA (hardly confirmation that he was not a UDA member).

Later, Tyrie rang Allan, who suggested that the bodyguard should apply immediately for the weapons certificate, indicating he (Allan) would find out to which police station Tyrie should apply. While he appreciated that the British government's policy was opposed to the proliferation of weapons, he believed this was 'a useful precedent in the context of other very delicate matters of which you [the

NOTE OF A MEETING BETWEEN MR ANDY TYRIE AND MR ALLAN AT LANESIDE
AT 18.30 HRS ON FRIDAY 21 MARCH

1.   Mr Tyrie came to Laneside for a private chat.   He was accompanied
by Mr James Creighton, his travelling companion.   Mr Tyrie made the
following points.

   a.   Personal security

   He was very concerned about his own safety.   He hoped that the
   Northern Ireland Office could help him (or as I suggested in
   preference Mr Creighton) to get a firearms certificate.   If not
   frankly he might have to make provision outside the law.   I said
   I would prefer not to know of this latter idea.

   b.   Constitutional Convention

   I indicated that an early announcement on the elections for the
   Conventions was likely.   In this connection, I emphasised
   once again the need for the UDA to make their views known
   whether it be through elected representatives or by other
   means.   Mr Tyrie was despondent about the possibility of the
   UUUC providing any real vehicle for the UDA's views to be made
   known.   He believed that the real problem was to have them
   properly articulated.   This required a research assistant
   and they were extremely keen to employ Mr David Burnside even thou
   the VUP had the first option on his services.   They would
   probably have to pay as much as £3½ thousand per annum  and they
   had not got that sort of money.   Could not the British Government
   help in some way?

   c.   Young Offenders

   Mr Tyrie was agreeable to seeing officials at the Northern
   Ireland Office once again but he questioned how useful such visits
   were unless he had access to his own people in H M Prison
   The Maze./  He foresaw great difficulty about the young offenders
   because although he had progressive views he was hearing from
   The Maze that a number of special category were digging their
   heels in;  they did not want to be divided up from their colleagues
   There would be an important selling job and any question of
   young offenders being segregated in cellular accommodation could
   raise great difficulties.   The Loyalists were on the whole much
   more compliant than the Republicans but they would fight very
   hard to retain special category except for the periods of work.
   So far as this was concerned the Northern Ireland Office might
   not be aware that a number of prisoners were making a good deal
   of money by private handicraft.   Indeed, he had heard of one
   man who was making £40 per week by making leather wallets.
   In connection with all this I attach a note which has been smuggled
   out of The Maze.   THIS SHOULD NOT BE DISTRIBUTED FURTHER SINCE
   WE HAVE HAD STRICTURES FROM MR PARKES ABOUT INFORMATION OBTAINED
   BY LANESIDE FROM H M PRISONS.

Could he now be
given a guarantee
that he would
be given such a
visit?

/ d.

CONFIDENTIAL

*NAUK, CJ4/3734, note of a meeting between James Allan and Andy Tyrie at
Laneside, 21 March 1975*

recipient] are aware'.[30] It would be extremely interesting to learn what these delicate matters were.

This memo reinforces the view that British officials were ambiguous about the arming of the UDA.

On 23 May Tyrie and John Orchin met with Allan. They provided assurances that the UDA was not responsible for recent sectarian assassinations and suggested that the UVF in Tiger's Bay was the likely culprit for recent killings in north Belfast.[31] However, while the UDA leadership was denying UDA involvement, a declassified document providing statistics on those charged with terrorist-type offences noted that 26 per cent of those charged between January and September 1975 'had UDA traces, according to Special Branch'.[32]

At the meeting there was also what is described in the minutes as 'some ribald discussion of Mr McKeague's proclivities'.[33] This may be a reference to John McKeague's claimed paedophilia – hardly a laughing matter for his victims. Chris Moore claims that McKeague 'was known to police as someone with a sexual appetite for young boys'.[34] Moore also said that McKeague was an informant for British Army Intelligence.[35]

The British were not alone in meeting with loyalists. An Irish government official, John McColgan, a counsellor in the Department of Foreign Affairs, held many meetings with people from various backgrounds in Northern Ireland, including UDA and UVF leaders. On 15 January McColgan met with UVF leader Ken Gibson. He noted he was meeting Gibson for the fourth time. Gibson warned him that the mood in the Protestant community, if the ceasefire were to break down, would be 'uncontrollably explosive'.[36]

On 21 May McColgan met with the UDA's Andy Tyrie, Glen Barr and Herbie McMorrow (Barr's assistant) in the Conway Hotel, Dunmurry, Belfast. The official noted that it had been eight months since his previous meeting with Tyrie and described him as looking 'slightly more seedy and down-at-heel'. Tyrie told McColgan he was suspicious that the IRA would resume its campaign in due course. Tyrie believed the British 'were only looking for an excuse to get out'. McColgan reported that at no time did Tyrie refer to the sectarian assassinations or the feud that was currently going on between the UDA and the UVF.[37] McColgan's assessment of Tyrie was that he was a man of considerable political awareness and shrewdness, and that he was personally involved in ordering sectarian killings. He did, however, add that Tyrie did 'seem to see the ultimate futility of such activity'.[38]

On 22 July McColgan met with John McKeague, commander of the RHC, which had come under the control of the UVF in 1973. McColgan said McKeague was regarded as one of the nastiest people in Belfast and referred to indications from 'reliable journalistic sources' that he was involved in some of the most gruesome 'romper room' sectarian killings.[39] McColgan noted that McKeague expressed a 'totally fundamentalist approach to life' and found it difficult to convey 'just how perfectly he fits into the stereotype of the mindless Protestant gunman'. McKeague boasted to McColgan of their 'sophisticated and accurate' intelligence-gathering.[40]

On the same day, McColgan met again with Glen Barr, who told him that the UVF was causing extreme difficulties and 'had become enamoured of sectarian violence'. He claimed that the UDA was 'genuinely' not engaging in 'much shooting at present' and that Andy Tyrie was happy that his units were under control.[41] The statistics show that there was some truth in this claim, as the vast majority of sectarian murders during 1975 were carried out by the UVF. According to McKittrick *et al.*, the UDA killed twenty people, while the UVF was responsible for 105 deaths.[42] The figures also suggest that the UDA was able to turn its campaign of violence on and off as it saw fit, and that Tyrie was in a position to impose control.

The British authorities' willingness to tolerate UDA illegality is again highlighted by a bizarre episode that occurred in the spring of 1975. After two UDA men (Hugh McVeigh and David Douglas) disappeared on 7 April, the UDA jumped to the conclusion that they had been abducted by the IRA. Three weeks later, the UDA announced it intended to kidnap about twenty Catholics and hold them hostage until the two UDA men were safely returned. A leading member of the SDLP, John Hume, who first revealed the kidnap plot in a *Sunday Press* article on 27 April, said the UDA's admission made clear 'beyond any shadow of a doubt, the nature of the organisation'.[43]

BBC Radio Ulster reported on 30 April that the UDA had confirmed its intention to kidnap Catholics, but it denied claims that the plan was to kill them at a rate of one per day until the missing men were returned. The UDA, however, dropped the kidnap plan when it realised that the UVF had abducted the two men as part of the loyalist feud.

In an internal NIO memo, headed 'UDA kidnap plot', Douglas Janes gave his view of this affair. Referring to Hume's role in revealing the plan, Janes suggested that he wanted to use the episode as a stick with which to beat the United Ulster Unionist Council (UUUC) for its links to the UDA, contending that the plan was dropped after the intervention of 'a prominent Protestant clergyman'.[44] He also referred to a *Belfast Telegraph* article the previous evening, which said that Tyrie told the newspaper's reporter it was twenty republicans, not ordinary Catholics, who were to be kidnapped, and it was the

UDA's plan to kill off a hostage a day. Janes doubted that the UDA statement 'revealed a criminal offence'.[45]

Janes advised that, in the wake of this episode, the NIO should deal with the Irish ambassador as follows: suggest that Hume's statement had been very irresponsible; explain that successive efforts had been made at the time to defuse an extremely dangerous situation; offer the view that the UDA had, in the event, acted with moderation; note that further speculation, especially in public, might be likely to arouse tensions and passions which could do much damage; suggest the Irish government think carefully about its intentions in this context; and stress that the NIO believed the UDA had no firm plan worth the name – its admission showed naivety which added credibility to its denial that it intended any killings (it's unclear what denial he is talking about).[46] The NIO's attitude to the UDA in the context of a plan to kidnap Catholics and possibly kill them was unprincipled. John Hume was blamed for his 'irresponsibility', while the UDA was portrayed as 'naïve' and it was even suggested it acted with 'moderation'.[47]

By the spring of 1975 the British authorities were beginning to feel pressure from a variety of sources on their response to loyalist sectarian killings of Catholics and the perceived failure of the security forces to investigate. Peter Taylor notes that the killings continued with growing intensity throughout the period of the IRA ceasefire, making it increasingly difficult for the IRA not to respond. He claims that one of the tactical purposes of the loyalist campaign was to push the IRA into breaking the ceasefire.[48]

On 9 April Cardinal Conway met Minister of State Roland Moyle. He admonished Moyle, saying it was 'intolerable that the Secretary of State should permit the UVF to remain a legal organisation while they were giving press conferences in the Shankill "at which they openly boast of killing Catholics'".[49] He suggested that talk by ministers of 'gang warfare and internecine killings dodged the issue and did not explain all the murders'.[50]

Cardinal Conway had in his possession a list of killings carried out by loyalists since May 1972. The source of this list is unknown, but it was possibly compiled by Fathers Denis Faul and Raymond Murray. The RUC had also compiled a list, which was passed to the cardinal by James Allan. Conway queried some omissions on the RUC list. In what appears to have been a bid to manipulate the statistics, the RUC had excluded killings carried out during a robbery or done in the 'heat of the moment'.[51] The RUC also claimed that there had been no sectarian murders before May 1972, which was, of course, untrue. The force continued to deny the truth about the fifteen people killed in McGurk's Bar and others killed by loyalists in 1971, while at least five Catholics were killed in sectarian attacks before May 1972, none of which took place during a robbery or 'in the heat of the moment'.[52]

On 16 May, further to the cardinal's meeting with Roland Moyle, NIO civil servant Bill Webster sent a memo to Moyle advising him against writing to the cardinal and explaining that the cardinal's view was that the NIO was minimising the significance of Protestant attacks on Catholics.[53] Webster believed the cardinal had 'a closed mind' and explained that Allan had been in touch with Conway regularly to discuss the situation orally – but they had always taken the view that it would not be in British interests to put anything down on paper. Allan agreed with Webster that it 'would be inadvisable to provide further ammunition to the cardinal' against themselves.[54]

Allan had sent a memo to Webster on 14 May on the 'problem of sectarian murders', which he viewed as mainly being directed at

Catholics. If these were allowed to continue, he stated, they would prejudice the possibility of a peaceful settlement and lead to the increasing alienation of the Catholic population.[55] He worried about international pressure, citing the current 'sensitivity of the government in Dublin and the Vatican'. Allan continued that 'the Catholic population', and indeed some Protestants, believed there must be 'some "Mr Big" directing Protestant murder gangs, particularly before elections'. He claimed they were very short of intelligence on exactly which organisation was behind those who were perpetrating the killings and ended by asking, 'Is it too fanciful to suggest that some loyalist politicians know more about this subject than they will say publicly?'[56]

Fearing for their international reputation, the British were reluctant to reveal the true statistics to the cardinal. There was a protocol in place to differentiate between sectarian and other murders. The Irish government was already seeking a sectarian analysis of the figures for the total number of house searches for arms, ammunition and explosive materials in a given period between Catholic and Protestant houses. John Hickman, second-in-command to the British ambassador in Dublin, wrote to Bill Harding, FCO, warning that such figures should not be made available to the Irish government even in confidence, 'because of the risk of their being quoted against us later, e.g. in proceedings at Strasbourg'.[57] An unnamed NIO official, in a briefing paper to Hickman in preparation for a meeting with Irish Minister for Foreign Affairs Garret FitzGerald, advised:

> Since the Irish have got hold of the figure of 350 [sectarian] murders
> (perhaps from Cardinal Conway or one of his associates) we may be
> forced to reveal the figure of 346. If that is so, use may be made of

the 56 cases already cleared and our hopes that the present increase in detection rates will reduce the number outstanding before too long. Beyond that we will probably not wish to go. If and when this material is used, I suggest that it should be given to the Irish ambassador in London for the Taoiseach rather than to the DFA [Department of Foreign Affairs].[58]

The briefing paper also provided some detail on those killed. It was noted that more Catholics than Protestants were victims of assassinations and that, as of 12 May 1975, 120 Protestants and 222 Catholics had been victims. (A column described as 'Other' contained four, giving the overall total of 346.)[59] As for the fifty-six murders described as 'already cleared', murder convictions had been obtained only in eighteen cases, and in a further five cases there were convictions for manslaughter; eighteen cases were still awaiting trial; there had been acquittals in three cases; and in the remaining twelve, charges had either been withdrawn or not proceeded with.[60]

When Secretary of State Merlyn Rees met with Minister Fitz-Gerald, he claimed that the internal organisation and method of operation of the 'Protestant paramilitary organisations differed significantly from that of the PIRA with its clearly articulated command structures.' He said that 'ICOing' (interning) the paramilitary leaders would not halt sectarian murders by 'individual Protestant travelling gunmen'.[61]

An internal NIO paper noted a slight upsurge in sectarian killings in April compared with March. It was suggested that the responsibility for killings in south Belfast seemed to lie with the Sandy Row UDA, while those in north Belfast were carried out by both the UDA and UVF. It was also noted that 'the UFF and the

Young Militants are pseudonyms adopted by the UDA to maintain their respectable front'.[62]

An interesting intervention in the British debate came from A. G. L. Turner, Guidance and Information Policy Department of the FCO, in a letter to NIO official Robin Masefield on 16 April, in which he expressed concern at Cardinal Conway's isolation of sectarian violence from 'the total spectrum of violence'. He articulated the view that the cardinal had overlooked the 'difference between provocation and retaliation'. He suggested that the IRA, as the 'provoking sect', was likely to initiate violence against public order generally. This led to retaliation by the 'opposing sect', which would probably be 'directly sectarian in nature', such as a bomb in a church.[63] Turner advised that one answer to Cardinal Conway's argument was that even as many as 350 sectarian murders formed only a small part of the total violence in Northern Ireland, which had seen some 1,200 deaths during the period in question.[64]

Turner's thesis did not sit easily with Frank Cooper's assessment of loyalist violence, which he set out in a paper in May 1975. Permanent Secretary Cooper, who, by then, had served three years in Northern Ireland, advanced the view that sectarian assassinations started from the loyalist side at times when they felt threatened. Cooper forwarded his paper to GOC Lieutenant General Sir Frank King and the chief constable on 15 May 1975. His conclusions were as follows:

> Waves of sectarian assassinations seem to start from the Protestant side. When the Protestants feel threatened (particularly those in the poorer areas of East and North Belfast) they turn to a campaign of murder. The criminal causes of the threat may vary but could generally be described as a fear as to whom is on top. But once unleashed

the Protestant backlash continues for a fair time until the immediate frustration has ceased. The campaign then tends to die away for the time being. This violence seems rooted in fear and frustration stemming as much from attitudes and emotions as anything else.[65]

In the body of the paper, he referred to upsurges in sectarian murders, giving some examples of when these upsurges had occurred, such as the suspension of Stormont, the time of republican 'no-go' areas and after the killing of Judges McBirney and Conaghan on 16 September 1974. Any 'advance' by the IRA or the minority community might lead to an upsurge in sectarian murder, he said, describing the UDA and UVF as seeing themselves as defenders of the status quo, threatened by, as they saw it, 'a culturally and socially inferior minority sub-group, which is identified by the Catholic religion. This justifies random attacks on Catholics as a group to "keep them down".'[66] Cooper used the well-worn catchphrase that many of these killings were carried out by people 'loosely tied to these groups'. In many cases, he argued, a psychopathic element was present.[67]

Cooper's paper on sectarian murders was discussed at a meeting between the secretary of state and several NIO officials on 28 May. It was noted that the army tended to leave the solving of sectarian murders to the RUC, so that it could concentrate on 'fighting the PIRA', which it saw as its main task. It was also noted that the RUC was hampered in dealing with sectarian (that is, loyalist) killings for the following reasons: shortage of CID staff; fears about its own safety if it pressed its inquiries too vigorously in hard loyalist areas; the inadequate degree of interchange of information between the CID and Special Branch; and the greater constraints which the courts and the DPP in Northern Ireland placed on the police in terms of the preparation and treatment of offenders.[68] This is official recognition at the highest level in the NIO that the RUC was unable, or perhaps unwilling, to pursue investigations in loyalist areas, and confirmation that information was not shared sufficiently between CID and Special Branch.

The newly appointed commander of Land Forces at HQNI, Scotsman Major General David T. Young, responded to the NIO paper on 5 June. He disagreed with the view that 'waves of sectarian violence started from the Protestant side'. He expressed his belief that 'waves of violence can stem from isolated acts of a random nature on either side and this can in turn be self-generating so causing the wave to grow'.[69] He believed that 'the Protestant community ... are frustrated by their suspicions that the PIRA are winning by devious tactics and that there will be a "sell-out" of them by the government'.[70]

The NIO was not convinced by Major General Young's response. It insisted its view was the correct one – the initiative in sectarian violence was taken by loyalist groups. A recent example was the upsurge in loyalist violence in February after the IRA ceasefire. It cited remarks made by the so-called Protestant Action Force (PAF) in the *Sunday News* of 25 May: 'Until Mr Rees announces details (of the secret dealings with the Provisionals) the PAF intends to continue with its campaign (of sectarian assassinations).'[71]

The FCO sent a letter to British embassies in August offering guidance on countering accusations that insufficient action was being taken against those involved in sectarian murders and how the subject should be presented publicly. It provided clarification that loyalist violence more commonly took the form of sectarian violence, while IRA violence was directed against the British economic system and the security forces. It was stated that the murders were undertaken by groups connected with the UVF and the UDA. There is no mention in the letter of the UFF. Embassies were advised that, for public consumption, they should suggest that some murders, which might appear to be sectarian, could be 'disciplinary' killings by the paramilitary organisations, or they might be carried out 'to pay off old debts' under the cloak of sectarian strife.[72]

Exact identification of killings, the letter noted, must always be tentative until police investigations were complete and charges brought. The advice continued that two 'commonly held illusions' amongst those who were critical of British policy in Northern Ireland was that only Catholics were the victims of sectarian murders and that few charges and convictions were obtained.[73] Statistics of charges and convictions were included, pointing out that Catholics were by no means the only victims, although the FCO conceded they were the majority. A claim was made that 'recently the trend has been for more Protestants to be the victims of assassinations'.[74] Propaganda was again being used as a tool to advise the embassies.

In December 1975 Frank Cooper advised the GOC, Sir David House, by producing a very different set of statistics:[75]

> If we turn to sectarian assassinations, the statistics show that in practice the Protestants take the greater share of the responsibility … our figures show that since 1972 Catholics have borne the brunt of sectarian murders. I think your own figures will bear this out, for every two Protestant victims there have been about three Catholic victims. Your figures show that there have been 686 Protestant bomb attacks since 1973. I'm sure you will agree that we must be equally resolute in our determination to catch and convict criminals from both communities. The IRA has to be emasculated – isolate them from the minority community.[76]

The Irish government expressed its concern about loyalist sectarian assassinations through John McColgan, Department of Foreign Affairs, when he met with James Allan on 17 April. McColgan put it to Allan that, despite the fact that they were 'no longer fighting the Provos, the Army had proved itself totally incapable of doing anything effective against Protestant violence'. Allan refuted the accusation 'very spiritedly' and promised that his assistant would provide McColgan with detailed figures on arrests, charges and convictions. 'Needless to say,' McColgan remarked, '*I never got such figures.*' When McColgan sought an update on the IRA ceasefire, Allan was, he recorded, 'totally uncooperative and stone-walling'.[77]

On 13 July McColgan and Allan met again, shortly before Allan's departure from Northern Ireland. He informed McColgan that he would remain on secondment from the Foreign Office for a further six months to produce a historical record of his time in Belfast. He would be replaced by Donald Middleton, former British chargé d'affaires in Phnom Penh. He explained that an extra first secretary was being sent by the Foreign Office to Laneside, increasing the strength of its staff there. Interestingly, Allan commented that 'Frank Cooper [PUS of state at the NIO from 1973 to 1976] runs the North of Ireland and not Merlyn Rees'.[78]

Later that month McColgan had lunch with Allan's successor, Donald Middleton, who spoke of Britain gradually reducing its commitment, and McColgan formed the impression that independence for Northern Ireland was being seen as the best possible option. Middleton had been joined in Laneside by another Foreign Office official, the former head of Chancery in Paris. He assured McColgan that he would find it 'personally repugnant' to have the army running the situation in Northern Ireland and, while that might have happened in the past, it would be extremely unlikely to occur in the future.[79]

On 11 September another meeting took place between the two men. McColgan reported that Middleton accepted that, if direct rule were to continue and internment (which was being phased out by the end of 1975) to be re-introduced, the British would have to find a more even-handed security policy – one that was seen to be impartial and fair to both communities. He disclosed that the re-proscription of certain organisations was being considered, namely, the UVF and the IRSP. The latter organisation, the political wing of the INLA, had, however, not previously been proscribed. He confided his hope that the fact that the UDA was not one of those to be immediately proscribed would 'take a lot of the sting out of reaction on the Protestant side'. A final decision had not yet been taken, but the thinking of the British was going in that direction.[80]

\*\*\*

In the early hours of 31 July 1975, members of the UDR and UVF shot dead three members of the popular Miami Showband and injured two others, one of them seriously. Two of the perpetrators were also killed at the scene when a bomb they were planting on the band's minibus exploded prematurely. The gang operated a fake VCP on the main Belfast–Dublin road at Buskhill, County Down. Their intention had been to plant a bomb in the band's minibus and allow the men to proceed on their journey from Banbridge towards Dublin, when the bomb would explode on the way, killing them all. The full details of the attack have been recorded elsewhere.[81]

On 24 August, in a similar attack using a fake VCP, two civilians were killed at Altnamackin (near Newtownhamilton) in the south of County Armagh, on their way home from the All-Ireland Football semi-finals in Croke Park, Dublin. The UVF, along with members of the UDR and RUC, were responsible.[82] Despite the widespread condemnation and shock at the killings, the UVF remained de-proscribed. The British were quick out of the traps to deny UDR involvement in the showband killings but had to swallow their denials when first one member of the regiment and then a second were charged with the murders.[83]

On 13 August the IRA attacked the Bayardo Bar in Aberdeen Street, Belfast. Peter Taylor claims this was in retaliation for the Miami Showband attack, as were the shootings in south Armagh on 5 September when the IRA killed five members of the Orange Order at Tullyvallen Orange Hall, near Newtownhamilton. These sectarian attacks by the IRA left the ceasefire in tatters.

At a meeting in Stormont Castle on 4 August, it was intimated that people in Britain found it strange that, while the IRA was proscribed, the UVF, which was responsible for the Miami Showband attack, was not.[84] The PUS warned that proscribing an organisation could 'raise expectations unjustifiably' about the action that could be taken against that organisation. He also warned that proscription of the UVF could have the effect of uniting Protestant paramilitary organisations and loyalist politicians.[85] MI5's Denis Payne stressed that the RUC was having new and encouraging successes in seeking out 'Protestant terrorists'. It was agreed that no immediate action should be taken, but that a public statement by the prime minister should point to the large number of UVF and IRSP members who had been charged in recent months.[86]

On 7 August John McColgan met with Bill Craig of the Ulster Vanguard Unionist Party. Craig had held several portfolios in the old Stormont Parliament, including the Ministry for Home

Affairs. He boasted to McColgan that he had easy and frequent access both to British Army Intelligence and to senior levels of the RUC. He indicated that 'there is an enormous central stockpile of arms on the Protestant side. These arms are not at the moment freely available even to people like Tyrie but are under control.'[87] He implied that he knew the identity of the man who controlled the arms and wished to leave McColgan in no doubt that 'the fire-power that was available on the Protestant side was almost unlimited'. He expressed shock at the Miami Showband killings and at the degree of sympathy and support at the funerals of the UVF men. He also claimed there had been a very large number of DUP supporters at the UVF funerals.

They went on to discuss the sectarian assassinations, with Craig advising that he had no doubt 'the Army was feeding information about individuals on the Catholic side to certain of the Protestant paramilitaries'. He was confident that loyalists had access to very highly confidential information, which 'was most unlikely to have been gathered by themselves'. He told McColgan that he was aware of several cases in which the British Army had set up Catholic victims 'for Protestant paramilitaries'.

In his report on the meeting, McColgan sounded a note of caution regarding Craig's claims. Other information provided by Craig led him to conclude that it was impossible to know what to take seriously and to distinguish which elements were merely to 'frighten Dublin'.[88]

On 26 August, two days after the Altnamackin killings, Webster noted in a memo that the press had received a statement from the UVF informing them that the PAF and RHC had been brought within 'the general umbrella' of the UVF.[89] The PAF had claimed responsibility for fifty-three killings of Catholics and the RHC was a proscribed organisation, so, Webster worried, was it likely the 'Catholic community' would increase pressure for the re-proscription of the UVF? The NIO expressed concern that this could lead to increased difficulties in meeting UVF representatives and to loyalist demands to re-proscribe Sinn Féin.[90]

Even before the Miami and Altnamackin killings, however, consideration was already being given to re-proscribing the UVF. In an internal memo dated 23 June 1975, it was suggested that it would be easy to proscribe the UVF; however, those it would be easier to prosecute for membership were the 'political' leaders whom they 'might want to talk to at some stage', while those it would be difficult to prosecute would be the 'hangers-on who do the murders and whose connections with the UVF are more shadowy'.[91] NIO official J. B. Bourn warned that if they were to proscribe the UVF and not the UDA, they might be seen as siding with one paramilitary organisation against the other. He concluded by saying, 'if we proscribe some of the UDA's subsidiary organisations, for example, the UFF and Young Militants, we may have all the Protestants around our necks'.[92] Bourn does not appear to have been on top of his brief, as the UFF had been proscribed since November 1973.

In an internal NIO memo dated 17 September, David J. Wyatt, MI6, informed Webster that a decision had been taken not to proscribe the UVF, but suggested cynically that they should 'keep it up our sleeves until we decide to take or are forced to take real measures in the security field against Republicans. We could then play this card (which has only a presentational value) in the even-handedness game.'[93]

***

On 2 October 1975 the UVF went on a murder rampage, killing seven Catholics (an eighth died later) and losing four of its
own members in a premature bomb explosion at Farrenlester, near
Coleraine, County Derry.[94] Four of the Catholics were killed by
the soon-to-be notorious UVF gang the 'Shankill Butchers'. After
this, the secretary of state had little choice but to re-proscribe the
organisation. The die was cast on 3 October using the urgency pro-
cedure, enabling the ban to come into effect at midnight.

In a speech to the House of Commons a month later, regarding
the re-proscription, Secretary of State Merlyn Rees said that the
UVF had been named as a proscribed organisation in 1973, but
recalled that in April 1974 he had told the House he intended
to bring forward an order to de-proscribe it. The reason was that
there were clear signs many of its members 'wished to find a way
back' to political activity and he was anxious that this should be
encouraged.[95] He had stated that this more constructive path would
be followed, and a political wing – the Volunteer Political Party
(VPP) – had been formed and entered the field in the October
general election.[96] Unfortunately, he said, it had become increasingly
clear during 1975 that 'a number of members of the UVF' were
deeply involved in sectarian violence.[97] Yet again, a distinction was
being made between the organisation and its members.

On 22 October a meeting was held in the secretary of state's
room in the House of Commons to discuss a proposal that rules
of evidence for courts in Northern Ireland should be changed to
make it easier to obtain convictions for membership of proscribed
organisations. The difficulty, however, was that the scheme would
have to be tied to proscription, and this would cause 'problems of
presentation'. The secretary of state noted that many 'terrorist-
type' crimes were committed by 'UDA members', but the UDA

was not proscribed and hence members of the UDA could not be imprisoned under the new scheme. He said he was very unhappy about the proposals and continued to feel that any such legislation would create great difficulties in the House of Commons.[98]

Frank Cooper remarked that it was true many special-category prisoners had, or claimed to have, UDA affiliations, but he persisted with the fiction that the UDA had not, as an organisation, been responsible for planning and carrying out acts of terrorism in the recent past.[99] It is interesting that Frank Cooper should make such a claim about the UDA in late October 1975. Just a few weeks later, on 29 November, two bombs exploded in public toilets in Dublin airport, killing airport employee John Hayes.

On 1 December the UDA military command issued a press statement to the Press Association, Belfast, claiming responsibility for the airport bombs.[100] On the same day, at a meeting in HQNI to discuss the security situation, reference was made to a letter which had been sent to the Irish minister for justice, Patrick Cooney, requesting closer security cooperation between the Gardaí and the RUC. Cooper commented on the UDA's claim and suggested that this might provide Mr Cooney with 'an incentive for an early reply'.[101] This very telling remark gives further insight into the cynical attitude of the British authorities towards law and order.

Hugh Smyth, spokesman for the UVF, met with the secretary of state on 19 November, several weeks after the re-proscription of the organisation, and asked if Laneside contacts could be renewed, having first declared that the secretary of state was right to proscribe the UVF. He insisted that the contacts would be 'bona-fide and genuine members of his welfare association who were quite separate from the UVF'.[102] In an internal memo Frank Cooper asked Donald Middleton to consider the request, remarking that he had no objection in principle provided 'we are not laying ourselves open to the charge of meeting people who have been proscribed and are members of a proscribed organisation'.[103]

In December John McColgan met with the Rev. (later Canon) William Arlow, the Church of Ireland minister who had been the main driving force behind the Feakle talks with the IRA a year earlier, which had led to the ceasefire. During the meeting, Rev. Arlow expressed serious concerns about the UDA. He told McColgan that the Irish government should be under no illusion but that the UDA had been responsible for a number of sectarian assassinations during the year. He said he was particularly worried about the close relationship and the level of trust that existed between the NIO and the UDA. He implied that there was 'an informal pact between the NIO and the UDA and that the British are giving considerable sums of money to UDA welfare organisations'.[104]

He also told McColgan a very disturbing story. He said he knew of a UDA member whom he 'could certify' as having been responsible for fourteen murders but who was still walking openly around Belfast. He was aware that somebody was prepared to go into court and give evidence against the UDA member, which would have ensured a conviction against him. This evidence was passed to the RUC but was not acted on, and the person offering the evidence 'had to be smuggled out of Ulster'. Arlow was involved in getting the man safely to Britain. The man, he explained, subsequently gave identical information to the British police, but, again, nothing was done and the UDA member was left at large.[105] He urged McColgan to press the British 'very hard' on what they were doing about the UDA. It was Arlow's view that, in the long term, the UDA presented a much greater danger than the UVF 'in the North but also for the South'.[106]

The authenticity of the story is hardly in doubt, coming from such a source – Rev. Arlow was a highly respected ecumenist and, in 1974, because of his reputation, had been recruited by the Irish Council of Churches 'to build bridges across the religious divide'.[107] Importantly, Arlow himself had been actively involved in making arrangements for 'the man' to flee Northern Ireland.

In April 1975 Seán Donlon had prepared a discerning and damning report for his minister, regarding the effect on the nationalist population of Northern Ireland of Britain's failure to confront loyalist violence. The report was compiled following his recent visit to the North and a series of meetings with nationalist politicians and members of civil society.[108] He began by recording that he had never seen the Catholic population so despondent. He expressed the view that the security forces 'had once more shown themselves' unable to deal with sectarian assassinations and bombings, even during 'a Provo ceasefire'. He claimed that every Catholic in greater Belfast and in the Portadown/Dungannon/Pomeroy triangle was a possible target for assassination, and he noted that there was 'considerable fear'. He argued that the release of all loyalist detainees in the middle of a campaign of loyalist violence had added to the fear. Donlon stated that he had been told repeatedly by the British authorities that the loyalist perpetrators of some of the most brutal assassinations had been detained, and he quoted the SDLP's Paddy Devlin: 'It is not easy to sleep peacefully when you know that the man who stabbed Senator Paddy Wilson over thirty times and mutilated his body is now free again.'[109]

This, Donlon commented, had convinced many that there was a return to the pre-1972 situation where internment was for the minority only.[110] He reported that 'there appears to be no minority confidence in Rees, who is seen as being motivated by an excessive sensitivity to the loyalist view on all matters, major and minor.'[111]

The year 1975 had begun with high hopes due to the IRA cease-fire. Despite numerous meetings with loyalist leaders, however, the British government had failed to halt the loyalists' escalating campaign of sectarian assassination, and instead attempted to minimise its extent when pressure was brought to bear by Cardinal Conway and the Irish government. James Allan was prepared to procure a firearms licence for Tyrie's bodyguard despite his leadership of an organisation engaged in murder. The UVF, although engaged in sectarian assassinations ever since its de-proscription in May 1974, was declared illegal only after it went on a rampage in October, and, of course, the UDA continued to be legal. The British government's continued failure to deal with loyalists in an even-handed way suggests that it contributed to the breakdown of the IRA ceasefire, which was another chance missed in ending the conflict.

# 7

# DISCRIMINATION IN 'SCREENING' AND THE POWER OF PROPAGANDA

The UDA ... either denies responsibility for sectarian murders ... or claims them in the name of the Ulster Freedom Fighters, a proscribed and essentially fictitious organisation.

*Internal British briefing paper on paramilitary organisations*[1]

The practice of screening the civilian population of Northern Ireland replicated similar measures in Kenya, Aden and elsewhere. It was introduced by Frank Kitson when he arrived in Northern Ireland in 1970. Screening involved the arrest by the army of individuals at home, on the street, or at VCPs; these individuals were then taken, usually to army barracks, to be interrogated by battalion intelligence officers. The intention was to build up extensive intelligence files on whole communities and collect mundane information about how many rooms were in a house, whether those who lived there worked or were unemployed, and the number of people living in a family home. The practice was finally ruled illegal in 1981.[2]

Declassified military documents paint an extraordinary picture of the impact of screening on nationalists. The statistics demonstrate that similar screening measures were not carried out in loyalist areas despite high levels of violence from loyalist paramilitary groups. This speaks volumes about NIO and British Army attitudes towards

Andy Tyrie, UDA commander from 1973 to 1988.
*Courtesy of Pacemaker Press International Ltd*

Tommy Herron, UDA brigadier from 1971 to 1973.
*Courtesy of Pacemaker Press International Ltd*

David Payne, UDA brigadier from 1974 to 1988.
*Courtesy of Pacemaker Press International Ltd*

Hugh Smyth, UVF spokesperson in the 1970s.
*Courtesy of Pacemaker Press International Ltd*

Tommy Lyttle, UDA brigadier from 1975 to 1990.
*Courtesy of Pacemaker Press International Ltd*

UDA Headquarters, Newtownards Road, Belfast.
*Courtesy of Pacemaker Press International Ltd*

A UDA march in Belfast in 1972.
*Courtesy of Pacemaker Press International Ltd*

A UDA press conference, *c.* 1980, with Tommy Lyttle, Glen Barr and John McMichael.
*Courtesy of Pacemaker Press International Ltd*

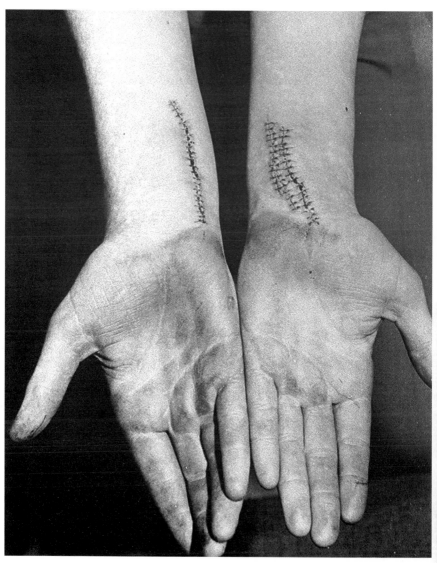

The slashed arms and wrists of Gerard McLaverty, the only
survivor of the Shankill Butcher gang.
*Courtesy of Pacemaker Press International Ltd*

A UVF member in front of a UVF flag.
*Courtesy of Pacemaker Press International Ltd*

View of the aftermath of the assassination of Shadow Secretary of State for Northern Ireland Airey Neave in a car-bomb attack on the exit ramp of the Palace of Westminster car park in London on 30 March 1979. *Photo by United News/Popperfoto/Getty Images*

'Look the other way'.
This cartoon was created by Ian Knox specially for this book.

loyalist violence. The official documents compare deaths, injuries and screening arrests. HQNI produced the statistics for all three army brigade areas in Northern Ireland accompanied by a religious breakdown of those screened.

It has been possible to compile a table from the official figures for screening arrests for an eleven-week period from 4 January to 20 March 1976:

## SCREENING

| Time Period | 3 Brigade | | 8 Brigade | | 39 Brigade[3] | | Total | Handed to RUC |
|---|---|---|---|---|---|---|---|---|
| | Catholic | Protestant | Catholic | Protestant | Catholic | Protestant | | |
| 04/01/1976–11/01/1976 | 11 | 3 | 4 | | 43 | 3 | 64 | 7 |
| 11/01/1976–25/01/1976 | 29 | | 29 | 2 | 90 | 2 | 152 | 24 |
| 25/01/1976–31/01/1976 | 6 | | 3 | | 34 | 4 | 47 | 1 |
| 31/01/1976–07/02/1976 | 16 | | 18 | 1 | 39 | 5 | 79 | 9 |
| 08/02/1976–14/02/1976 | 7 | | 22 | | 27 | | 56 | 3 |
| 15/02/1976–21/02/1976 | 7 | | 11 | | 32 | | 50 | 1 |
| 22/02/1976–28/02/1976 | 6 | | 19 | | 41 | | 66 | |
| 29/02/1976–06/03/1976 | 6 | 4 | 4 | | 23 | | 37 | |
| 07/03/1976–13/03/1976 | 6 | | 26 | | 28 | 1 | 61 | 1 |
| 13/03/1976–20/03/1976 | 3 | | 16 | | 29 | | 48 | 2 |
| Total | 97 | 7 | 152 | 3 | 386 | 15 | 660 | 48 |

The table shows that of 660 persons screened during this time, 635 (or 96 per cent) were Catholic, while twenty-five (or 4 per cent), were Protestant. Only forty-eight of those screened were handed over to the RUC, presumably because there was some evidence of illegal activities in these cases.

When examined, the figures for responsibility for deaths and injuries covering roughly the same period (from 1 January to 29 March 1976) show very starkly how discriminatory towards the Catholic population the practice of screening actually was. During this period republicans killed forty-three people (nine members of the security forces and thirty-four civilians), while they were responsible for injuring 110 people (forty-seven security-force members and fifty-three civilians). Loyalists killed thirty-six people (all civilians) and injured 115 (all civilians). In percentage terms, of those killed, republicans were responsible for 54.4 per cent, while loyalists accounted for 45.6 per cent. Republicans were responsible for 49 per cent of total injuries, while loyalists accounted for 51 per cent. (This is the only period for which we have a weekly breakdown.)[4] There is a stark imbalance between the figures showing the religion of the victims of screening and the figures showing where the responsibility for murders and injuries lay.

For the period from 6 September 1975 to 20 March 1976 (just over six months) a total of 1,994 persons were screened. Of this number, 1,876 were Catholics and 118 were Protestants.[5] No equivalent official figures for responsibility for killings and injuries are available for these dates. According to *Lost Lives*, however, during the same period 100 people (56 per cent) were killed by republicans, while seventy-eight (44 per cent) met their deaths at the hands of loyalists. Again, the disparity between screenings and responsibility for lives taken is significant.[6]

Meanwhile, the authorities continued to deny that the main loyalist paramilitary group, the UDA, was carrying out an assassination campaign aimed at the same civilian population that was being subjected to harsh security measures such as the screening outlined above. Throughout the conflict, the British government's official position was that the UDA was not proscribed because it did not carry out sectarian assassinations and bombings. These were invariably claimed in calls to news organisations and The Samaritans by anonymous voices using the UFF soubriquet.[7] Thus, the UFF was illegal, while the UDA was not.

The British authorities, however, made no pretence in private to uphold this public fiction, and the non-proscription of the UDA remains a decades-long scandal. For example, in an internal British briefing paper headed 'A Guide to Paramilitary and Associated Organisations', dated 2 September 1976, their state of knowledge could not be clearer. The UDA is described as follows:

> The UDA is the largest and best-organised of the Loyalist paramilitary organisations. It tries to maintain a respectable front and, to this end, either denies responsibility for sectarian murders and terrorist bombings or claims them in the name of the ULSTER FREEDOM FIGHTERS (UFF), *a proscribed and essentially fictitious organisation* which is widely known to be a nom de guerre for the UDA.[8]

Andy Tyrie, the UDA's leader, or 'Supreme Commander' as he liked to call himself, was described in the briefing paper as a pragmatist who would like to convert the UDA into a mass movement under his leadership, but his main difficulty was his constant need to keep in step with his rank and file who were far more militant than he was. It was observed, however, that Tyrie was not 'averse to killing

Catholics, even those who have no Republican connections, if he thinks it necessary at any particular point in time.'[9]

Despite this internal acknowledgement, the UDA was not proscribed until 1992, and the UFF was publicly and officially exposed as a fictitious organisation only in December 2012, in Sir Desmond de Silva's *Report of the Patrick Finucane Review*.[10] Tyrie himself was not arrested or questioned about any of the hundreds, if not thousands, of illegal acts in which the group he commanded was involved.[11] A memo of the NIO to the ECHR described the UFF untruthfully as 'a new terrorist organisation'. The index to 'A Guide to Paramilitary and Associated Organisations' made it very clear that the UFF was a pseudonym for the UDA, but even today, newspapers still refer to the UFF.

In the same 'Guide to Paramilitary and Associated Organisations' of September 1976, the UVF is described as 'not a cohesive entity; the notorious mid-Ulster UVF, responsible for many sectarian murders and bombing atrocities, is only loosely under Brigade staff control'.[12] It is undoubtedly true that the mid-Ulster unit of the UVF, which included a number of UDR and RUC officers, carried out some of the most notorious killings of the conflict, and it has been contended by Colin Wallace that the unit was 'largely autonomous'.[13] The unit – which included members commonly referred to nowadays as the Glenanne Gang – carried out a spate of sectarian murders between 1972 and 1977, mainly in Counties Armagh and Tyrone, but also in County Down. South of the Irish border the gang carried out the Dublin and Monaghan bombings and those at Dundalk (see Chapter 8 for more details) and Castleblayney,[14] and the killing of IRA member John Francis Green.

In the aftermath of the killing of ten Protestant workmen in Kingsmill, south Armagh, in January 1976 by the IRA, the gang planned a retaliatory gun attack on Beleek's Catholic primary school, intending to kill thirty children and their teacher. This claim was made on separate occasions by two former members of the gang, both of them police officers – one in an interview with the author and the other on a BBC *Spotlight* programme.[15] There is a credible claim, however, that this scheme was vetoed by the UVF leadership in Belfast, as they feared it would prompt outright civil war, which indicates that the mid-Ulster unit of the UVF did, ultimately, come under the control of its headquarters in Belfast.[16]

On 18 August 1975 Seán Donlon, assistant secretary at the Department of Foreign Affairs, sent a handwritten note to his minister, Garret FitzGerald, informing him that the garda commissioner had received confidential information that four members of the RUC in the Portadown area were also members of the UVF and one of them was actually engaged in the murder investigations in the Murder Triangle area.[17]

This information was passed to Minister of State Stan Orme by the Irish ambassador in London two days later. The ambassador reported back to Donlon that Orme was clearly quite taken aback by this information and said that, if correct, this would be a serious situation. He stated that there could be no question of such joint membership 'being tolerated for a moment'. He assured the ambassador that the matter would be 'fully investigated with great urgency'. Orme suggested that any further useful information would be appreciated, but the ambassador replied that he could offer nothing more. Orme was returning to Belfast the following day and promised to 'set enquiries in train immediately'.

In his telegram to Donlon, the ambassador expressed the view that 'one could imply from his remarks' that the minister of state 'would not altogether exclude the possibility' of an RUC member also being a member of the UVF. Orme said the UVF was a source of great concern to the secretary of state, as it could be a serious threat to security and 'this was an added reason why Rees would not tolerate for a moment involvement of RUC members in the UVF'.[18]

Despite the assurance to the ambassador of immediate action, it was indicated at a further meeting in September between the NIO and Donal O'Sullivan that it was difficult for the authorities in Northern Ireland to do much in the absence of any additional information. The chief constable had been informed and the 'Special Investigations Squad which dealt with questions of police loyalty had been asked to look into the allegation discreetly, but so far had come up with nothing'.[19] The British used this lack of detailed information to claim inability to investigate the allegation.[20] As a result of this failure, the Glenanne Gang was permitted to act with impunity for more than five years during the 1970s; its reign of terror halted only in 1978 when one of its members, RUC officer William McCaughey, suffered a nervous breakdown and began talking.

\*\*\*

Arguably, the most depraved gang of sectarian killers operating during the conflict was the UVF unit known as the Shankill Butchers. It terrorised Catholics on the streets of Belfast, under the leadership of Lenny Murphy and his two lieutenants, a man dubbed 'Mr A' by Martin Dillon, and Murphy's brother, John. It specialised in torture and 'cut-throat' murders. The gang conducted its campaign between October 1975 and May 1977. It was responsible for at least twenty-four killings between these dates, eight of which were of Protestants – four civilians, two UDA members and two UVF members. The sixteen Catholics killed were all civilians.[21]

It has been argued that the RUC's ultimate holding of the gang to account through the courts was an example of the force rigorously and impartially investigating loyalist sectarian murders. When the course of the police investigation is examined closely, however, it is clear that this is far from the truth. One has to wonder if the gang would ever have been brought to justice if one of their victims, Gerard McLaverty, had not survived.

Edward McIlwaine, one of the Shankill Butchers gang, who lived at Forthriver Crescent in the Glencairn estate, was a serving member of 10 UDR, its Belfast City Battalion.[22] One of 10 UDR's bases was Girdwood Barracks on the Crumlin Road, and in 1977 (while the Shankill Butchers gang was operating in the area) it became the focus of an internal investigation into fraud, corruption and subversion.[23] The investigation revealed that at least fifteen members of a UVF unit had been based at Girdwood over a period of years.[24] According to the report of the military investigation, at least seventy members of 10 UDR had loyalist traces 'and this has since grown'. Despite fears that there was 'serious penetration' of the battalion throughout the city of Belfast, the media and public were kept in the dark about the security investigation until the discovery of the relevant declassified files in the National Archives UK in Kew.[25] The internal investigation was dropped due to the unease it was causing within the regiment.

McIlwaine went on the run after the arrests of other members of the gang in May 1977, and was eventually detained on 13 June that year. Dillon cites James Nesbitt, the senior investigating RUC officer based in Tennent Street police station, as contending that McIlwaine had been dismissed from the UDR before his arrest, but Dillon himself believes his dismissal came about 'as a result of a communication from the police that he would shortly be questioned about serious crimes'.[26] According to contemporary newspaper reports, McIlwaine had served in 10 UDR from April 1974 until 1 August 1977. The UDR claimed he was discharged for 'poor attendance' several weeks after he was arrested and charged with kidnapping.[27]

McIlwaine was sentenced to fifteen years' imprisonment for the attempted murder and kidnapping of the Shankill Butchers' last Catholic victim, Gerard McLaverty. The serious penetration of 10 UDR by the UVF at the height of the Butchers' murder campaign is an issue that has yet to be investigated independently.

\*\*\*

From the beginning of the conflict, propaganda was a very powerful weapon in the British arsenal. One particular element was the denial of knowledge of the identity of the perpetrators of a particular attack when they knew full well that loyalists were responsible; another element was blaming republicans or, occasionally, even the victims themselves for loyalist attacks.

On 9 October 1971 a no-warning UDA bomb exploded at the Catholic-owned Fiddler's House pub in Durham Street at the bottom of the Falls Road. A forty-five-year-old Protestant woman, Winifred Maxwell, from the Shankill Road, was killed, and nineteen people were injured. In response to a question in the House of Lords following this attack, Lord Windlesham claimed that the police were not yet able to establish responsibility for this and other recent bombings. This prompted Lord Kilbracken to ask, 'My Lords, does the noble Lord think it likely that a member of the IRA would blow up a Catholic public house?' Showing a keen awareness of the contradictions in security policy, Kilbracken went on to ask if loyalists were now to be interned.[28]

The most infamous example of the security forces blaming a loyalist attack on republicans is that of the bombing of McGurk's Bar on 4 December 1971. McGurk's is notorious for good reason given the horrific death toll – fifteen men, women and children – and the subsequent flawed reports from the HET and police ombudsman. Reference has already been made in Chapter 4 to the disinformation disseminated after the attack, and official attempts to claim that the UVF attack was an IRA own goal have been explored in greater detail elsewhere.[29] Crucial to understanding the motivation of those who pointed the finger of blame at republicans was the issue of internment and the Irish state case that was lodged with the ECHR less than two weeks after the attack. As has been noted, one aspect of that complaint was the allegation that the UK was discriminatory in its one-sided internment policy.

The bomb that exploded on that December evening in the quiet community pub had the potential to blow apart a central tenet of official security policy – that there was only one source of violence, namely the IRA. From a British perspective, therefore, it was sometimes pragmatic to deny loyalist violence. McGurk's was not an isolated case.

The explosion of a car bomb outside Kelly's Bar, at the junction of the Whiterock and Springfield Roads in nationalist west Belfast, on 13 May 1972 marked the start of an unprecedented wave of violence, which left eight people dead at the hands of loyalists. John Moran, a student working in the bar, died as a result of the blast, and more than sixty people were injured. As casualties were being ferried from the scene, loyalist gunmen on rooftops in the nearby Springmartin Estate opened fire, killing Tommy McIlroy.

A soldier on duty at a nearby observation post claimed that two men had emerged from a vehicle and entered the bar. The bomb exploded shortly afterwards. Secretary of State William Whitelaw told parliament some days later: 'The evidence suggests that the bomb exploded prematurely whilst those intending to use it elsewhere were either inside the bar [the McGurk's lie regurgitated] or were returning to their vehicle from the bar.'[30] He claimed that loyalist gunfire did not begin until 'some forty minutes after the explosion at Kelly's Bar' and that 'the facts did not support the theory that the bomb was planted by Protestant extremists'.[31]

The following account is written in the British Army watch-keeper's log:

> Kelly's Bar explosion – 2 chaps were seen to arrive in the car behind by the OP behind the Henry Taggart Hall. 8 minutes later [they] came out of the bar, stood beside car and must have been killed when the bomb exploded.[32]

The real facts were that the bomb car had been hijacked earlier that day on the Shankill Road; two men parked the car outside Kelly's Bar and immediately fled the scene in a second vehicle. The HET, wound up before its final report could be delivered to the bereaved families, informed them in the interim that it was without doubt a loyalist attack and that the incoming gunfire directed at the rescue operation was timed to coincide with the explosion – not forty minutes later, as claimed by Whitelaw, who had clearly been wrongly advised. The senior HET officer investigating the events of the day believes that the testimony given by the soldier who claimed that the bombers entered the bar is deeply flawed. Questions about why the British Army issued a series of demonstrably false statements minimising the role of loyalist gunmen have yet to be answered.

On 25 March 1973 George Potsworth, a forty-five-year-old

machine-packer, was shot and paralysed when he was accosted by at least two men near the Shore Road, Belfast, while walking home. He died more than two years later on 20 May 1975 from complications arising from the shooting. On 5 February 1976 a detective sergeant told the inquest into his death that the attack site, a bridge under the M2 motorway, was an ideal spot for a robbery, adding that George was 'a Protestant in a Catholic area'. The Potsworth family was told by the RUC that the IRA was responsible. It was only when they received the HET report concerning George's death in 2010, thirty-five years later, that they became aware that the gun used in his shooting had been recovered during a house search in April 1975 and had belonged to the UVF. This crucial piece of evidence, the murder weapon, had been destroyed by the RUC in November 1975.[33]

Francis McCaughey, a thirty-five-year-old farmer from Aughna-cloy, County Tyrone, was seriously injured when a booby-trap bomb exploded in a cowshed on his parents' farm on 28 October 1973 as he entered the building to milk their cows. He died a week later from his injuries. The bombing was claimed by loyalists, and it later emerged that the attack was carried out by members of the Glenanne Gang. The HET has confirmed that loyalists were responsible.[34] Despite overwhelming evidence to the contrary, a barrister representing the NIO at Francis' inquest suggested to the jury: 'You may feel this was probably a booby-trap set up for soldiers who would be searching buildings such as this.'[35] Soldiers had occasionally searched the shed in a general sweep, perhaps once every six months, but Francis entered the building twice a day to milk his cows.

Martin Crossen was shot dead on 29 January 1976 while helping out in a Catholic-owned off-licence on the Antrim Road, Belfast. Two men entered the premises, threw a duffle-bag bomb on the floor and then opened fire, killing Martin and injuring another person. After the killers fled in a stolen car, Martin was carried outside – as was the unexploded bomb, which one of the off-licence owners flung into the middle of the road.

In the immediate aftermath, a witness came forward; he provided the registration number and description of the getaway car and detailed descriptions of the suspects. This witness attended voluntarily at North Queen Street RUC station and offered to view photograph albums and attend an identity parade. The HET confirmed that he was never shown photographs of suspects, nor was he asked to attend an identity parade. Hours after his visit to the police station, he received an anonymous threatening telephone call.[36]

The owners of the off-licence were shown photographs, and one of them picked out a suspect – who turned out to be a republican. It seems the owners were never shown photographs of loyalists who were active in north Belfast at the time, only those of republicans.[37]

According to the HET, there were a number of indicators that this was a loyalist attack. Months earlier, the UVF had threatened to attack Catholic-owned businesses on this very stretch of the Antrim Road, known as 'Murder Mile' because of the high number of loyalist assassinations. The getaway car had been stolen on the Shankill Road, a loyalist area. Hours after the attack on the off-licence, a UVF gang had thrown another 'duffle-bag' bomb into the Catholic-owned Stanley Bar, seriously injuring five people and demolishing the building.[38] Loyalists also bombed Kelly's Bar in the Short Strand on the same day, and killed forty-year-old Joseph McAlinden in north Belfast that night.

An RUC officer told the Crossen inquest in July 1976 that there was 'no suggestion who was behind the murder'.[39] Yet during that January six people had already been killed by loyalists in north Belfast before Martin Crossen's murder.

On 3 July 1976 bombs exploded at hotels in Dublin, Killarney, Rosslare and Limerick. The attacks, in which there were no fatalities or injuries, were clearly intended to damage the growing tourism sector in the Republic. They were claimed by 'Captain Black' of the UFF. Notwithstanding the obvious implication that loyalists were involved given the location of the targets, the GOC told the prime minister, 'Despite the claim of responsibility from UFF, the bomb attacks in the Republic on 3 July seem likely to have been the work of the PIRA.'[40] It would appear that the RUC either did not share this view or, more likely, the GOC didn't believe it himself, since the same briefing document records that the RUC had 'visited' the homes of several UVF suspects 'following the bomb attacks in the Republic'.[41] This extensive security briefing of the prime minister by the GOC included statistics for bombings, murders, arms finds over the previous six months, and even detailed descriptions of IRA funerals. What is striking is the absence of any reference to the sectarian campaign of the Shankill Butchers gang being waged on the streets of north Belfast at that time.

On 29 July 1976 three men – Joseph Watson, Daniel Mc-Grogan and Thomas Hall – died and thirty others were injured when a no-warning bomb exploded at a crowded bar in Anderson-stown, a nationalist area of west Belfast, as customers watched TV. The barman gave evidence of a stranger entering the bar, carrying a box; he said the stranger disappeared suddenly, after ordering a drink. Despite this indication that this was a planned attack and, therefore, probably a loyalist bombing, the RUC told the inquest in May 1977 that Special Branch believed the explosion had been caused by a bomb 'in transit'. According to McKittrick *et al.*, it was a UVF bomb.[42]

As in the case of the bombing of McGurk's and Kelly's bars, the bizarre implication was that republican bombing teams, bombs in hand, routinely stopped off for a pint *en route* to their actual target.

It is valid to ask if the false attribution of attacks, and the smearing of victims, was an unforeseen consequence of the chaos that was Northern Ireland in the 1970s, or something more sinister. Were the RUC and British Army overwhelmed, and did they, sometimes, innocently get it wrong in the 'fog of war'? The evidence points to a resounding no. Of the hundreds of declassified documents from the MoD, NIO, Prime Minister's Office and other departments that have been studied, not a single document has emerged in which the opposite case is made – that victims of an IRA bomb were victims of a premature explosion of their own devices, i.e. loyalist paramilitaries who were culpable in their own deaths. Not a single document has emerged suggesting that an IRA attack in a loyalist area was in fact a loyalist 'own goal'.

It is one thing to speculate on the source of a particular attack where there is, genuinely, little information. It is entirely another to create an elaborate lie – very elaborate in the Kelly's Bar case – in order to downplay, or even deny, loyalist violence. This provides further evidence of the extent to which propaganda was used to present a false picture of incidents by blaming republicans for loyalist bombings and shootings. The effect of such propaganda was to further diminish nationalist trust in the state.

# 8

# CIVIL WAR? THE 'OFFICIAL' ARRIVAL OF THE SAS AND 'ULSTERISATION'

We remain reluctant to outlaw an organisation [UDA] of such large size, many of its members being of a quite non-violent disposition, though no doubt they would turn willingly enough to violence if HMG seems likely to commit the ultimate betrayal.

*P. W. J. Buxton, NIO official[1]*

A deadly escalation in the conflict on both sides in the last weeks of 1975 and the first week of 1976 would have a serious and long-lasting impact on security policy in Northern Ireland.

On 19 December 1975 the notorious Glenanne Gang carried out two coordinated attacks, one across the border in Dundalk (which left two men dead) and another in Silverbridge, County Armagh (in which two men and a boy of fourteen lost their lives). In the final hours of that year, an INLA attack on a hotel in Gilford, County Down, killed three people. These killings were followed by three more attacks in the early days of the New Year, which left sixteen men dead.

The Glenanne Gang carried out two attacks on 4 January, killing three members each of the Reavey and O'Dowd families in south Armagh. The IRA's response was swift and terrible. On the following evening, a minibus containing Protestant workers (and one Catholic) travelling home to Bessbrook from Glenanne was stopped at Kingsmill and the eleven Protestant workmen were mown down, while the sole Catholic was ordered to leave the scene. One of the victims, Alan Black, who sustained eighteen gunshot wounds, somehow survived.[2]

The British government's first reaction was to declare County Armagh a 'Special Emergency Area'. Then, on 12 January, the 'Spearhead Battalion', a British Army infantry battalion kept at readiness to deploy at twenty-four hours' notice, as well as two battalions of the UDR, were sent there, and troops of the SAS – who had been deployed undercover much earlier in the conflict – were officially moved there from Dhofar, where they had been fighting for the Sultan of Oman. The British prime minister announced the arrival of the SAS in Northern Ireland in the House of Commons that day.

In high-level meetings to discuss the crisis, the sole focus was on the IRA, despite the two-sided nature of the recent violence. On 11 January, at a meeting in Chequers, which was attended by the prime minister, the secretary of state for Northern Ireland, the defence secretary and the GOC, among others, the discussion centred on the IRA.[3] The GOC remarked that the 'dirty men' in south Armagh were the IRA and that 'no pressure should be put on people north of the border', that is loyalists. 'This,' he said, 'would be the wrong response and would disillusion them.'[4]

In the midst of this security crisis, Andy Tyrie was invited to Laneside by Donald Middleton following a telephone call from the Derry UDA leader Glen Barr. Barr had confided to Middleton that he and Tyrie were 'drifting apart'. Tyrie, along with John Orchin and Jim Craig, met with NIO officials Middleton and John Bard on 19 January 1976. The two-hour meeting gave Tyrie the opportunity to expound on recent political and security developments. He had the effrontery to declare that the UDA would strongly oppose cabinet appointments for SDLP politicians. He appreciated that 'Catholic' politicians should be in government but believed that cabinet positions would be a step too far. The recently completed Report of the Northern Ireland Convention had recommended a 'committee system' in an attempt to involve 'opposition' parties more closely in government. Tyrie remarked that this system would give the SDLP an opportunity to 'serve an apprenticeship'.[5] His remarks reflect the position of the UUUC.[6]

Tyrie expressed concern about the security situation but said he was heartened by the prime minister's statement and the actions that followed. He believed that the security forces should now be given 'free rein to demolish [the] PIRA'.[7] He observed that the statement and the arrival of the SAS 'were indicators that a hard line was now being taken', and this pleased him. He commented that 'the wheel has now turned full circle, from the use of the B-Specials, through Mr Whitelaw's soft line approach to mobilisation of the UDR and the introduction of the SAS', and he expressed satisfaction that the security forces had at last recognised 'who the enemy was and were going on the offensive'.[8]

Tyrie was also worried by 'Republican penetration' of government bodies, such as the Housing Executive and the Post Office. Three UDA clubs had recently been damaged by bombs, and Tyrie made the questionable claim that these bombings could only have occurred with the help of 'PIRA supporters within the Housing Executive, probably in the Inspectorate'.[9]

The tone of the record of this striking encounter is suggestive of a meeting between equals, rather than between senior officials of a democratically elected government and the spokesman for a loyalist gang responsible for many sectarian murders by January 1976.

The beginning of March saw the ending of Special Category Status for loyalist and republican prisoners, introduced by William Whitelaw in June 1972 in the lead-up to the first IRA truce, and its replacement by a policy known as 'Ulsterisation' and 'criminalisation'. The new strategy was two-fold. 'Ulsterisation' meant that the British Army would gradually disengage from Northern Ireland and be replaced with members of the local forces – the RUC and UDR. The objective was to confine the effects of the conflict, as much as possible, to Northern Ireland.[10] According to Richard Bourke, 'criminalisation' would avoid acknowledging the political motivation and nature of the conflict – such a replacement policy was required to change the perception of the conflict as a colonial war into that of a campaign against criminal gangs – hence prisoners could no longer be given prisoner-of-war status.[11] The new policy also led to the British authorities growing more dependent on the RUC and the UDR, and, as a result, it became even less likely that loyalists would be confronted. The local forces could be pushed only so far in policing their own community.

*\*\**

In August 1976 the GOC, Sir David House, drafted a nine-page report entitled 'A Personal Review of the Security Situation in NI'.[12] He noted that the IRA was responsible for more overall casualties (of security forces and civilians) than loyalists, but warned that 'under a designation of strictly inter-sectarian incidents, the trend developed last year, and has continued into this, of Protestant extremists, under the arguable pretext of retaliation, causing more civilian casualties than PIRA.'[13] He went on to describe the levels of violence as 'disturbingly high' and noted that the statistics for the previous twelve months 'throw a disturbing and disappointing light on the security situation.' While admitting that this wasn't the time for the introduction of 'emotive draconian anti-IRA measures', he proposed that the secretary of state should conduct a high-level study to identify 'reasonable emergency measures for the speedier and easier conviction and imprisonment of the guilty'.[14] Although the reference to 'conviction' of the guilty indicates due process, one of three possible courses of action being suggested by the GOC was a return to detention (without trial) in one form or other.[15]

The tone of the GOC report, which focused firmly on the IRA, with only a brief reference to loyalist violence (noting that loyalists had killed more civilians), supports the view that from the perspective of HQNI there was only one enemy – the IRA. This is exemplified by the fact that the GOC blamed the IRA for bombings in the Republic of Ireland in July, even though it was clear that the attacks had been carried out by loyalists.

In December 1976 following on from the GOC's suggestion, a working group was set up to undertake a high-level study of the report.[16] Chaired by the MoD's A. W. Stephens, it comprised senior RUC, MoD, HQNI and NIO officials, including the head of RUC Special Branch, ACC Slevin. There was concern that knowledge of the study might emerge into the public domain. In a letter from Stephens to Slevin, the MoD official notes that 'it is regarded as very important that the existence of this study should not become known publicly or even widely within official circles, for obvious reasons'.[17] It would have been politically explosive had information leaked out that a working group had been established to consider even the possibility of a reintroduction of internment without trial.

When the working group delivered its twenty-three-page report, entitled 'Contingency Study of Preventive Custody' to the secretary of state in January 1977, the chairperson explained that it had interpreted its task as follows:

> To test the validity of the underlying assumption that the removal from circulation of some of the leading organisers and perpetrators of violence who are currently at large would have the right effect of significantly reducing the amount of violence that was going on;

> To assess not only the scope for alternatives to detention for this purpose but also the likely outcome of further recourse to detention itself.[18]

The report makes clear that one of the options considered was 'executive detention', which allowed for the secretary of state to sign detention orders on the basis of 'intelligence' where no evidence was available that could be put to a court, as had been the case in 1975 before internment was phased out.[19] However, the conclusion reached was that a reintroduction of internment would be politically possible only in the advent of a dramatically worsening security situation.[20]

These discussions are relevant because of the organisations to be targeted if detention was reintroduced. In the early 1970s the British and unionist governments tried to explain their decision not to intern loyalists (until early 1973), by downplaying the involvement of loyalist paramilitaries in violence. This explanation – one that was also posited to the ECHR – was a monumental deception, and this spurious claim could not be made in late 1976.

The report of the Contingency Study discussed the various options for 'ensuring the imprisonment of persons organising or carrying out acts of terrorism in Northern Ireland who cannot be successfully prosecuted under the existing law'.[21] In a section entitled 'The Nature of the Violence', it argued that:

> one of the most worrying outbreaks of violence in recent months was the succession of tit-for-tat inter-sectarian murders in the area of North Belfast. There are good grounds for thinking that, especially on the Protestant side, attacks of this kind are generally *not* planned centrally and carried out under orders, but are the work of individuals acting independently.[22]

This mirrored the evidence given by former Chief Constable Shillington to the ECHR in defending the earlier decision not to intern loyalists discussed in Chapter 4: 'The behind-the-scenes organiser was not so apparent in Protestant activities because they were more freelance. It was more individuals acting without an overall direction'.

Having apparently established that loyalist violence was random and 'tit-for-tat' in nature, the Contingency Study then went on to suggest that this lack of central planning or direction was 'not the general pattern'. Examples of coordinated IRA attacks were outlined, including those on members of the UDR and RUCR in a 'small area north-west of Lough Neagh'. Reference was made to the brigade and battalion staffs of the PIRA and the implication is clear that the IRA might be vulnerable to some form of 'executive detention', whilst loyalists were less so.

The study outlined the possible impact of a reintroduction of internment and noted:

> While it is not axiomatic that a resort to executive detention on a limited scale would be followed by a reaction similar to 1971, we

think it would encounter strong and widespread hostility among the Catholic community as a whole (unless it was applied to Protestants only) and probably among some elements of the Protestant community as well.[23]

Even though the report expressed anxiety about perceptions of the initial detention operation – 'difficult questions would arise over making the initial detention operation an even-handed one between Republicans and Loyalists, particularly if the operation followed a period of intense PIRA-inspired violence' – the real target of 'executive detention' becomes more obvious later in the document, where the observation was made that:

> There would be opposition from the families of those detained, from the SDLP, from the Irish Government, from the less institutionalised but well-established Official IRA, from the Peace People and from the Alliance Party. While the DUP is not of comparable relevance, past experience suggests that it too would join the opposition.[24]

Lest there be any doubt, the Contingency Study of Preventive Custody went on:

> Having examined the problem closely in the light of RUC and Army views, we are sceptical of detaining 50–100 leading members of the Provisional IRA ... we suspect that to be reasonably sure of seriously weakening the organisation's capacity to inflict violence it would be necessary to detain something of the order of 500.[25]

Finally it concluded: 'If detention were reintroduced, on whatever scale, the minority community as a whole could be expected to react strongly. Waning sympathy for Provisional IRA would be revived ...'[26]

Other than the references above, there is no mention of loyalist violence, and no reference whatsoever to the loyalist paramilitary organisations in the documents relating to this study.

The group convened in December 1976 and reported the following month. In the previous twelve months, 308 people had been killed. Republicans were responsible for 163 deaths (53 per cent), while loyalists killed 126 people (41 per cent). The British Army and RUC killed sixteen, while responsibility for three further deaths is unknown.[27]

It would appear that one of the other options examined in the Contingency Study was actually adopted. The law on the admissibility of confessions was changed and incorporated into the Northern Ireland (Emergency Provisions) Act 1978. Confessions could be accepted as evidence, provided the judge was convinced that they had not been obtained as a result of torture, or inhuman or degrading treatment. Peter Taylor writes that the change in the legal definition gave RUC interrogators a latitude they had not previously enjoyed.[28] This new flexibility resulted in numerous dubious convictions.

***

In 1977 the British authorities were making vigorous efforts to prove a link between Sinn Féin and the IRA so that the re-proscription of Sinn Féin might be considered. In July 1978 the RUC produced a 294-page report of their investigation into these links. This investigation had not begun because of a crime having been committed, nor with a belief that specific offences were being committed by known suspects. Rather, there was 'a feeling' that the links between the PIRA and Sinn Féin were such that at least some members of Sinn Féin were implicated with the PIRA in a criminal manner and that, through a detailed investigation, the 'Godfathers' might be 'brought to book'.[29] As a result, a lengthy operation was put in hand to 'build up a mosaic' of information about certain premises, people who frequented them and activities within them. This was achieved through observation, searches of the premises, seizure of documents and interviews with suspects.

A report on the investigation, prepared by NIO official P. W. J. Buxton and dated 19 October 1978, reveals that the Sinn Féin offices at 170 Falls Road were under observation, along with two other premises, between 26 September 1977 and 27 April 1978, the object being to prove the link 'between Provisional Sinn Féin and the PIRA'.[30]

Whether the RUC should continue with lengthy investigations into Sinn Féin was an operational matter for the chief constable according to Buxton, but considerable resources had already been devoted to the pursuance of the case. The investigation had so far not brought the RUC 'any closer to the men of violence or those who direct them'.[31]

From the information adduced, the RUC was able to bring cases against certain individuals in respect of alleged criminal offences. Searches had been carried out on 15 December 1977 and 27 April 1978 at 85 and 170 Falls Road and at a printing company in Lurgan. Despite an extensive investigation, Buxton stated that the facts as presented by the chief constable did *not* bear out the claim 'that Sinn Féin was not a political party or autonomous body in their own right but were an integral and important part of the republican movement, at the centre of which was PIRA'.[32] In other words, Buxton considered the evidence didn't support the view that

Sinn Féin and the IRA were inextricably linked. He said the case showed there were links between some individuals in Sinn Féin and some in the IRA, although the nature of those links was not always clear. He contended that this did not, of itself, indicate that the two organisations were anything other than autonomous bodies that worked together on some matters but remained, in legal terms, independent of each other. There was nothing to show that Sinn Féin came under the same command structure as the PIRA. He also said that if the case against the accused succeeded, it did not mean that all Sinn Féin members were 'tarred with the same brush' or were part of 'a PSF [Provisional Sinn Féin]/PIRA conspiracy'.[33]

While the authorities were at great pains to find grounds for the re-proscription of Sinn Féin, the exact opposite was the case regarding the UDA. In a memo to the PUS dated 29 April 1977, Douglas Janes agreed that:

> The note on the UDA is very much on the lines that I had envisaged after my brief talk with [name redacted] that we have shied from proscribing the UDA in the past despite the anomaly because it could be counter-productive.[34]

He continued that their one chance of removing this anomaly could arise if the UDA were clearly involved in violence in the context of the strike. He felt sure this would be a chance they should not miss, and hoped they could be poised ready to take the opportunity if it arose.[35]

The loyalist strike referred to above, which was a complete failure, was organised to urge the restoration of devolved government to Northern Ireland under a system of simple majority rule, and to force the British government to introduce tougher security measures against the IRA.[36] It is bizarre that the NIO should have been waiting for the UDA to be involved in strike-related violence to act against the organisation, when it had already killed more than 200 people by April 1977.[37] The comment by Janes gives the impression that he was keen to proscribe the UDA, but this view is not evident in other documents, and the UDA remained legal. The possible implication is that the NIO could tolerate individual sectarian murders of Catholics, however many, but found any violence intended to subvert its own policies – such as a strike – unacceptable.

In his October 1978 report on Sinn Féin, Buxton made reference to the UDA as follows:

> Minority opinion, even outside the close Republican Movement, would feel, given the existence of a sizeable innocent PSF membership – that the Government was acting discriminatorily in proscribing PSF while leaving the UDA untouched. There is little real force in the argument, seeing that the UDA is entirely quiescent at present, and its violent wing, the UFF, already proscribed. But the feeling would nonetheless tend to alienate a wider section of Catholic opinion. For the reason given, we could not possibly recommend UDA proscription today.[38]

It is true that the UDA was relatively inactive in 1978, as far as responsibility for murders was concerned – two deaths during the entire year. However, this figure increased to nine the following year (42 per cent of all loyalist killings occurred during the years 1972–6). In the case of other illegal activities, it was business as usual. The overall death toll for 1978 was, at eighty-eight, the lowest figure since 1970.[39]

Buxton again expressed concern about the UDA in July of the following year – not about its illegal activities, but rather about the possibility that the Home Office might, at the behest of the Scottish Office, consider proscribing the organisation in Britain. Proscription of the UVF was under consideration there, following a trial of UVF members in Edinburgh. The Glasgow trial of UDA members for firearms and other offences, however, had caused Buxton to think that the case for proscribing the UDA in Britain was almost as strong. He had explained that, while proscription of the UVF would merely bring Britain into line with Northern Ireland, proscription of the UDA there would cause considerable problems for the British authorities:

> We remain reluctant to outlaw an organisation of such large size, many of its members being of a quite non-violent disposition, though no doubt they would turn willingly enough to violence if HMG seems likely to commit the ultimate betrayal. If the UDA were outlawed in GB, our own proscription of the UFF would look rather thin, however legitimate a defence in practice. [Several lines redacted].

> In the light of these arguments, it seems possible that the Scottish Office will not ask the Home Office to proceed further with proscription of the UVF, still less the UDA. They will keep us in touch with their thinking.[40]

The term 'ultimate betrayal' is usually understood by unionists and loyalists to refer to the possibility of the British government's agreeing to a united Ireland. While this may be the correct interpretation, in contrast, in the context of these documents, it may simply refer to the proscription of the UDA.

To Buxton's relief, two months later, Miss C. J. Stewart of the Home Secretary's Private Office confirmed that the home secretary had agreed that the UDA and UVF should not at present be proscribed in Britain.[41]

In July 1979 NIO official N. R. Cowling prepared a briefing, updating descriptions of loyalist paramilitary organisations. He wrote that, in general, they were a working-class response to the perceived threat to the 'Protestant way of life' by the IRA, the Republic of Ireland and the Catholic Church. He noted that they had perpetrated sectarian murder and violence in both Northern Ireland and the Republic of Ireland and had the capacity to do so again. They had demonstrated their ability to bring normal life to a halt in the UWC strike of 1974. He claimed that members of these organisations were also involved in criminal activities other than terrorism and were a considerable threat to HMG's authority and to law and order. The UDA was described as follows:

> The UDA is easily the largest loyalist paramilitary group and is believed to have adherents in most areas of the Province. It evolved out of vigilante groups formed in September 1971 to patrol Protestant areas and met Protestant demands for a 'third force' to be set up independent of the British Army and RUC. UDA members played a prominent and active part in [the] UWC strike of 1974 ... and also in the 1977 UUUC[42] stoppage when they were widely criticised for alleged intimidation of the Protestant workforce. Since the failure of the 1977 strike, the UDA has not been much in evidence on the streets and its leader, Andy Tyrie, has turned his attention to more political pursuits ... The new-found political emphasis of the UDA should not be allowed to obscure its determination to oppose any moves towards the re-unification of Ireland – if necessary by militant means.[43]

The UFF is described thus: 'This group is believed to be an under-cover organisation of the UDA and has been responsible for a number of sectarian terrorist attacks. It is a proscribed organisation.'[44]

The UVF is explained thus:

> Formed in 1966 by extreme Protestants opposed to a short-lived improvement in relations between Belfast and Dublin marked by meetings between the NI Prime Minister, Terence O'Neill, and Seán Lemass. Took its name from the original UVF raised by Carson in 1912, but apart from its name there is no connection between them. During 1966 the UVF conducted a campaign of sabotage against water and power installations and murdered a number of Catholics. [The campaign of sabotage was waged in 1969, not 1966.] Gusty Spence and other UVF leaders were sentenced to long periods of imprisonment. Terence O'Neill described the UVF as a 'sordid conspiracy of criminals against an unprotected people'. Since 'the troubles' began in 1968, the UVF has been responsible for some of the most vicious and brutal sectarian murders and violence. The notorious Shankill Butchers convicted in 1979 of the murder of twelve innocent Catholics were all members of the UVF. Since 1966, with only a brief break, the UVF has been a proscribed organisation.[45]

It is interesting to note that the author of this paper, when describing the UDA, omits any reference to its campaign of sectarian murder and even his description of the UFF is minimal in its allusion to sectarian killings.

It is clear from the official papers that the British authorities saw republicans as the sole enemy. In January 1976 the immediate response to the upsurge in violence was to deploy the SAS to County Armagh, and, as the GOC's remarks at the meeting in Chequers implied, the covert regiment would be used against republicans only. Two months later the policy of 'Ulsterisation' and 'criminalisation' was introduced, which, again, was aimed mainly at republicans. In August the GOC commissioned a study that gave serious consideration to the reintroduction of internment. This, too, was aimed solely at republicans. In 1977 an attempt was made to gather evidence against Sinn Féin so that consideration might be given to re-proscribing it. In contrast to this attitude towards republicans, NIO officials were concerned at the possibility of the UDA being proscribed in Britain and loyalist violence was played down or ignored. These double standards failed to appease the loyalists and they continued with their campaign of violence.

# 9

# UDA MURDERS OF
# HIGH-PROFILE REPUBLICANS

The UDA is not an avowedly terrorist organisation, nor has there
been evidence that, as an organisation, it has been responsible for
terrorist acts.

*Nicholas Henderson, British ambassador to the USA*[1]

In the year following the murder of Airey Neave, the shadow
secretary of state for Northern Ireland, by the INLA on 30 March
1979, the UDA began to target and kill high-profile republicans.
This entirely new development could well have been in retaliation
for Neave's death, or it may have been the UDA's response to the
H-Blocks crisis.[2] Outrage at these deaths and the continuing legal
status of the UDA began to emanate from many quarters.

While there are a number of conspiracy theories regarding responsibility for the death of Airey Neave in the car park of the Palace
of Westminster, considerable evidence exists that it was carried out
by the INLA. These theories range from left-wing republican sympathisers in Westminster to a disgruntled MI6/CIA group.[3] However, as the INLA claimed responsibility, it was inevitable that the
organisation would be proscribed, especially after Airey Neave's close
friend and colleague Margaret Thatcher came to power in May 1979.
On 25 July Minister of State Michael Alison moved the proscription
order in the House of Commons:

First, it is an affront to public sensibilities for the law to countenance an organisation openly and avowedly dedicated to criminal violence and the overthrow of civil authorities. ... Public confidence in civil order and in the rule of law is undermined when such an organisation, with such openly avowed and flaunted objectives, can exist with no legal impediment.

Second, the Government believe that proscription would damage the organisation's structure and effectiveness. It may be helpful to remind the House that the effect of proscription is not only to make it an offence to belong or to profess to belong to a proscribed organisation. It is also an offence to solicit or invite financial support for it, or knowingly to make or receive financial contributions on behalf of the organisation.[4]

The proscription of the INLA meant that the only paramilitary organisation that remained lawful was the UDA. Much of what Michael Alison said about the INLA applied equally to the UDA, but British determination not to proscribe the UDA continued.

After the random sectarian murders of two Catholics, Alexander Reid and John Morrow, in January and February of 1980, in June the UDA killed John Turnly and Miriam Daly, both members of the National H-Blocks Committee, which was campaigning on behalf of republican prisoners. Rodney McCormick, a former prisoner, was killed in August in the mistaken belief that he was a member of the INLA. Ronnie Bunting, a founder member of the INLA, and Noel Lyttle were killed in October. Three of those killed had connections to the IRSP, the political wing of the INLA. In January 1981 the UDA attempted to kill Bernadette and Michael McAliskey at their isolated County Tyrone home, but, despite being shot several times, both survived. Bernadette McAliskey was a prominent member of the National H-Blocks Committee and had previously been a member of the IRSP. In a number of quarters, these attacks are believed – because of the failure of the police to bring the perpetrators to justice – to have been the British establishment seeking retribution for the death of Airey Neave through their proxies in the UDA.[5] Through the elimination of its intellectual leadership, the IRSP was badly disabled, and the organisation never recovered – it was severely weakened both politically and militarily.[6]

The details of the killings do go some way to supporting the view that retaliation against the INLA might have been a motive. The first to die was John Turnly, a forty-four-year-old former British Army officer who came from a landowning unionist background. By the time of his death, however, he was an avowed republican, a member of the Irish Independence Party and an elected councillor. He was killed on 4 June while being dropped off by his wife to a meeting in Carnlough, County Antrim. He was shot nine times with an SMG and a pistol. While Turnly had no known connection to the IRSP, one of the gang members subsequently convicted of killing him, Robert McConnell, told police that Turnly had been killed on the instructions of high-ranking officers in the UDA, who had informed them that he was a member of the INLA.[7] Immediately after Turnly's murder, a witness driving along the Ballymena–Carnlough road had seen two men in circumstances which suggested they might have just set fire to a getaway car; these men had then escaped in a blue Ford Escort van.

Martin Dillon reproduces the police statement of Robert McConnell, who was eventually convicted of Turnly's murder, as follows:

When I was about to get into the van two cars passed on the Coast Road. I saw one of these cars slowing up and the driver looking over. I stood in front of the number plate so that he wouldn't get the number. We got into the van and headed for Ballymena.[8]

In response to the information from the witness, UDR patrols set up VCPs in the area. At 9 p.m. McConnell, who was driving a blue van, was stopped. He had two passengers – his brother, Eric, and William McClelland. They were searched, as was the van, but nothing was found to link them to Turnly's death. The UDR patrol, however, contacted Larne police station and was instructed to detain them.

An RUC patrol arrived on the scene and asked the three men to 'accompany' it to Larne RUC station. Robert McConnell was known to one of the officers, and the three were allowed to drive to Larne in their own vehicle, not under arrest.[9] This officer stated that the men were asked to account for their movements that evening, and that they and their van were searched but 'nothing but a smell of fish' was found. He continued: 'I informed Sergeant [name redacted] of these facts and he spoke to the three men.'[10] The available police statements in the court papers make no reference to alibis being checked or swabs taken to check for firearms residue, nor is there any mention of fingerprints being taken. A detective 'observed nothing suspicious and authorised the release of the men'.[11]

On the day following Turnly's death, the witness who had observed the men escaping in the blue van provided police with a written statement containing a 'reasonable description' of the two men he had seen and described one of the men as having a 'pock-marked' face.[12] Despite this apparently useful information, no progress was made in tracking down the culprits, and they killed again. On 24 August they were lying in wait for Rodney McCormick, a former prisoner, as he returned home with his wife, and he was shot dead as he was about to enter his home.[13] This killing further supports the retaliation motive, as the gang incorrectly believed McCormick to be a member of the INLA.

As well as proceeding with the Turnly and McCormick murder investigations, the RUC was also investigating other terrorist crimes in County Antrim, and suspicion fell on, among others, the McConnell brothers and William McClelland. A link was then made between the Turnly and McCormick killings. In September 1980 twenty-nine men were arrested and charged with various crimes including murder, attempted murder, robbery, possession of firearms and causing explosions. The twenty-nine included two serving members of the UDR, as well as the McConnell brothers and McClelland. It has very recently come to light that William McClelland had served in the UDR from mid-1975 until late 1978,[14] and in the prison service from 7 August 1978 to 22 April 1979.[15] These highly relevant facts were not disclosed during the trial.

McClelland's membership of the prison service is particularly relevant as the HET has confirmed that the gun used to kill Rodney McCormick was also linked to the attempted murder of a Catholic prison officer in Newtownabbey in May 1980. The officer had been shot six times in the back but had survived. Moreover, the McCormick family has confirmed that Rodney was released from prison in early January 1979. McClelland's employment in the prison service coincided with his incarceration.

The McConnells and McClelland admitted their responsibility for both the Turnly and McCormick murders and were sentenced to life imprisonment on 10 March 1982.[16] After they were sentenced, Robert McConnell stunned the court by delivering a speech claiming he had been working for the SAS. He told the court he had been stopped one day near Cushendall by a van containing a number of men. He later learned they were all members of the SAS, and their leaders were Sergeant Tom Aiken and Corporal McGow.[17] He claimed that the first job he was asked to do was to plant a listening device in a Cushendall bar where Gerry Adams was said to meet people.[18] McConnell carried out that instruction, and the SAS men subsequently discussed republican leaders with him, particularly John Turnly, Miriam Daly and Bernadette McAliskey. He said the SAS men had provided him with weapons, uniforms and information on how to obtain intelligence-gathering equipment. He concluded by stating he wanted the court and the public to be aware that information concerning Turnly and the others was fed to him by the British intelligence services.[19]

There is no way of knowing if McConnell was telling the truth. It was claimed that he had not mentioned anything about the SAS during his questioning or trial. He could not hope for a reduction in his jail term, as he had already been sentenced. Perhaps he felt let down by his SAS handlers.

Suspicions of state involvement at some level were fuelled by a detective's admission during the trial regarding 'sensitive information' he had been given. A report published in the *East Antrim Times* stated:

> Another mysterious part of the trial was the 'sensitive information' a detective said had been given during interviews by Eric McConnell. The Detective Chief Inspector in charge of the case considered the information so sensitive he told the detective to destroy his notes on the interview and to re-write them. He admitted he had never ordered notes to be destroyed before or even heard of it happening.

It seems clear it was not thought 'safe' to keep the notes in police files. The detective said the information was not connected with the murders but was under investigation and could lead to charges.[20]

These interventions raise further serious questions about the British authorities' relationship with the UDA. After the convictions of these men, they knew that this perfectly legal organisation was in the business of targeting and assassinating elected representatives. Clearly the RUC, the courts and the prosecution service would have had access to McConnell's interviews. According to court documents, in one of these he admitted: 'All these guns and ammunition were handed to me by high ranking officers in the UDA. These top men are from the Belfast area and I don't want to give names.'[21]

According to the statement of an RUC superintendent who interviewed William McClelland (also convicted of the Turnly and McCormick murders): 'We discussed the big chiefs in the UDA and their feelings towards subject (McClelland) and how much or how little they worry about him and his well-being.'[22]

There is no reference to the UFF anywhere in the available court documents. However, it appears that counsel had been briefed otherwise. The *East Antrim Times* reported: 'At trial … the Counsel for the prosecution told the court that "the murder was a UFF operation". The Crown went on to claim that "the outlawed UFF was the military wing of the legal UDA".'[23]

Clearly, this was a falsehood. The accused had themselves admitted that the killings were planned and organised by senior members of the UDA – with no mention of the UFF. Therefore, Barry Shaw, the director of public prosecutions, and the chief constable, John Hermon – whose officers had carried out the investigations – had to be aware that this claim was false.

If John Turnly was a relatively easy target, Dr Miriam Daly was not. For safety reasons, she, along with her husband and ten-year-old twins, had moved from Stranmillis to Andersonstown in west Belfast. On 26 June, just three weeks after the death of John Turnly, and after intense military activity in the area, the killers entered her house. They cut the telephone line and tied her up while they waited for her husband to come home. When he failed to arrive, they used a cushion to muffle the sound of the shots they fired at her. They had probably also intended to kill her husband, Jim, who, like his wife, was a member of the IRSP.[24]

The killing of IRSP members Ronnie Bunting and Noel Lyttle, on 15 October, also suggested a high level of professionalism. At about 1 a.m., two masked men sledgehammered their way into a house deep within the Andersonstown area which, unlike Miriam Daly's, was not on a main road and was, therefore, even less accessible. The gunmen knew exactly who they were looking for and in which bedrooms to find them. Ronnie Bunting's widow, Suzanne, later recalled the precision and professionalism of the killers' movements as they shot her husband in one bedroom and then his friend, Noel Lyttle, who was sleeping in the same room as their infant son.[25] The Buntings' two daughters were sleeping in another bedroom.[26]

The attempt on Bernadette McAliskey's life came three months later. On the morning of 16 January 1981 three gunmen arrived at the remote family home outside Coalisland, County Tyrone. Like the Buntings', the McAliskeys' front door was smashed in by sledgehammers. Michael McAliskey was shot four times, while Bernadette was pursued into the couple's bedroom and shot eight times. According to Paul Routledge, Andrew Watson – a former member of the UDR – stopped shooting only when the magazine of his nine-millimetre Browning pistol was exhausted. The couple miraculously survived the terrifying experience. Outside their home an undercover army unit of paratroopers, believed to be SAS, was dug in. They saw the gunmen arrive but made no attempt to stop them. They arrested them as they were leaving. One of the soldiers was said to have then administered first aid to Bernadette, saving her life.[27] Obviously, if the would-be killers had been prevented from entering the house, there would have been no necessity to save her life. All three culprits were members of the UDA.

In the cases of John Turnly and Bernadette McAliskey, it was clearly UDA members who carried out the attacks. Both were easy targets, living as they did in the countryside. Miriam Daly and Ronnie Bunting were a different matter; their homes were located in the republican heartland of Andersonstown. The killers in both these cases had sophisticated intelligence about their victims. The only survivor of these murders, apart from the Bunting children, was Suzanne Bunting, who was seriously injured in the attack.[28] She was adamant that the killers were members of the SAS rather than loyalist paramilitaries, because the attack was too well planned 'by men who were cool and calm and knew what they were doing'.[29] Furthermore, a detective sergeant from Andersonstown RUC station told Miriam Daly's inquest at Belfast Coroner's Court that 'he had never known a loyalist gang to go into the Andersonstown area to perform a shooting before'.[30]

These were carefully and meticulously planned attacks in which the perpetrators had considerable knowledge of the location and layout of the homes of their victims. Whether Ronnie Bunting and Noel Lyttle (and possibly Miriam Daly) were killed by the SAS – as claimed by Suzanne Bunting – or by the UDA, it is likely that whoever carried out the killings had assistance from the security forces, as evidenced by their ability to move in and out of a nationalist enclave with such ease.

Even before the murders of Bunting and Lyttle, the political affairs division of the NIO was becoming increasingly concerned at the UDA's involvement in 'sectarian terrorism'.[31] In an internal NIO memo of 7 November, Stephen Leach noted that an article in *The Times* of 12 September 1980 was a 'serious assessment of the pressures on the UDA towards sectarian terrorism on one hand (represented by the UFF) and political expression on the other (represented by the NUPRG [New Ulster Political Research Group]'.[32] It is clear the recent surge in 'UDA-sponsored violence' was prompting Leach to reconsider whether he should agree to an NIO meeting with Glen Barr, having firmly rebuffed him earlier in the year.[33]

In the same memo, on the one hand, he suggested that if Barr were seen to be taken seriously by the government, the UDA leadership would be less inclined to sanction acts of terrorism. On the other hand, he worried that any meeting with Barr would probably not remain private and could prove politically damaging to ministers, given the UDA's involvement in terrorism. Leach contended that the organisation 'seems to be confused and reacting with more than its usual recklessness to the issues posed by the Maze hunger strike'.[34] Once again, an official was expressing a benign view of the UDA's behaviour, using words such as 'confused' and 'reckless', as if the UDA members were children who did not know any better. He felt the authorities had to do something because both the SDLP and the Alliance Party were calling for the proscription of the UDA. The NIO needed to head off these demands by securing a significant reduction in UDA terrorism.[35]

\*\*\*

It appears that the recent violence had provoked not just domestic, but international unease, with the US government expressing concern at the deaths – and the UDA's involvement. On 4 November 1980 the British foreign secretary, Lord Carrington, sent a briefing telegram to the British embassy in Washington, stressing he had no evidence of a UDA claim of responsibility for the murders. He said it would not be 'in character' for the UDA to make any such claim as it would invite proscription.[36] Carrington confirmed that Andy Tyrie had never been held for questioning by the RUC and, possibly to give Tyrie a spurious cloak of respectability, pointed out that he [Tyrie] had attended a seminar in Boston in 1975. Carrington said three loyalist organisations were proscribed – the RHC, the UFF and the UVF – and claimed that it wasn't possible to state how many loyalist prisoners had been convicted of terrorist-type offences as they were not classified separately (as was noted previously, separate records were indeed kept).[37]

Carrington advised the Washington ambassador of the 'line to take' – a line that was extremely disingenuous:

> 'The UDA have not claimed responsibility for these killings … the UDA as an organisation has never admitted to the use of terrorist violence to achieve its aims. Three men have already been charged with the murder of John Turnly and police investigations continue into the murders of Ronnie Bunting, Noel Little [*sic*] and Miriam Daly.' … The three men charged … are believed by the police to be members of the Ulster Freedom Fighters (the unadmitted terrorist wing of the UDA). It is believed that all the murders mentioned are the work of either the UVF or the UFF. The Government prefers to use its powers to proscribe named organisations as sparingly as possible. Thus both the PSF and the IRSP remain legal organisations,

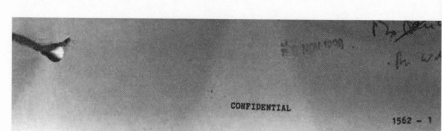

CONFIDENTIAL

1562 – 1

OO WASHINGTON
OO BIS NEW YORK
GRS 477
CONFIDENTIAL
FM FCO 041611Z NOV 80
TO IMMEDIATE WASHINGTON
TELEGRAM NUMBER 1733 OF 4 NOVEMBER
AND TO IMMEDIATE BIS NEW YORK
NORTHERN IRELAND: UDA
YOUR TELNO. 4445 OF 31 OCTOBER

1.   WE HAVE NO EVIDENCE OF A CLAIM BY THE UDA THAT THEY WERE
RESPONSIBLE FOR THE MURDERS OF RONALD BUNTING, NOEL LITTLE,
MIRIAM DALY OR JOHN TURNLY.   ON PAST FORM IT WOULD NOT BE IN
CHARACTER FOR THEM TO MAKE ANY SUCH CLAIM, WHICH WOULD INVITE
PROSCRIPTION.

2.   HOWEVER, THE UDA ISSUED THE FOLLOWING STATEMENT ON
29 OCTOBER IN RESPONSE TO THE HUNGER STRIKE CAMPAIGN:
     'THE UDA WILL NOT BE DRAWN INTO A SECTARIAN WAR BUT WILL
     USE EVERY MEANS AT ITS DISPOSAL TO ELIMINATE THOSE WHO
     POSE A THREAT TO THE STATE OF ULSTER AND ALL ITS PEOPLE.
     THE UDA IS NOT TO BE SEEN AS A THREAT TO ALL MEMBERS OF
     THE H-BLOCK CAMPAIGN BUT IS ONLY INTERESTED IN ELIMINATING
     ACTIVE PROVISIONALS IN THE MOVEMENT'.

3.   IT IS CONFIRMED THAT ANDY TYRIE HAS NEVER BEEN HELD FOR
QUESTIONING BY THE RUC.   IT IS KNOWN THAT HE ATTENDED A SEMINAR
IN BOSTON, USA IN 1975.

4.   THREE 'LOYALIST' ORGANISATIONS ARE PROSCRIBED UNDER THE
NORTHERN IRELAND (EMERGENCY PROVISIONS) ACT 1978:
          THE RED HAND COMMANDO
          THE ULSTER FREEDOM FIGHTERS
          THE ULSTER VOLUNTEER FORCE

5.   IT IS NOT POSSIBLE TO STATE HOW MANY 'LOYALIST' PRISONERS
HAVE BEEN CONVICTED OF TERRORIST-TYPE OFFENCES AS PRISONERS
CONVICTED OF SUCH OFFENCES ARE NOT CLASSIFIED SEPARATELY.   HOWEVER
THE NUMBER CURRENTLY IN PRISON IS WELL OVER 200.
LINE TO TAKE.

*NAUK, CJ4/3963, telegram sent to the British Embassy in Washington by Lord
Carrington, 4 November 1980, p. 1*

CONFIDENTIAL

1562 - 1

6.   WE SUGGEST YOU TAKE THE FOLLOWING LINE, BESIDES DRAWING ON
PARAGRAPHS 1-5 ABOVE:-
    'THE UDA HAVE NOT CLAIMED RESPONSIBILITY FOR THESE KILLINGS.
    THE POLICE INVESTIGATE ALL ACTS OF VIOLENCE WITH A VIEW
    TO BRINGING THE PERPETRATORS TO JUSTICE IRRESPECTIVE OF
    RELIGION OR POLITICAL OR PARAMILITARY AFFILIATION.   THERE
    HAVE BEEN MANY CONVICTIONS FOR MURDER IN NORTHERN IRELAND
    WHERE THOSE CONVICTED ARE KNOWN TO HAVE HAD 'LOYALIST'
    AFFILIATIONS, BUT THE UDA AS AN ORGANISATION HAS NEVER
    ADMITTED TO THE USE OF TERRORIST VIOLENCE TO ACHIEVE ITS
    AIMS.   THREE MEN HAVE ALREADY BEEN CHARGED WITH THE MURDER
    OF JOHN TURNLY AND POLICE INVESTIGATIONS CONTINUE INTO THE
    MURDERS OF RONALD BUNTING, NOEL LITTLE AND MIRIAM DALY.'
NOT FOR DISCLOSURE.
7. THE THREE MEN CHARGED WITH THE MURDER OF JOHN TURNLY ARE
BELIEVED BY THE POLICE TO BE MEMBERS OF THE ULSTER FREEDOM
FIGHTERS (THE UNADMITTED TERRORIST WING OF THE UDA). IT IS
BELIEVED THAT ALL THE MURDERS MENTIONED ARE THE WORK OF EITHER
THE UVF OR THE UFF. IN GENERAL, THE GOVERNMENT PREFERS TO USE
ITS POWERS TO PROSCRIBE NAMED ORGANISATIONS AS SPARINGLY AS
POSSIBLE. THUS BOTH THE PSF AND THE IRSP REMAIN LEGAL
ORGANISATIONS, IN SPITE OF THEIR CLOSE LINKS WITH PIRA AND INLA
RESPECTIVELY.   THE RELATIONSHIP BETWEEN THE UDA AND THE UFF IS
NOT DISSIMILAR.

CARRINGTON

| LIMITED | PS/PUS | ADDITIONAL DISTRIBUTION |
|---|---|---|
| RID | SIR A ACLAND | NORTHERN IRELAND |
| NAD | CHIEF CLERK | |
| OID | MR ADAMS | |
| IPD | MR BULLARD | |
| WED | MR FERGUSSON | |
| NAED | LORD N G LENNOX | |
| NEWS DEPT | MR BRAITHWAITE | |
| SECURITY DEPT | | |
| PUSD | | |
| PS | | |
| PS/LPS | | |
| PS/MR HURD | | |
| PS/MR RIDLEY | | |
| PS/MR BLAKER | | |

CONFIDENTIAL

*NAUK, CJ4/3963, telegram sent to the British Embassy in Washington by Lord
Carrington, 4 November 1980, p. 2*

in spite of their close links with PIRA and INLA respectively. The relationship between the UDA and the UFF is not dissimilar.[38]

On 24 May 1982 this suggested line was taken by the British ambassador, Nicholas Henderson, when he wrote to Congressman Hamilton Fish, US House of Representatives, in an attempt to counter an approach by the Irish National Caucus (INC). The INC was an Irish-American lobby group founded by Rev. Seán McManus in September 1974 to counterbalance British influences in the United States Congress and government. Henderson referred to a newsletter which had suggested that Fish, with other members of Congress, were planning to write to US Secretary of State Alexander Haig asking the US government to demand that the British government proscribe the UDA and the 'Third Force'.[39] He noted that the INC had claimed the British government had encouraged loyalists to use terrorism to maintain the British connection. One example provided, he said, was the attempted murder of Bernadette McAliskey, but the facts were very different.[40]

When the McAliskeys were attacked in January 1981, he wrote, 'not only were their lives saved by the prompt medical aid administered by British soldiers', but those responsible had been arrested by the soldiers and had subsequently been charged and convicted. Henderson listed the proscribed organisations as 'PIRA, INLA, UVF and UFF'. He then went on to claim:

> The UDA is not an avowedly terrorist organisation, nor has there been evidence that, as an organisation, it has been responsible for terrorist acts. Provisional Sinn Fein is in a similar position, and is similarly not proscribed even though it makes no secret of its links with and support for the PIRA.[41]

The British ambassador made no mention of the fact that those convicted of the attempted murder of the McAliskeys were members of the UDA, nor that British soldiers had allowed them to access the McAliskey home and arrested them only on their exit from the premises.

An official in the public-affairs branch of the NIO informed a colleague, Richard Davies, Law and Order Division, that he had altered a paper on the UDA 'in advance of seeing the line adopted in the Fish reply'. He recorded that he had omitted the arguments about 'proscription leading to mass defiance and leading fringe members into more direct terrorist activity'. He declared: 'I simply do not believe it.'[42]

The British government was well aware, and had acknowledged privately as cited above, that the UDA and the UFF were one and the same organisation and the relationship between them was not in the least similar to the relationship between Sinn Féin and the IRA. As is noted from the HET report into the death of Rodney McCormick, the perpetrators of John Turnly's murder told police it was the UDA that organised it. They made no mention of the UFF. But it seems as if even senior British government ministers were prepared to defend the UDA.

In November 1980 Michael Canavan of the SDLP wrote to Jonathan Margetts at the NIO, informing him that the SDLP had passed a unanimous resolution calling for the UDA to be proscribed.[43] He submitted evidence linking the UDA with 'para-military terrorism'.[44] This triggered a memo from C. Davenport of the Law and Order Division, Stormont House, to the private secretary of the secretary of state. Davenport agreed that a check of their records against Canavan's evidence showed that some of the incidents recorded in his letter did have a basis in fact. He stated that the nub of Canavan's case for proscription was that the UDA and the UFF were synonymous. Davenport then proceeded to vacillate on this issue by arguing:

> Although they are of course closely linked, it has been the UFF, already proscribed, which has claimed terrorist attacks and it was the UFF which held the 'hooded and armed' press conference. Canavan's evidence adds nothing to our present knowledge of the UDA's relationship with terrorism, on the basis of which Secretary of State has decided not to proscribe the organisation at this time.[45]

Davenport sent a further memo to the private secretary on 28 January 1981, following the attempted murder of the McAliskeys. He had received another letter from Michael Canavan on 18 January requesting a meeting with the secretary of state to discuss the proscription of the UDA. Davenport suggested that the secretary of state should meet Canavan and explain the 'impartiality of the Government's security policy and its application'. He commented that Canavan was 'a vehement and at times virulent critic of the UDR and RUC' and some of his past statements had done nothing 'to calm tensions between Protestants and Catholics'.[46]

Davenport added that the secretary of state could draw Canavan's attention to the fact that twenty-seven Protestants had already been charged that month, three of them for attempting to murder the McAliskey family. He remarked: 'It is this sort of action which will curb and prevent violence by so-called loyalists more effectively than proscription of the UDA.'[47] The tendency of senior NIO officials to reproach anyone who complained about UDA violence was remarkably consistent.

The reaction of the Alliance Party to the killings was to complain to the ECtHR. The party's security spokesman, John Cousins, wrote to the ECtHR on 4 November about the continuing legal status of the UDA 'which still enjoys the full protection of the law', despite repeated requests to successive secretaries of state by him on behalf of the Alliance Party and despite the fact that 'the UDA continues to make statements threatening the lives and property of citizens of the UK in Northern Ireland'.[48] He pointed to the various organisations that were already proscribed and believed that the continuing 'favoured status' enjoyed by the UDA amounted to an unfair and partial application of the law. He wrote that he intended to make a formal application in due course.[49]

John Cousins also wrote to the secretary of state, Humphrey Atkins, the following day, suggesting that Atkins must be greatly concerned by recent statements from the UDA and UFF (which he regarded as purely 'a flag of convenience' for the UDA) and the recent actions of the UFF, including several assassinations and assassination attempts.[50] He informed the secretary of state that he had decided to petition the ECtHR on the matter, but would be happy to withdraw his application if the UDA were to be proscribed.[51]

A paper on the UDA was prepared in response. The author, NIO official A. C. Stott, noted that the UDA was 'an organisation *sui generis*' (stand alone, separate). On the one hand, it was not a straightforwardly political organisation, on the other hand, 'although conceiving of violent actions as part of their contingency plans', the UDA itself had not admitted carrying out any attacks to date.[52] He stated that 'violent attacks which we believe to be UDA-associated are traditionally claimed by the proscribed UFF'. Unlike the IRA, the UDA had no long and 'glorious' history, so there would not be the same reluctance to re-form under another, unproscribed, banner. The security arguments for proscription were not, therefore, substantial.[53]

On the political side, the argument against proscription was that there would be a strong loyalist reaction – it would be seen as uneven-handed while Sinn Féin remained unproscribed. The possibility of large numbers of 'ordinary' UDA members, not personally involved in terrorist acts, being brought before the courts would also produce its reaction, he said, before concluding that 'as long as the UDA refuses to acknowledge terrorist acts the balance seems to be against proscribing it'.[54]

The idea of proscribing the UDA was discussed by NIO official J. M. Burns with the RUC's deputy chief constable, Michael Mc-Atamney, who confirmed that the RUC was still of the view that there was no point in proscription. Burns suggested that they:

> could all be made to look fools if the UDA chose to defy the ban by holding some sort of mass march and the police could not possibly arrest or charge those who took part and the ban would be seen to be dangerously ineffective.[55]

This alarming comment indicates clearly that the British government was unwilling to confront UDA violence in a determined manner.

In a briefing for the secretary of state on the Alliance Party demand for the proscription of the UDA, it was noted that, as a deterrent, such a move might well backfire, making those on the fringes of the UDA opt for full participation. The civil servant noted that there was also a danger that the security forces would have difficulty in coping with any mass defiance of the law that proscription might provoke, adding that neither the RUC nor the army saw any worthwhile operational advantage in proscribing the

UDA; indeed the police considered that it would be more likely to cause additional problems.[56]

On the loyalist side, the authorities could expect a significant reaction, both from politicians and from the ranks of UDA sympathisers. If nothing else, it would almost certainly provoke demands for comparable action against certain republican organisations for which proscription would not only be unattractive on its own merits but would further exacerbate tensions.[57]

If the UDA were to start claiming responsibility for terrorist attacks, that would put a different complexion on the matter. The nature of the organisation would be clear to all, and there would be a strong political presumption towards such action. The signs were, however, that the UDA had been worried by the possibility of proscription and did not, at least for the time being, intend to take a more violent role 'as an organisation', although some of its members might 'sporadically' carry out sectarian attacks.[58] It was noted that in light of the recent spate of loyalist attacks on republican activists, in which some 'disinterested' Catholics had been injured, the NIO had been considering anew the possible proscription of the UDA.[59]

An internal NIO memo of 10 November 1980 advised against meeting with Glen Barr, who had by this time established the NUPRG, advocating an independent Northern Ireland. J. A. Daniell suggested that it was difficult to imagine the UDA rank and file eschewing 'the traditional paramilitary weapons of intimidation, assassination and street violence in favour of a political philosophy which few of them really understand and which threatens the existence of the union'.[60] He believed that the 'present upsurge' in loyalist violence would be highly unlikely to be stemmed as a result of official contact with Glen Barr. Daniell observed that sectarian violence was running at a higher level than for some time 'with the

UDA/UFF sponsored killings playing a prominent role. The UDA is careful not to associate itself with the killings, which means that pressure for the organisation's proscription can at the moment be resisted.'[61]

Daniell advised that Leach had broached the possibility of officials making contact with Glen Barr but warned that 'we must seek to avoid the intrigue and misunderstandings surrounding the old Laneside days'.[62] Although this might give the impression that meetings with the UDA ceased after Laneside was closed down by Secretary of State Roy Mason, this was not the case.[63] A closed file is held by the National Archives, Kew, which is entitled 'UDA: Meetings and contacts with UDA leadership 1976–1979'. This file will not be opened to the public until 2052.[64]

An NIO official, in an internal memo dated 22 January 1981, advised that she had received a telephone call from John Cousins, Alliance Party, again pressing for the proscription of the UDA. Cousins had informed her that he had passed information to the RUC that at least one of the men charged with the attack on the McAliskeys – Watson – had attended a meeting at a UDA centre two days before the attack, and that John McMichael had been present.[65]

On 2 February 1981 Leonard Figg, the British ambassador in Dublin, in a telegram to the Foreign Office on proscribing the UDA, reported Irish media reactions to Andy Tyrie's statement that the UDA was a counter-terrorist organisation that would be prepared to pursue terrorists across the border. Figg advised that this had been reported prominently in all newspapers in the Republic and on RTÉ television. The reports, he said, were accurate, but he expressed anxiety that they had put UDA proscription once again on the political agenda.[66]

Demands for the immediate outlawing of the UDA came from several quarters after the conviction of three members of the organisation for the murders of John Turnly and Rodney McCormick. There were also strong demands for a public inquiry after Robert McConnell's dramatic statement from the dock, claiming he had 'teamed up' with two named SAS soldiers.[67] The SDLP's Michael Canavan accused the UDA of being a major contributor to terrorist crime: 'It highlights the failure of the British Government to proscribe that organisation despite its appalling record of sectarian atrocities. Their activities have been condemned by many judges and have scandalised public opinion.'[68] Fr Denis Faul and Seamus Close of the Alliance Party were also loud in their criticism.[69]

In February 1981 the MP for Fermanagh/south Tyrone, Frank Maguire, joined the chorus of those demanding the proscription of the UDA. His letter prompted an internal NIO memo which discussed an article from the *New York Daily News* that Maguire had enclosed with his letter.[70]

On 19 December 1980 Michael Daly, a reporter with the *New York Daily News*, had written of a telephone conversation he had with Sam Duddy, the UDA's press relations officer, at UDA headquarters. Daly expressed astonishment that the UDA was actually listed in the telephone directory – an organisation which he claimed had 'at the last count slaughtered some 500 Roman Catholics'.[71] Noting that 'the UDA is the only terrorist organisation in Europe listed in a telephone book', he went on to write that, unlike the IRA, the UDA was not outlawed and that the British Army's major operations against the group 'have been limited to soccer matches between paratroopers and UDA gunmen'.[72]

Daly added that, while the IRA was pursued by soldiers, UDA leaders operated openly out of a Victorian house at 279 Newtownards

Road. When Daly had rung the premises, Sam Duddy had answered the phone. He described Duddy as having served, 'for a number of years as a fingerman for a hit squad in north Belfast'. Daly's article explained that the leader of this squad, known as 'The Window Man', was a burglar with a penchant for shooting Catholics through their bedroom windows.

During the call, Duddy suggested that tensions created by the IRA hunger strike 'may keep the Window Man very busy'. He told Daly, 'We can be ruthless when it comes to the part. We have sought out and eliminated certain people in the past. We make no apologies about it.'[73]

Daly enquired if the British Army would interfere, to which Duddy replied, 'I would like to think the security forces know who their friends are. They know where they can get a cup of tea.'[74]

Duddy suggested to Daly that some insight could be gained by reading the UDA training manual. Daly reports that the first section 'indicates that the UDA's violence is closely supervised by the leaders who operate without interference by the British at the house on the Newtownards Road'. The next section of the manual dealt with explosives, and Daly used the example of the Dublin and Monaghan bombings.[75] This was, of course, incorrect, as the UDA was not responsible; however, in the 1980s and up to 1993 when Yorkshire Television exposed the real culprits, it was widely believed that the UDA was responsible.[76]

The memo's author, D. F. E. (Frances) Elliot, sought comments on the UDA press officer and his remarks 'especially his reference to the so-called UDA training manual'. Clarification was also sought on whether or not the UDA had openly claimed responsibility for any of the murders referred to in the article.[77]

The RTÉ documentary *Collusion* revealed in June 2015 what

many journalists had suspected for years: that Sam Duddy, described as a senior UDA figure, was also an agent for 'some branch'
of the security forces. The programme reported that Tommy Lyttle, a former UDA leader who died of a heart attack in 1995, left
behind a tape in which he named Duddy as an agent. He had also
stated that the UDA 'was riddled with informers'. The RTÉ programme also claimed that Duddy was behind the MI5 propaganda
campaign against Pat Finucane.[78]

***

It was not only MPs and political parties who were discussing
proscription of the UDA. At the trial of one of the killers of
Alexander Reid, the judge also raised the issue. Reid, a twenty-
year-old Catholic, was killed in a random attack by a UDA gang on
3 January 1980 when he and a friend hailed a taxi, which then took
a route along the Shankill Road before halting outside a loyalist
club. His friend managed to escape, but Reid was beaten to death
with a brick and a concrete block. According to McKittrick *et al.*,
UDA members in the club had been discussing 'getting a Roman
Catholic'.[79] One of those convicted of the killing in February 1981
was Stanley Millar Smith. The trial judge, Mr Justice Murray, in his
judgement, included the following:

> The facts in this case are quite horrifying. Alexander Reid, an
> unsuspecting young man, from a Roman Catholic area of the city,
> was delivered by a Shankill Road taxi-driver into the hands of a
> gang of young UDA thugs on the Shankill Road. They first of all
> attacked him with fists and feet and rendered him unconscious or
> nearly so and then some of the gang dragged him up to a nearby

covered alleyway where they savagely battered the defenceless young man to death by repeated blows to his head by a brick and concrete block. It is in my view important that these facts should be clearly stated in open court so the public may know of, and I hope ponder deeply, the horrors which are perpetrated in this country. It is one thing for the citizen to read in his paper of the finding of a body in an alleyway on a dark night. It is quite another to be faced with the horrifying details of the killing and see, as I have done, photographs of the broken and bleeding body of the victim.

There is much talk nowadays of counter-terrorism and retaliation for IRA atrocities. Such talk in my view is dangerous in the extreme since it leads to the sort of vicious sectarian murder of an innocent young man which is before the court today … It is not for me to enter into a policy question on whether the UDA should be added to the list of proscribed organisations but I refer to the fact that the papers in this case contain a clear indication that a plot to carry out a retaliation killing of a Catholic was being hatched in a UDA club on the night that young Alex Reid was murdered.[80]

The secretary of state and the NIO were so concerned, not it would seem by the horrific killing of Alexander Reid, but at the judge's words of condemnation of the UDA, that they requested a transcript. An internal memo was sent by J. M. Burns to the secretary of state's private secretary on 5 February 1981 in response to a request for advice. He advised that the main requirement was to 'damp down the issue' and, despite Justice Murray's remarks, there was still little evidence of expectation on the question of proscription. He relayed the message that the chief constable's view was that the best approach was to say nothing.[81] Burns believed that was unrealistic because the secretary of state had already said publicly that he would consider the question of proscribing the UDA, and, therefore, must at some stage announce the outcome of his deliberations. He advised that it would be better for the secretary of state 'to make his own low-key announcement … at a time of his own choosing'. There would also be an advantage in diverting attention by saying the statement had been referred to the police. No reason should be given for the decision.[82] This comment illustrates the utter cynicism of the NIO's approach.

MI6 officer David Wyatt, in an internal memo on 12 February, informed the permanent under-secretary that the chief constable was pressing for a meeting between Secretary of State Humphrey Atkins and Glen Barr.[83] Wyatt, however, warned against any such meeting, declaring ominously: 'UDA/UFF gunmen, with the full blessing of Tyrie, are going to continue murdering identified Republicans.'[84]

In a memo to J. F. Halliday at the Home Office, civil servant Mike Hopkins referred to the announcement by Humphrey Atkins on 6 February that he had decided not to proscribe the UDA but would keep the matter under review. He wrote that the arguments weighed substantially against proscription. Significantly, he said: 'A good deal hangs on the fact that the UDA do not claim responsibility for terrorist attacks and, as long as that remains the position, the political arguments are also balanced against proscription.'[85] Even at this stage, ministers were still prepared to keep their heads firmly in the sand.

Evidence was mounting of UDA involvement in assassinations. In *Smashing H-Block*, US author and academic F. Stuart Ross writes that, nine days after the funeral of IRA hunger-striker Bobby Sands on 7 May 1981, the *Belfast Telegraph* reported that the UDA had displayed in an east Belfast office a photograph of a section of the crowd attending the funeral. It was shown with a caption asking people if they recognised anyone in the picture. That same night, Patrick Martin, a thirty-seven-year-old husband and father from Crumlin Road, Belfast, was shot dead in his bed by the UDA – the justification put forward was that he had attended the Sands funeral.[86]

# 10

## RUC RAIDS ON UDA HEADQUARTERS EMBARRASS THE BRITISH GOVERNMENT

> In terms of the politics of proscription [of the UDA], we have always regarded the existence of such denials as more important than their accuracy.
>
> *C. Davenport, NIO official*[1]

On 26 May 1981, at the height of tensions over the IRA/INLA hunger strike,[2] the RUC searched the headquarters of the UDA in Newtownards Road, Belfast, and discovered the following weapons: one Thompson sub-machine gun, six home-made Sten guns, a .45 revolver and 550 rounds of ammunition. According to official records UDA man Robert McDevitt was arrested, while Andy Tyrie was merely interviewed. However, *The Irish Times* stated that two men were arrested along with Tyrie.[3] The discovery prompted a debate amongst top civil servants, ministers and the chief constable. If involvement in outright sectarian murders was not sufficient cause to ban the UDA, would catching the organisation red-handed, with a deadly arms cache in its headquarters, be enough? Surely a Rubicon of sorts had been crossed?

This certainly triggered a flurry of internal memos between senior NIO officials. Assistant Secretary Stephen Boys-Smith, wrote to P. W. J. Buxton about the arms discovery, noting Buxton's views at a meeting with the secretary of state the previous day regarding UDA proscription.[4] Buxton had told Humphrey Atkins:

> The UDA is not now engaged in violence although it might be ready to resort to or encourage violence in extreme situations. The organisation reflects certain strands of the thinking of the Protestant community and it would be a substantial step to proscribe it.[5]

This statement was simply untrue. The UDA was, at that time, engaged in violence. In March, it killed Paul Blake, a Catholic, and – just ten days before the arms find – another Catholic, Patrick Martin. Buxton also ignored the high-profile attempted murder of the McAliskeys (see Chapter 9).

Some senior NIO officials had certainly been expecting an upsurge in UDA violence in response to the election of IRA hunger-striker Bobby Sands in the Fermanagh/south Tyrone by-election held on 9 April 1981. David Blatherwick had written to D. J. Wyatt in April stating that they were aware 'that the UDA is currently considering a major escalation in violence as a response to Sands' victory'.[6]

At a meeting on 1 June Atkins expressed concern that the police had failed to make arrests following the discovery of the arms and had not sought extensions of detention while pursuing their enquiries. Justifiably, he worried that the police would not be seen to have acted as might have been expected had a similar discovery been made elsewhere, rather than at UDA headquarters.[7]

In a note to John Blelloch, deputy secretary, NIO, dated 3 June, Buxton reported on his questioning of the chief constable, Sir John Hermon, the previous night about the failure to bring charges; he had put it to Hermon that he could have used Section 9 of the Northern Ireland (Emergency Provisions) Act 1978 to do so.[8]

Buxton had advised that Section 9 provided that when arms were found 'in premises of which a person was the occupier and which he habitually used otherwise than as a member of the public', that might be accepted as sufficient proof of illegal possession of arms, unless the person could prove ignorance. The section reversed the onus of proof – under Section 9 a person was not presumed innocent until proven guilty, but rather had to prove their innocence. Hermon had agreed that it had proven useful in other cases. In what appears to be a barely veiled criticism of the chief constable, Buxton advised Blelloch that 'Hermon still needs to focus on the continued possibility of laying charges'.[9]

It was a busy time for Buxton. In a long memo to the secretary of state's private secretary, he discussed the arms discovery and echoed the secretary of state's regrets that it was dealt with at divisional level without reference to RUC headquarters.[10]

Either Andy Tyrie had very strong powers of persuasion, or the RUC regarded arms finds in the loyalist community very differently from arms finds in the republican community. After the local detective chief superintendent had taken him and the relevant UDA keyholders in for questioning, they had satisfied their interrogators they had no connection with or knowledge of the arms and were soon released without charge, including McDevitt. Buxton reported that the chief constable had conceded that it might have been 'convenient' to hold them for a couple of days, but, he added, the action taken, 'professionally speaking', was defensible.[11] He explained that the UDA was a tenant of the property, not the owner, and the NIO had been unable to establish the status of other properties in which the UDA had an interest. He argued that if the UDA were proscribed, it would cause the organisation no difficulty to 'declare themselves under another name' and re-register properties under that name.

Buxton then presented the pros and cons of proscription. Points in favour were that statements by Andy Tyrie in recent months had come close to admissions of direct involvement in the 'direction of terrorism'.[12] In *The Washington Star* the previous week, Tyrie had defended assassinations and taken responsibility for 'the small offensive unit called UFF'. The arms find at UDA headquarters lent tangible credence to these statements. Inaction by the government would put its credibility and that of the RUC at risk when they claimed an even-handed approach to law enforcement, he said. Proscription would please the Irish government and Irish-American circles and might act as a 'sweetener' to the 'beleaguered Catholic community'.[13]

The points against proscription were that Tyrie had played a 'generally helpful' role in stabilising loyalist opinion. If the UDA were to be proscribed, he would lose control, creating a 'second front' for the security forces when they were fully stretched on the main front, combatting the IRA. They could expect disturbances in Protestant areas, just when the marching season was beginning; the conviction of UDA wrongdoers would be more difficult, given the 'general disaffection' and drying up of intelligence sources. It would alienate the 'Protestant community', even those who had no sympathy with the UDA; the organisation had just unveiled some worthy plans for a new political movement – proscription would probably nip that in the bud.[14]

Buxton imparted the views of Hermon, who he said was firmly of the view that this was an inopportune time to proscribe the UDA. In Hermon's view, two conditions would have to be satisfied – the politico-security scene must be quiet (meaning that the hunger strike crisis must be past), and the UDA should have developed politically to a point 'where the mass of dormant membership and the "social welfare/community worker" elements had been syphoned off, leaving a rump of hard men (loosely speaking the UFF) and an ordinary criminal fringe ripe for proscription'.[15]

The chief constable had warned Buxton that, if the government decided to proceed with proscription, it could not count upon his support, and he hoped to be given the chance to state his views before a final decision was taken, preferably at a meeting with the secretary of state. Although not quite a veto, this does seem to be the chief constable exerting an undue influence on government policy. If ministers decided not to proscribe for the moment, Hermon would be glad to be quoted in support of the decision. His chief argument was the 'demonstrable efforts of the RUC to bring members of the UDA to book and the obstacles which proscription would place in their way in the future'.[16]

Buxton agreed that a strong argument could be advanced about the prosecution of UDA members and suggested it was proof of the RUC's *bona fides* in claiming an even-handed approach and no sanctuary for the UDA. He suggested that, in security terms, proscription would be counterproductive and politically would tend to aggravate rather than ease intercommunal tensions and provoke demands for similar action, which they would be very reluctant to take at present, against 'supposedly similar' republican organisations. He concluded by recommending that the secretary of state should not proscribe the UDA but should keep the matter under close review, agreeing with Hermon that if Atkins felt unable to accept his recommendation, he should invite the chief constable to present his case before a final decision was made.[17]

Boys-Smith, in a most revealing memo, wrote to Blelloch on 5 June, reminding him of a remark by Atkins that proscription would 'deprive the security forces of the access which they presently had to those members of the UDA who were also active in terrorism'.[18]

C.R.   DESKBY  10.25   s e c r e t   35/47/03   (14)   ...

25 JUN 1981

Mr Blelloch (M)

c.c.  PS/SOS (B) — M
PS/Mr Alison (B&L)
PS/PUS(B&L) - M
Mr Marshall
Mr Moriarty
Mr Wyatt — M
Mr Ranson — M
Mr Davenport — M
Mr Harrington
Mr Blatherwick — M
Mr Chesterton
Mr Buxton — PT

PROSCRIPTION OF THE UDA

You spoke to the Secretary of State on 3 June about the
proscription of the UDA in the light of          note
of 2 June and Mr Buxton's note of 3 June.  Mr Buxton and
Mr Wyatt were also present.  The Secretary of State noted
that proscription would deprive the security forces of
the access which they presently had to those members of the
UDA who were also active in terrorism.  He appreciated too
that proscription would alienate sections of the Protestant
community but was unlikely at least in the long run to do
much to impress the Catholic community, bearing in mind
that its practical effects would be limited.  He agreed in
the light of discussion that it would not be right at present
to proscribe the UDA.

The Secretary of State expressed his concern about the way
in which the discovery of arms at the UDA headquarters and
the associated police action would be interpreted, especially
if the UDA was not proscribed.  He feared that the Government
and police would not appear impartial, and that even if there
were good reasons for not bringing prosecutions they were not
ones which would necessarily be widely understood in the
Catholic community or generally in Great Britain or elsewhere.

The Secretary of State agreed that he would meet the Chief
Constable later in the day.  He would say that, given the
Chief Constable's advice, he would not at present seek to
proscribe the UDA;  he would express his concern about how
moderate Catholics and people generally outside Northern
Ireland might interpret recent events;  and he would urge
the Chief Constable to take action to ensure the security
forces and so by implication the Government were seen in a
better light, minimising the effect of his decision not to
seek proscription.

*NAUK, CJ4/3963, memo to John Blelloch from Stephen Boys-Smith, 5 June 1981,
p. 1*

SECRET

The Chief Constable called on the Secretary of State at 4.30.
You were also present.  The Secretary of State made the
following points:-

1.  He noted that the Chief Constable was opposed to
    proscription at this stage and that he thought
    it would be unhelpful to the preservation of security.
    He accepted this advice.

2.  He was concerned about the perception of events both
    as it bore on the discovery of arms and the subsequent
    arrests, on the continuing police investigations, and
    on the possibility of proscription.  He had to have
    in mind the questions which would be asked of him in
    Parliament and by his colleagues and others in Great
    Britain.  He also needed to consider a wider view
    which would be taken of the Government   and the
    security forces. He noted the Chief Constable's wish
    that the RUC should be seen as an impartial and pro-
    fessionally competent force.

3.  He was ready to answer the suggestion that the UDA should
    be proscribed because of the misdeeds of a few of its
    members, and he thought that he could do so effectively.
    But the discovery of arms at the headquarters created
    a different situation.  The UDA as a whole was seen to
    be involved and questions about its future were bound
    to be raised.  Many, for example, would assume that
    the Chairman and officers could be held responsible;
    this might particularly be the case with those who
    knew of Section 9 of the Emergency Provisions Act 1978.

4.  In these circumstances he believed that there would be
    less criticism if arrests were made or if there were
    prosecutions.  He appreciated that there could be pro-
    secutions only if there was a reasonable chance of
    conviction, but he believed that a legitimate prosecution
    which failed in the courts might well be better than
    no prosecution at all.

In the light of these points the Secretary of State emphasised to
the Chief Constable the sensitivity of the situation as he saw it
and the importance of  taking  action  which would minimise the
harmful    reaction in Northern Ireland, Great Britain and elsewhere to which he referred.

The Chief Constable made the following points:-

1.  He confirmed that he did not believe proscription at the
    present time was right.  Most UDA members did not act
    illegally and the organisation was not active in violence.
    Only a small core of its members were involved in terrorism
    or illegal activities and they were not a sufficient
    reason for proscription.  There was a good record of success
    against Protestant extremists which would be hindered

*NAUK, CJ4/3963, memo to John Blelloch from Stephen Boys-Smith, 5 June 1981,
p. 2*

E.R.

SECRET

rather than helped by proscription.

2.  In his view the immediate aftermath of the discovery
    of arms had been badly handled by his officers and he
    had taken steps to ensure that the same would not
    happen again.   The release of the 3 suspects had been
    premature, given the context in which arrests had been
    made, and the decision had not been referred to a suitably
    senior level in the Force.   But intelligence confirmed
    that the decision was nevertheless correct and that the
    suspects had not been involved.

3.  He assured the Secretary of State that he wished the
    RUC to be seen as an impartial and professional force.
    He appreciated the sensitivities to which the Secretary
    of State referred.   The key to ensuring the RUC were
    seen to be impartial was continuing hard work in in-
    vestigating those who broke the law.   It was possible
    to show that much was being done to deal with Protestant
    as with other offenders, and these efforts should not be
    diverted by pressures of the moment.

4.  He did not believe that charges could be brought against
    the officers of the UDA, notwithstanding Section 9 of
    the 1978 Act.   Nor did he wish to prosecute if he be-
    lieved there would be an acquittal.

5.  He had already directed that efforts should be made to
    identify those who might be involved and to arrest and
    detain them for question.   He had also directed that
    full use should be made of all available intelligence to
    this end.   He assured the Secretary of State that the
    enquiries were being pursued urgently and energetically.

In the light of a full and robust discussion the Chief Constable
assured the Secretary of State that he remained alert to the
difficulty over presentation and to the need for the RUC to be
seen to be impartial.   He would ensure that every effort was
be made to arrest offenders and that the whole affair was capable
of presentation in a way which reflected the sensitive issue of
public perception of the security forces to which the Secretary
of State had referred.

*S.W. Boys Smith*

S W BOYS SMITH
5 June 1981

SECRET

*NAUK, CJ4/3963, memo to John Blelloch from Stephen Boys–Smith, 5 June 1981,
p. 3*

As can be seen from the de Silva report into the murder of Pat Finucane, around 85 per cent of all UDA intelligence information was coming from the various branches of the British security forces at this time.[19] Clearly the 'access' worked in both directions, and to the UDA's benefit. According to a BBC *Panorama* programme, Lord Stevens, during his investigations, arrested 210 loyalist paramilitary suspects, of whom 207 were agents or informants for the state.[20]

A document included in de Silva's report, headed 'Collusion between the security forces and loyalist paramilitaries', observes that the flow of intelligence to the UDA increased significantly around the time of the Anglo-Irish Agreement:[21] 'However, it is assessed that research of intelligence dating from previous years would be likely to reveal a similar picture to that given in the attached document.'[22] Boys-Smith appreciated that proscription would alienate sections of the 'Protestant community' and agreed that it 'would not be right at present to proscribe the UDA', although he noted that Atkins had again expressed concern at how the discovery of arms at UDA headquarters and the associated police action would be interpreted, especially if the UDA was not proscribed. 'He feared the Government and police would not appear impartial, and that, even if there were good grounds for not bringing prosecutions, they were not ones which would necessarily be understood in the Catholic community or generally in Great Britain or elsewhere.'[23]

The chief constable, he advised, had called on the secretary of state later that day. Atkins remarked that Hermon was opposed to proscription 'at this stage' as he 'thought it would be unhelpful to the preservation of security'. He accepted the chief constable's advice but told Hermon he was 'concerned about the perception of events', both in terms of the discovery of arms and the subsequent arrests and about the continuing police investigation.[24] Boys-Smith commented that the secretary of state had to be mindful of 'the questions which would be asked of him in Parliament and by his colleagues and others in Great Britain'. While he was ready to answer the suggestion that the UDA should be proscribed 'because of the misdeeds of a few of its members' and he had up to then believed he could do so effectively, the discovery of arms created 'a different situation'. The UDA as a whole was seen to be involved, and Atkins worried that 'questions about its future were bound to be raised'. Many people would assume that the UDA's 'Chairman' (Tyrie) and other officers could be held responsible; 'this might be the case particularly with those who knew of Section 9 of the Northern Ireland (Emergency Provisions) Act 1978'.[25]

Boys-Smith observed that Atkins had suggested the criticism would be muted if there were arrests and prosecutions. He appreciated that prosecutions were only possible if there was a reasonable chance of conviction, but believed 'a legitimate prosecution which failed in the courts might be better than no prosecution at all'. He stressed to Hermon the sensitivity of the situation and the importance of taking action which would minimise the harmful reaction.

The chief constable reiterated that he did not believe UDA proscription at the present time was the right way to go and asserted:

> Most UDA members did not act illegally and the organisation was not active in violence. Only a small core of its members was involved in terrorism or illegal activities and they were not a sufficient reason for proscription. There was a good record of success against Protestant extremists which would be hindered rather than helped by proscription.[26]

Hermon conceded that 'the immediate aftermath of the discovery of arms had been badly handled by his officers' – the release of the three suspects 'had been premature, given the context in which the arrests had been made, and the decision had not been referred to a suitably senior level in the Force … He did not believe that charges could be brought against the officers of the UDA', notwithstanding Section 9 of the Northern Ireland (Emergency Provisions) Act and was opposed to prosecutions that would result in acquittals. He had assured Atkins that enquiries 'were being pursued urgently and energetically' to try to identify those who might be involved and to arrest and detain them for questioning.[27]

While politicians such as Atkins might have claimed ignorance of the true nature of the UDA, no such excuse was available to Hermon. As chief constable, he had full access to Special Branch intelligence and would have been well aware of the widespread involvement of the UDA in assassinations, bombings, extortion and intimidation.

In the month before the arms find, NIO official D. F. E. (Frances) Elliot drafted a letter to a Mr McNamara of Liverpool in answer to his letter requesting the proscription of the UDA, dated 25 March. Ms Elliot explained that the secretary of state was not, at present, going to proscribe the UDA. She wrote that the decision was based:

> on the difference between an organisation *as such* being engaged in terrorist activities (as for example, the PIRA or the UFF, both of which are proscribed) and individuals (who also happen to be members of an organisation) committing crimes.[28]

This oft-repeated disingenuous and subtle distinction was based on two false premises. First, the UFF was not a separate organisation but merely a cover name for the UDA. Second, it assumes that 'individuals' who carried out acts of terror were acting alone and were not being directed by leaders of the UDA.

Michael Canavan of the SDLP persisted in his efforts to have the UDA proscribed. On 1 June he wrote again to the secretary of state with new information to bolster his case, referring to seventeen members of the UDA convicted of terrorist offences; an Ulster Television *Counterpoint* programme detailing UDA gun-running from Scotland; the judicial comments, not only of Justice Murray at the trial of the killer of Alexander Reid, but also of Justice McDermott (3 April), Justice Rowland (18 April) and Justice Doyle (24 March and 28 May); and armed attacks on at least five persons, one fatal.

Having taken the decision not to proscribe the organisation, officials struggled to decide whether or not to inform Canavan of this. In a remarkably cavalier response to Canavan's dogged and justifiable concern, C. Davenport of the Law and Order Division of the NIO advised against informing him, noting that 'interest in the UDA has gone off the boil'.[29]

On 10 August, in response to a letter from Don Concannon, the Labour shadow spokesman on Northern Ireland, concerning the arms find at UDA headquarters, Under-Secretary of State Michael Alison replied that he understood from the chief constable that, despite 'a thorough and exhaustive investigation', the police had not secured evidence which would justify the mounting of a prosecution.[30] Meanwhile, in the midst of all the concerns within the NIO regarding the arms find, the UDA announced hastily the establishment of a new political party, the Ulster Loyalist Democratic Party (ULDP), amid fears that the UDA might be proscribed. It replaced the NUPRG, ousting Glen Barr, but nevertheless continued for a time to promote an independent Northern Ireland.[31]

NIO official Stephen Leach commented caustically on the party in a memo to his boss, David Blatherwick, on 4 August, responding to a June query from him as to whether there might be 'any benefit in opening "political" contacts with the UDA'.[32] Leach was one of the officials who had favoured developing links with Barr but had been overruled. His advice to Blatherwick was:

> although the UDA had allegedly formed a new political party, replacing the NUPRG, there was little evidence that it had much objective existence … its existence was announced rather hurriedly at a time when proscription of the UDA was being widely discussed.[33]

He noted that the new party's leader, John McMichael, was the UDA's south Belfast commander and 'had nothing of Barr's political pedigree'. He advised Blatherwick that the time for 'nurturing political seeds in [the] UDA' had passed and recommended that no action be taken to initiate contacts.[34]

The new party did not enjoy any electoral success. Its first foray into politics saw John McMichael securing only 1.3 per cent of the vote in the 1982 by-election in south Belfast.

***

C. Davenport, in an internal memo to another official, commented on the fresh calls being made, yet again, for the UDA's proscription on the grounds that the UDA and UFF were 'one and the same' after the UFF claimed responsibility for the murder of Eugene Mulholland – a twenty-five-year-old married father of two children – on 19 September 1981.[35] He noted that Gerry Fitt and the Alliance Party had issued statements. However, Davenport insisted that nothing had changed.[36] He commented that, following the

**CONFIDENTIAL**

.R.

Mr Blelloch
Mr Buxton
Mr Wyatt
Mr Blatherwick
Miss MacGlashan

MR FERGUSSON

THE UDA

Following the murder of Eugene Mulholland, claimed by the UFF, and the latter's reported "death list" of Republicans, there have been fresh calls for the proscription of the UDA, on the alleged grounds that the two organisations are one and the same. Gerry Fitt is reported to have said that proscription should be the new Secretary of State's "most urgent task", and the Alliance Party, who have pressed the point before, may take it up in their meeting with him today.

2.   Unless these calls for proscription are to continue - which they may not unless there are more sectarian murders claimed by the UFF - I would not be disposed to offer Ministers unsolicited advice on the subject.  It may well be, however, that we shall be asked for advice, particularly if the Alliance Party raise the matter today. I think it would therefore be worth your dusting off our previous submission on the matter and considering whether anything has changed since then in the balance of the argument.  At first sight, it does not seem to me that it has.  In particular, I see that, following the UFF claim over the Mulholland murder, the UDA have reportedly denied any connection with the other organisation.  In terms of the politics of proscription, we have always regarded the existence of such denials as more important than their accuracy.

C.D.

C DAVENPORT
Law and Order Division
Stormont House
22 September 1981

*NAUK, CJ4/4198, memo to George Fergusson from C. Davenport, 22 September 1981*

UFF claim of responsibility, the UDA had reportedly denied any connection with the UFF: 'In terms of the politics of proscription, we have always regarded the existence of such denials as more important than their accuracy.'[37] This statement suggests that Davenport, a senior civil servant in Stormont's Law and Order Division, considered it most important that the UDA should continue to deny involvement in murders even though the organisation was responsible.

David Blatherwick had not accepted Leach's advice on contact with the UDA/ULDP and, in October 1981, sought the opinion of David Wyatt, MI6's man in Belfast. He began by noting that 'In recent years neither Ministers nor officials have had direct dealings with persons or organisations involved in paramilitary activity.' He reminded Wyatt that this had 'not always been the case'.[38] Until the arrival of Roy Mason as secretary of state in September 1976, Laneside (shorthand for the section of the NIO responsible for observing political developments) had met both republican and loyalist groups on a regular basis. One of Mason's first acts had been to close down Laneside, which had been home to Frank Steele and Michael Oatley.[39]

Blatherwick noted that in the course of 1980, this firm restriction on not meeting persons or organisations involved in paramilitary activity had been 'relaxed slightly' in respect of Hugh Smyth of the Progressive Unionist Party (PUP) – 'an organisation close to the UVF' – who had met the secretary of state as part of a delegation of smaller political parties. Blatherwick remarked that the UDA was not proscribed, although he accepted that the leadership of the new organisation, the ULDP, was 'heavily involved in UDA paramilitary activities' and was 'little more than the shop window for a fairly nasty organisation'.[40] Moreover, although Mason had closed down Laneside, meetings at some level of government with the UDA leadership continued, as is borne out by the closed NIO file in Kew.

Blatherwick set out his argument in favour of initiating contact, pointing out that 'the UDA/UDLP is a much larger and more amorphous organisation than the UVF/PUP or indeed PIRA/PSF and has roots and considerable influence in loyalist working-class areas'. He believed it would be desirable to be in a position to speak to them directly, as this would 'increase our knowledge of attitudes in a section of opinion which could become increasingly important (especially if Ministers proposed to follow policies which set unionist teeth on edge).'[41] He argued:

> whether we like it or not, the UDA is a political as well as a para-military body, in a way neither PIRA nor the UVF, for example, are. … the UDA/ULDP are fairly sensible on many political issues, and have a good grasp of the grass roots. We might hope to tap support which at present goes partly by default to the DUP.[42]

He advised Wyatt that it should be made clear that they would not talk to those 'involved in terrorism', suggesting that Councillor Sammy Millar or Billy Elliot – an unsuccessful candidate in a recent by-election – might be suitable as they were 'clean'. He remarked that he would very much like the Public Affairs Branch to be authorised to approach them and others not involved in terrorist activities, warning they should be 'circumspect with people like Tyrie himself, who is not "clean"'.[43]

These extraordinary comments were made at a time when the UDA was heavily involved in terrorism as well as widespread extortion, robberies and intimidation.

E.R.

~~CONFIDENTIAL~~

1. M. Perkins

2 0 OCT 1981

PAB/1126/RE

cc: Mr Buxton
Miss MacGlashan
Mr Chesterton
Mr Davenport

Mr Wyatt

*This is getting into dangerous territory, just as sectarian tit for tat killings are on the increase. If we talk to UDA officially I cannot see why we should continue to refuse to talk to PSF.*

CONTACT WITH LOYALIST GROUPS

2. Please file.

Mr Blackwell

B~~en~~ 20/10

1. In recent years neither Ministers nor officials have had direct
dealings with persons or organisations involved in paramilitary activity
This has not always been the case.  Until the advent of Roy Mason as
Secretary of State Laneside, the part of the NIO with responsibility for
keeping in contact with political affairs in the Province, met both
Republican and Loyalist paramilitary groups on a regular basis.  It is
worth examining our current practice and the case, if any, for change.

2. In the course of 1980 the very firm restrictions were relaxed slightl
in one respect.  Councillor Hugh Smyth of the PUP, an organisation close
to the UVF which Ministers and officials had hitherto shunned, met the
then Secretary of State (Mr Atkins) as part of a delegation of smaller
parties.  Mr Smyth and his colleagues have since come to Stormont several
times on their own.  The only rule we have applied is that they should
not bring with them persons involved now or in the past in terrorist
activity (though one frequent visitor, Jim McDonald, is subject to an
exclusion order from Great Britain under the PTA and another, George
McDermott, who met Lord Gowrie on 14 October, is described as the UVF's
"official photographer"!)

3. I do not believe there is a case for changing our policy towards
the proscribed organisations (PIRA, INLA, the UVF, UFF, RHC etc).  To
deal with them would arouse great and justifiable anger in the community
here and in the rest of the UK.  It would lend encouragement to terrorism,
and it would undercut the position of the political parties committed to
democratic politics.  But there are border areas.  The PUP (or rather,
individuals belonging to or associated with it) is one example.  The UDA
is another.

4. The UDA is <u>not</u> proscribed, and it has over recent years played with
the concept of setting up a political wing.  The most ambitious attempt,
the New Ulster Political Research Group (NUPRG), collapsed in the summer.
A new organisation, the Ulster Loyalist Democratic Party (ULDP) was set

CONFIDENTIAL

-1-

*NAUK, CJ4/3963, memo to David Wyatt from David Blatherwick, 19 October
1981, p. 1*

on paper in August. One Councillor (Sammy Millar, from Belfast who fought the May election on a NUPRG ticket) has joined it. It fought a by-election in August, winning (or personating) over 1000 votes. But its leadership is heavily involved in UDA paramilitary activities and it is little more than the shop window for a fairly nasty organisation.

5.  The disadvantages of direct contact with the UDA or the ULDP are similar to those of contact with proscribed organisations and are set out above. But there would be possible advantages:

(a)  the UDA/ULDP is a much larger and more amorphous organisation than the UVF/PUP or indeed PIRA/PSF, and has roots and considerable influence in loyalist working class areas. To be able to speak to them direct would increase our knowledge of attitudes in a section of opinion which could become increasingly important (especially if Ministers propose to follow policies which set unionist teeth on edge).

(b)  though it would be wrong to exaggerate the point, we might hope through direct contact to explain what the Government is doing and get messages through which might help on some occasions. For example, in May this year Andy Tyrie, the UDA leader, played a useful and constructive role, together with the WP-RC, Paddy Devlin and others, in scotching Provo plans for a major sectarian confrontation in Belfast. It would have been useful to have had direct contact with him then. Similar occasions may arise in the future.

(c)  whether we like it or not, the UDA _is_ a political as well as a paramilitary body, in a way neither PIRA nor the UVF, for example, are. Tyrie uses his political influence; he writes articles, talks to other politicians, and is very much part of the Belfast political scene. (We know that he is keen to open a channel of communication with Government.)

(d)  we might hope (though I fear with little confidence) to encourage the UDA towards a political rather than paramilitary role (which Tyrie professes to want).

NAUK, CJ4/3963, memo to David Wyatt from David Blatherwick, 19 October 1981, p. 2

**L.R.**

CONFIDENTIAL  *Doc 93*

(e)  the UDA/ULDP are fairly sensible on many political issues, and
have a good grasp of the grass roots. We might hope to tap
support which at present goes partly by default to the DUP.

6.  In my view it would be useful to establish links, providing we made
it clear that we would not talk to people involved in terrorism. After
all, the UDA is <u>not</u> proscribed, and we do consort with the PUP. One or
two ULDP members (eg Councillor Sammy Millar; Billy Elliott, the
unsuccessful candidate in the by-election) are "clean" (and many are a
good deal cleaner than Jim McDonald of the PUP).

. . I would very much like PAB to be
authorised to approach them, and others who are not personally involved
in terrorist activities. This would be in line with our dealings with
the PUP, whom I am sure Ministers would like to continue to meet. But
we should be circumspect with people like Tyrie himself, who is <u>not</u>
"clean". And we should avoid a situation where Ministers are not willing
to meet people whom officials see.

*S.J. Leach.*

· D E S BLATHERWICK
Political Affairs Division

19 October 1981

-3-

CONFIDENTIAL

Blatherwick's memo initiated a number of responses. P. W. J. Buxton wrote to Wyatt, noting Blatherwick's 'putting the case for PAB [Public Affairs Branch] to re-open contacts with UDA on Laneside-style lines.' Buxton said his specific interest in this was 'avoidance of proscription of UDA', since he, like the chief constable, believed that this would be a hindrance to their security policy.[44] Unsurprisingly, he was sceptical of Blatherwick's argument that the UDA was distinctive in the context of being political as well as paramilitary, noting that 'whatever the artificiality of the distinction between PIRA and PSF, the latter has today some claim to political reality'.[45] If they were to initiate contacts with the UDA, it would lead to opening contact with Sinn Féin. Buxton regarded this as an unattractive proposition, as, he noted, there were already suspicions they had been dealing with republicans to end the hunger strike.[46] It is strange that Buxton should refer to 'the artificiality of the distinction between PIRA and PSF', as it was he who had compiled the report into the links between the two organisations just three years earlier, in 1978. His conclusion was that they were not 'inextricably linked'.

Davenport also wrote to Wyatt on the same date, commenting that, with the exception of Owen Carron, they did not talk to Sinn Féin because they were 'unable to draw a satisfactory dividing line between political leaders of PSF and terrorist leaders of PIRA'.[47] He pondered the fact that a lot of people thought the UDA ought to be proscribed, more so, 'oddly enough', than those who thought that Sinn Féin should be. He believed they knew fairly clearly which members of the UDA ran the UFF, but there was no simple dividing line. He doubted the value of such contacts if the actual leader of the UDA – Andy Tyrie – was to be excluded.[48]

Leach wrote to Wyatt the following day commenting on Buxton's and Davenport's memos, which he believed made a convincing case against official contact with Sinn Féin. Regarding the UDA, however, Leach came down on the side of Blatherwick, arguing that the cases of Sinn Féin and the UDA were not parallel and saying that the views of Buxton and Davenport did not refute Blatherwick's arguments. He argued:

> PSF is widely known to be the creature of an illegal terrorist organisation which is dedicated to achieving radical constitutional change through violence. Of course contacts with them would cause great anger and would serve no purpose, since no one believes they can be reached through argument. The UDA is in a different category. Contact with them would not carry the same emotive charge than if it became public that we were talking to the Provies; the UDA are not exploding car bombs in the middle of London, *and go to some lengths to avoid acknowledging responsibility for the violence they do commit* [emphasis added]. Many Catholics assume we have discrete contacts with the UDA already and express more distaste at the fact that Hugh Smyth and his UVF associates actually meet Ministers. To get the real measure of the difference, try to imagine Gerry Adams visiting Downing Street. Of course, contacts with the UDA would entail some political risks but they would also have political benefits which Blatherwick listed.
>
> In the last analysis the prospects for political development in Northern Ireland depend crucially on the way the loyalists behave. Whether we like it or not, the UDA is an organic expression of working-class loyalism and carries considerable influence in that community. It was UDA muscle in 1974 which torpedoed the closest thing we have yet had to a political settlement. The UDA leadership is much keener now than it was then to find a real political role.

Surely it makes sense to open up contacts (through 'clean' ULDP figures) to enhance our knowledge of, and to act directly upon, this very important variable in the equation.[49]

This is an extraordinary U-turn by Leach. His note contrasts sharply with his comments only two months previously, when he had advised Blatherwick he was utterly opposed to meeting with the UDA, describing their new political party, the ULDP, as having little objective existence. His main objection to talking to Sinn Féin seems to stem from the fact that the IRA was exploding bombs in London.

Leach was obviously aware that the RUC had spent seven months in 1977–8 investigating Sinn Féin to try to ascertain the closeness of its links with the IRA and had failed to establish 'that Sinn Féin was not a political party in its own right'. Sinn Féin had, by October 1981, already enjoyed electoral success on both sides of the border. He correctly described the UDA as 'an organic expression of working-class loyalism', but ignored the fact that it had no mandate.

In a memo to Wyatt, Blatherwick proposed contacting Billy Elliot (despite the fact that he had served an eighteen-month prison sentence in 1974–6 for an arms offence) and Dessie Dowds (an independent loyalist councillor from Newtownabbey who had 'strong UDA links').[50] Blatherwick's determination won through in the end. He phoned Elliot to arrange a meeting. Elliot enquired if he could bring the deputy commander of the UDA, John McMichael, and UDA spokesman Tommy Lyttle along, but Blatherwick 'demurred'. He asked if he could bring Andy Tyrie, but Blatherwick again 'demurred'.[51]

It was eventually agreed that Elliot would be accompanied by Mary McCurrie, the ULDP headquarters secretary. Blatherwick and Leach met them in a Belfast hotel on 19 November. Elliot told the officials that the party wanted to set up an assembly 'ideally in a sovereign state of Ulster expressing a separate Ulster identity' and that direct rule was inadequate. He spoke heatedly about how Rev. Ian Paisley had 'led people to the brink' in the past only to desert them and let them take the consequences. He wanted the officials to meet Tyrie and McMichael, but Blatherwick explained it would create problems as they were both leaders of a paramilitary organisation. Blatherwick reported that the meeting was friendly and amicable and he hoped that he and Elliot could keep in touch.[52]

On the following day, Blatherwick met with Dessie Dowds who, he wrote, was 'close to paramilitaries'. He informed Wyatt in a memo that Dowds had raised a number of specific points about personal weapons for the security forces, noting that Dowds' son was a member of the RUC. Dowds, too, was scathing of Paisley, claiming he had betrayed his followers in the past and would do so again. He recalled that Gusty Spence had told him when he was a prison visitor that before Spence and 'his friends' set out on their murder expedition they had had a meeting with a number of people, including 'a Reverend gentleman'. Blatherwick believed, 'from hints dropped', that he was sure Spence was referring to Paisley, but Paisley had kept 'safely out of the firing line'.[53]

The New Year of 1982 saw the chief constable expressing concern about the disillusionment and isolation of the UDA, for which he believed the government was responsible.[54] In a memo to Buxton dated 12 January, Boys-Smith advised that he and the secretary of state had met with Hermon earlier that day, when the chief constable had informed them of intelligence he had received 'during the course of the day about the future intentions of the UDA, and of McMichael in particular'. Hermon explained that the organisation was becoming disillusioned 'because it was unable to make a political impact'. It had, therefore, 'decided to adopt a more violent tactic and to seek to assassinate leading members of the PIRA. Targeting was good,' Hermon said, 'and there existed a list of 15 people.' He commented that 'Although the police had taken certain preventive measures they might not be wholly successful, especially because of the difficulty of exposing the source of the information.' He expressed the view that it would be extremely unfortunate if 'at a time when [the] PIRA was under pressure from the security forces' there were to be a series of murders carried out by the UDA/UFF which might well 'provoke a reaction'.[55] In the event, these murders were not carried out.

Boys-Smith understood that the chief constable was ascribing the sense of disillusionment which had prompted 'the development of this new tactic' largely, if not wholly, to 'the Government's failure to recognise the UDA as a legitimate political organisation'. Hermon had complained to the secretary of state that ministers did not meet McMichael, although they did meet Seamus Lynch, a former leader of the OIRA. Hermon regretted the increase in the UDA's isolation. For his part, he would like to see it 'brought into the political fold, although he was at pains to point out that a decision on this point was none of his business'.[56]

While the '"healthy cultivation" of McMichael could have security implications', Hermon said chillingly that he feared nothing could now be done to stop the attempted murders of republicans if the UDA acted quickly. He told James Prior, the secretary of state who had succeeded Atkins in September 1981, that 'He had his own communications, outside Special Branch, with somebody "influential with the UDA", which he had made use of recently; he would consider making use of them again on this occasion.'[57]

E.R.

LONDON COPIES BY MUFAX

PWJ8

10 1

12 JAN 1982

N.I.O. BELFAST

CC   PS/SOS (B&L) M
     PS/Lord Gowrie(B&L) M
     PS/Mr Woodfield (B&L) M
     Mr Marshall M
     Mr Bielloch
     Mr Wyatt
     Mr Doyne Ditmas
     Mr Angel M
     Mr Harrington M
     Mr Blatherwick
     Mr Gilliland

Mr Buxton

MEETING WITH THE CHIEF CONSTABLE: UDA

I am circulating separately, and necessarily more widely, the note of
yesterday's discussion with the Chief Constable. I have confined to
this note the comments the Chief Constable was making about the UDA.

2. The Chief Constable said he had received intelligence during the
course of the day about the future intentions of the UDA and of
McMichael in particular. The organisation had become increasingly
disillusioned because it was unable to make a political impact. It
had therefore decided to adopt a more violent tactic and to seek to
assassinate leading members of the PIRA. Targeting was good and
there existed a list of 15 people. Although the police had already
taken certain preventive measures they might not be wholly successful,
especially because of the difficulty of exposing the source of the
information. It would be extremely unfortunate if at a time when the
PIRA was under pressure from the security forces there was a series
of UDA/UFF murders which might well provoke a reaction.

3. As best I was able to understand, the Chief Constable appeared to
ascribe the sense of disillusion which had prompted the development of
this new tactic largely if not wholly to the Government's failure to
recognise the UDA as a legitimate political organisation. He pointed
out that Ministers did not meet McMichael although they did, for
example, meet Seamus Lynch, a former leader of the Official IRA. He
believed it was unfortunate to increase the UDA's sense of isolation.
For his part he would like to see them brought into the political fold
although he was at pains to emphasise that a decision on this point wa
none of his business. The 'healthy cultivation' of McMichael could ha

*NAUK, CJ4/4198, memo to P. W. J. Buxton from Stephen Boys-Smith, 12 January
1982, p. 1*

SECRET

F.R.

security implications although he feared that nothing now done was likely to have an effect on the attempted murders if the UDA/UFF decided to act quickly. He had his own communications, outside Special Branch, with somebody 'influential with the UDA' which he had made use of recently; he would consider making use of them again on this occasion.

4. The Secretary of State noted the Chief Constable's points and undertook to consider them. He has, as you know, already received advice on Ministerial dealings with the UDA. He would be glad of the views of officials on the case the Chief Constable has now put forward. The Chief Constable clearly attached a great deal of urgency to the matter and you will no doubt be able to determine whether he was right to do so in the light of the assessment you and others make of what he has said. But I imagine the Chief Constable may return to this at the meeting of SPM scheduled for 18 January and I think the Secretary of State will need at least an initial comment by then, either as part of the briefing or separately.

S.W. Boys Smith

S W BOYS SMITH
Private Secretary
12 January 1982

SECRET

PD

*NAUK, CJ4/4198, memo to P. W. J. Buxton from Stephen Boys-Smith, 12 January 1982, p. 2*

Boys-Smith informed Buxton that the chief constable clearly attached a great deal of urgency to the matter, and he believed it would be necessary to prepare an initial response to him by 18 January when a further meeting was scheduled.[58]

Roy Harrington, private secretary to the secretary of state, wrote to Buxton on the same topic the following day, expressing his disapproval of Hermon's views. He referred to a comment he had received from Harold Doyne-Ditmas, MI5's director and co-ordinator of intelligence in Northern Ireland during this period, and went on to warn that ministerial 'encouragement' of the UDA would not be viewed favourably abroad, especially in the United States.[59] He stated that 'rather unrealistically' the UDA is seen as the 'Protestant equivalent' of the IRA and noted that the British government's failure to proscribe it was 'from time to time' the subject of criticism. Harrington claimed that these considerations added to the strength of the case against a closer relationship with any paramilitary organisations, but he said Seamus Lynch and the Republican Clubs/Workers' Party could not be put into that category any longer, because by 1982, the OIRA was, by and large, defunct.[60] It is interesting to note that the head of MI5 in Northern Ireland was very much involved in these machinations.

In a memo to Boys-Smith, Wyatt noted that they had been 'round the course' with the chief constable many times on the issue of meeting with UDA leaders and that Hermon had produced 'intelligence' to support his views. He said that this 'intelligence', on closer examination, turned out to be something 'slightly different', suggesting he didn't believe the chief constable actually had intelligence to support his views. He reminded Boys-Smith that what was being proposed by Hermon was that ministers should meet men 'who are known to be engaged in criminal conspiracy to murder those of the opposing faction'.[61] Wyatt appears not to have had a very high regard for Hermon.

Wyatt, who was clearly under no illusion that the UDA leaders were up to their necks in directing violence, put his view bluntly: these people were only on the streets 'rather than in HMP Maze' because they were careful not to pull the trigger on those they condemned to death. He was largely in agreement with the views of Harrington and confirmed that officials 'on a deniable – but fairly widely known – basis' had met with UDA leaders frequently in the early 1970s. However, he said it had become clear that nothing could 'transmute' the UDA 'even partially' into a political organisation.[62]

Stressing that there was no evidence to suggest UDA members saw violence as being forced upon them by the absence of political channels, he said nothing had changed since the early 1970s in that regard. Even if it could bring it about, he opined, the British government did not want the UDA campaigning 'with a ballot box in one hand and an Armalite in the other'.[63] Wyatt strongly recommended that the secretary of state should deal with the UDA as the PUP/UVF or indeed the OIRA/Republican Clubs/Workers' Party had been dealt with – ministers should not meet men whom they knew to be engaged in violence. In the case of the UDA that meant meeting only those who were elected representatives with 'clean records', but who had some access to UDA leaders. He recommended that this 'low level' contact should continue through officials in the Public Affairs Branch.[64]

These discussions between senior civil servants in the NIO, which continued over many months from May 1981 – when the arms raid on UDA headquarters took place – until the following January, are very enlightening. While there were disagreements among them about whether or not to renew contact with the UDA, and all seemed opposed to the chief constable's views, not one of them recommended the proscription of the organisation. They were as one in that course of action.

On 14 April 1982, less than a year after the previous RUC raid on UDA headquarters, the RUC carried out a further raid. It seized documents containing details and photographs of IRA suspects as well as information on judges, magistrates and police officers. Six men were arrested: Andy Tyrie, John McMichael, Samuel McCormick, Edward Martin, John McClatchey and Robert McDevitt. They were charged with conspiring to have in their possession records and documents containing information which would be useful to terrorists between March 1981 and April 1982. The police had found 150 identifiable fingerprints in relation to the accused. All pleaded 'Not guilty'.[65]

More information emerged later that month, at a bail hearing for Tyrie and McMichael, at which their application was refused. Both men were accused of conspiring to possess information likely to be useful to terrorists between 25 July 1977 and 15 April 1982. They were also charged with conspiring to possess firearms and ammunition with intent to endanger life between 11 May 1981 and 15 April 1982. The judge was informed that the charges were based on documents and arms found during three separate raids on UDA headquarters. It emerged that as well as the raids of 26 May 1981 and 14 April 1982, an earlier raid on UDA headquarters had taken place on 26 July 1977.[66] The documents included the names of lawyers and prison wardens. There were names and addresses of alleged PIRA, OIRA and UVF members, as well as police and army lists and photographs of suspects. Other papers were plans of republican areas and pubs, minutes of Ulster Army Council meetings, particulars of people who visited prisoners on remand, a book entitled *The Terrorist's and Assassin's Bible* and manuals of sub-machine guns and on the manufacture of bombs.[67]

Both Judge Peter Cory and Sir Desmond de Silva QC reported that Pat Finucane was being targeted by the UDA in 1981, and de Silva reported that a second defence solicitor, Oliver Kelly, was also being targeted in that year.[68] It is not known, however, whether the documents seized in the 1982 raid contained the names of people subsequently killed by the UDA, such as Pat Finucane or many others.

Shortly after the May 1981 raid, RUC Special Branch had received intelligence that the UDA intended to kill Oliver Kelly. According to de Silva, the deputy head of Special Branch (Brian Fitz-simons) ruled out warning Kelly because 'RUC relations with Kelly are strained'.[69] The RUC apparently believed that he had some involvement in the breakout of eight IRA prisoners from Crumlin Road gaol on 10 June 1981. There was a change of heart when Kelly became 'directly and constructively involved' in discussions regarding the hunger strikes, and the director of intelligence made a decision to arrest selected UDA members to protect Kelly's life.[70]

In the course of the 1982 hearings, crown counsel said that, during the May 1981 raid, a sub-machine gun, a pistol and hundreds of rounds of ammunition had been recovered and, in the recent search, police had discovered a large quantity of ammunition, gun parts and bomb components. He continued that, for the two men, who were senior officers of the UDA, to claim they had no knowledge of what was found during the raid was 'stretching credulity'.[71]

Blatherwick and Leach met with members of the ULDP on 4 May 1982. The ULDP delegation included William Methven, Mary McCurrie and Billy Elliot. Methven was very critical of the arrests of the UDA leadership. He complained that having made sincere efforts to develop as a political party and to influence the UDA away from 'paramilitary activity', the ULDP was 'shattered' by the arrests on what Methven described as 'clearly trumped-up charges'. He indicated his belief that the arrests had been politically motivated and said it was 'most suspicious' that the arrests had followed quickly after the UDA's stated intention to 'unmask the real facts about [the] Kincora [Boys' Home scandal].' He described Tyrie and McMichael as 'moderates' and suggested that they would be replaced by 'the wild men'. Blatherwick denied that there had been any political interference.[72]

A month after their arrest in mid-April, both Tyrie and McMichael were given bail at a second court appearance, despite the prosecution's claim that the fingerprints of both men had been found on confidential police documents giving the details of people's information. Prosecuting counsel told the court that thousands of documents had been seized in the three raids. On the police raids in May 1981 and 'last month' detectives had discovered that the UDA's entire intelligence files had been renewed and updated since their initial raid in July 1977.[73]

The RUC had also found a biographical file including the names of judges, lawyers, prominent Catholics and 'moderate' Protestants known to socialise with Catholics. It was claimed that these names appeared to constitute an assassination list. In addition, the police recovered a number of weapons and an official army photograph album. Counsel for the defence asked why it had taken five years to bring charges.[74] At a later stage, de Silva reports, the Force Research Unit (FRU), an intelligence-gathering undercover unit of the British Army, through its agent Brian Nelson, 'extensively updated and disseminated targeting material to other loyalist paramilitaries, which they subsequently used in their efforts to carry out terrorist attacks'.[75]

Despite the evidence, the two men were granted bail and released on 14 May as a result of the intervention of three clergymen, who described Tyrie as 'a moderating influence against more extreme elements in UDA'.[76]

On 15 April 1983 charges against five of the men – John McMichael, Sammy McCormick, John McClatchey, Edward Martin and Robert McDevitt – were withdrawn by the DPP at Belfast Magistrates' Court. The charge against Andy Tyrie was not withdrawn, however, and he was remanded on continuing bail. A solicitor for the men said there had been an unacceptable delay on the part of the RUC and DPP in processing the cases. A solicitor for the DPP said she could not comment on what had caused the delay but promised that the charge against Tyrie would be dealt with expeditiously.[77] The case against Tyrie did not come to trial until 25 February 1986. It took just one hour for Tyrie to be tried and acquitted of the charge of possessing documents found during the police raid in April 1982.[78] This was despite the fact that the prosecution had claimed that his fingerprints had been found on some of the papers.

It is important to note that the relevant National Archives file contains only one official document which makes a passing reference to the arrests. The other documents contained in the file are newspaper articles which have been referred to above. A number of documents have been removed from the file and retained by the National Archives in Kew, but it is unclear whether or not these papers relate to the arms and documents discovery.[79]

Internationally, concerns continued to be raised about the failure to proscribe the UDA. In a self-serving paper prepared by David Hill for the FCO to rebut claims by the US-based INC, under the heading of 'UDA' Hill wrote that the UFF was a *nom de guerre* used by the 'military wing' of the UDA for its terrorist operations: 'although its policy is decided by an Army Council whose members are also leaders of the UDA, the UDA leadership publicly denies association with the UFF and Andy Tyrie is known to discourage random sectarian attacks'.[80] Hill referred to the UDA as a declining force and suggested that the muted response to the recent arrest of Andy Tyrie and other leading UDA members was 'symptomatic of their standing in the Protestant community'.[81]

\*\*\*

In the early 1980s reviews of emergency legislation were under-taken – in 1982 Sir George Jellicoe, a politician, diplomat and busi-nessman, reviewed the Prevention of Terrorism Act, and in 1983, Sir George Baker, a judge, was tasked with reviewing the Northern Ireland (Emergency Provisions) Act. During the course of his re-view, Jellicoe sought reasons for the decision not to proscribe the UDA. In August 1982 the NIO sought the advice of the RUC in the matter. In his reply, Chief Superintendent R. J. K. Sinclair pro-vided a note on the UDA and the criterion for proscription, which was:

> that a given organisation has demonstrated that the sole purpose of its existence is the commission of terrorist violence. The UDA does not meet this criterion. Although a number of UDA men have been convicted over the years of serious crimes, the great majority of its members are not involved in terrorism and confine themselves to participation in the UDA's social or, less frequently, political activities.[82]

Sinclair claimed that only a small percentage of UDA members became involved in the commission of crime or acts of terrorism 'and those that do are usually found to have dual membership of UFF'.[83]

Once again, there is double-speak on the UFF. The facts are that, by the end of 1981, the UDA had killed 267 people and injured hundreds more.[84] Would such a criterion apply to any other paramilitary organisation? The word 'demonstrated' is significant, as, clearly, the UDA had not claimed responsibility for any of the 267 deaths, with the exception of the death at Dublin airport in November 1975. As has been shown repeatedly, this was the real criterion for the non-proscription of the UDA.

Both the UDA and the UVF remained dangerous and unpredictable deadly forces throughout the 1980s and 1990s, and even into the 2000s. Links between the security forces and the UDA grew ever closer during the 1980s. The notorious UDA agent for the FRU, Brian Nelson (yet to come to public notice) was responsible for, among others, the killing of Pat Finucane. It remains a mystery as to why Nelson was recruited in 1984 (and re-recruited in 1987) by the FRU at a time when the number of UDA murders was lower than it had been for many years. In the years following Nelson's recruitment, however, the number of UDA murders increased exponentially. Gordon Kerr, the commanding officer of the FRU, justified his re-recruitment of Nelson to de Silva as follows:

> there was a desperate need for operational intelligence on the Protestant terror groups, who were successfully targeting individuals for assassination on a seemingly ad hoc basis … We, in the FRU, decided that if we could persuade Brian Nelson to return to Northern Ireland we could re-instate him as Intelligence Officer in the UDA and gain valuable intelligence on UDA targeting.[85]

The British authorities did eventually lose their long battle to keep the UDA lawful. The organisation was proscribed on 10 August 1992, but only after Nelson had been convicted of several murders and attempted murders that April, and after the broadcast of a BBC *Panorama* programme on 8 June, which made claims of Nelson's involvement in further murders and conspiracies.

In his December 2012 report on the murder of Pat Finucane, Sir Desmond de Silva disposed of any lingering doubts that the UFF was a separate organisation. He stated: 'It quickly became apparent to me that the notion of a separate UFF was in fact a fiction, though that is not to say that certain members of the UDA were not significantly more militant and violent than others.'[86]

De Silva examined just a sample of intelligence relating to leaks from the security forces to the UDA in the greater Belfast area between January 1987 and September 1989, and found 270 separate incidences of leaks. He notes that MI5 estimated that in 1985 the UDA had thousands of items of intelligence material and that 85 per cent of this was drawn from security force sources.[87] He included in his report Brian Nelson's statement to the Stevens investigation, dated 15 January 1990, in which Nelson described the UFF as follows:

> As the UFF is a proscribed organisation, which means it's illegal, any murders carried out by the Military wing of the UDA are claimed under the banner or flag of convenience of the UFF. For the UDA to publicly claim a murder would risk it also being proscribed. Therefore, whenever a murder is committed, there's normally the Senior Military Commander of the Unit that participated in the murder and, after clearance from the Inner Council, claims the murder in the name of the UFF.[88]

Volume II of de Silva's report, containing original documents, also has a 'loose minute' dated 29 September 1989 sent from Stormont House Annexe – names of sender and receiver redacted – which comments on a paper prepared for the Stevens investigation by the deputy head of Special Branch, Brian Fitzsimons.[89] The loose minute's unknown author stated there was no doubt that UDA and UDR links were significant. The author continued:

> Moreover, given the differing sizes and nature of the UDA and UVF (the latter being a proscribed organisation) we would expect there if anything to be more scope for contact between the security forces and the UDA than the UVF.[90]

This suggests that, because of the legal status of the UDA, better opportunities existed for contact between the organisation and the RUC and UDR.

Many contradictory remarks and different stances by senior NIO officials are evident in these internal memos, as these officials wrestled with the problems caused by the arms discoveries in UDA headquarters. The discoveries created huge difficulties for them in their continuing efforts to maintain the organisation as a legal entity. The officials apparently agonised over whether or not to renew contact with the UDA. However, as has been noted, there is good reason to suspect that meetings with the UDA leadership had been ongoing through the years at some level of government and with the security forces, bearing in mind the closed file at Kew that refers to such meetings from 1976–9, and Boys-Smith's memo to Blelloch quoting Humphrey Atkins as remarking that proscription would deprive the security forces of the access they had to those members of the UDA who were also active in terrorism.

The views of the RUC's chief constable, John Hermon, as reported in these memos, are very disturbing. The force's top police officer suggested that he knew the UDA was planning to kill fifteen leading members of the IRA but was doubtful that he could do anything about it because it would compromise his source.

For more than three decades a myth was perpetrated on the British and Irish people that the UDA was a benign organisation. No British government minister, no civil servant, no member of the security forces or services has ever been held to account for this disinformation.

# CONCLUSION

The documents analysed in this book reveal a relationship between the British government and loyalist paramilitaries that can be described as collusive. This association undoubtedly intensified into the 1980s and 1990s, as the de Silva report and the police ombudsman's report into the murders of Raymond McCord Junior and others by the Mount Vernon UVF clearly demonstrate.

From the outset, decisions were taken at the highest level by the British Army to treat loyalist paramilitaries differently from republicans, not merely by encouraging their cooperation with the security forces but also by using them as an auxiliary force. The UDA was given its head in patrolling its 'own areas' in uniform, often wearing masks; the authorities went so far as to turn a blind eye to the UDA's patrolling with arms and even permitted joint patrolling with British troops. There was a great reluctance to intern loyalists, the British government even undertaking to implement a special 'Arrest Policy for Protestants' (see chapters 2 and 3).

In the 1970s, regarding the ECHR case Ireland v United Kingdom, the British government was prepared to understate the loyalist sectarian assassination campaign before the commission and the ECtHR, not only to protect its international reputation, but also to justify its decision not to intern loyalists. At the hearings associated with the case, both the UDA and the UVF were portrayed as being undisciplined, unstructured organisations without proper leadership, with uncontrolled 'lone gunmen' running around like headless chickens killing people at random – yet the government knew the opposite to be the case (see Chapter 4). Descriptions such as 'impromptu Protestant hooligans', 'freelance', 'a handful of people in the UDA', 'groups of criminals', 'semi-autonomous', 'individual travelling Protestant gunmen', 'loosely tied' and 'hangers-on' are all terms scattered throughout the documents, which were intended to distance the loyalist killers from their organisations. Subtle distinctions were made between republican and loyalist paramilitary organisations to justify the differential treatment of political violence between the two communities; these distinctions were also made between acts of terror carried out by 'individuals' and those directed by leaders of an organisation.

In the early days of the UDA's existence, huge intimidatory marches by its members, wearing masks and uniforms and carrying cudgels, were not discouraged, and widespread disruptive protests by loyalists were tolerated. Loyalist leaders – even those who were suspected of having committed serious offences (including sectarian murder) – had easy access to senior NIO officials and even to the secretary of state for Northern Ireland, as well as to the RUC and army at the highest levels. According to NIO officials' own analyses, at times when loyalists perceived that the 'Catholic community' had gained an advantage, they reacted violently. On these occasions, government officials were at pains to placate them.

Members of the UDA were permitted to hold joint membership with the UDR. By allowing this, the British inflamed the situation – enabling loyalists to acquire weapons legally and to obtain military training and dossiers of information on nationalist targets. Moreover, although UDR weapons had begun to 'go missing' as early as 1971, this problem was not dealt with effectively, which allowed the loyalist paramilitaries to intensify their weapon 'thefts' and become more daring by carrying out raids on armouries. The British authorities' analysis was that the main source of all loyalist weapons was the UDR, and the regiment was 'the only source of modern weaponry'.[1]

Despite its knowledge of loyalist responsibility for a high percentage of sectarian killings during the 1970s, the British government batted away all concerns and complaints from the Irish government, the SDLP and the Catholic Church, even criticising them for expressing concern.

There was a continuous imperative to maintain publicly the implausible fiction that the UDA was separate from the UFF. This myth was sustained for twenty years. Yet, numerous statistics compiled on responsibility for murders, attempted murders and weapons possession make not a single mention of the UFF, only the UDA and UVF. These statistics, however, were for internal consumption only.

During the UWC strike of May 1974, the failure of the British prime minister, Harold Wilson, to mount a military challenge confirmed to the loyalists that violence and intimidation paid off. At the same time, it had a hugely alienating effect on the nationalist population, undermining their trust in the authorities still further (see Chapter 5). This alienation began in the summer of 1970 when the British Army imposed a curfew on the Falls Road that lasted for thirty-four hours. The nationalist community had since then witnessed the one-sided nature of internment; the detention of a small number of loyalists was merely a cosmetic exercise, as is borne out by the figures – only 5.4 per cent of the total came from the loyalist community. Internment was followed by Bloody Sunday in January 1972 and Operation Motorman six months later (see Chapter 2).

Seán Donlon's report on the despondency and fear in the nationalist community in 1975 owing to an upsurge in sectarian assassinations is further evidence of Britain's failure to apply the rule of law impartially or to protect 'its citizens'. Donlon's scathing comments that the security forces 'had once more shown themselves' to be unable to deal with sectarian assassinations and bombings, 'even during a Provo ceasefire' (see Chapter 6), are very striking.

In May 1974 the British government was determined to de-proscribe the UVF, outwardly accepting the falsehood that the organisation was on ceasefire, while knowing full well that it was involved in sectarian killings. The de-proscription legislation was permitted to come into force despite UVF responsibility for the Dublin and Monaghan bombings in the interim (see Chapter 5). Any proposed arrests around the time of de-proscription were to be vetted by senior NIO officials at Laneside. All efforts and demands by the SDLP, Alliance Party, Irish government, Catholic Church and members of civil society in Northern Ireland to have the UDA proscribed were strongly and consistently resisted and rejected. Bizarrely, the criterion for proscribing the UDA was that it had to *claim responsibility* for shootings and bombings. Whether or not it was actually guilty of carrying out the attacks was irrelevant.

It is clear that the then chief constable, John Hermon, was determined to resist the proscription of the UDA and threatened the NIO in January 1982 that if the secretary of state were to decide to proscribe the organisation, he could not rely on his support. More inappropriately, the former chief constable showed great empathy towards the loyalist paramilitary organisation, suggesting it should be brought into the 'political field' and seeking the 'healthy cultivation' of John McMichael. Having obtained intelligence from a UDA source that its intention was to kill leading IRA members, Hermon expressed the view that he was unlikely to be able to prevent these murders as it would compromise his source (see Chapter 10).

The practical consequences of the proscription of an organisation meant that the organisation became unlawful – it could not operate or recruit openly, it could not fundraise or invite support, and it could not have a base or hold public meetings. Convictions for membership carried a penalty of imprisonment. If the British government had seen fit to proscribe the UDA, this would have sent a powerful message to the nationalist community that sectarian murders were being taken seriously. Because the UDA was allowed to remain legal, young loyalists were encouraged to view the organisation as a legitimate option, and the fact that members (especially in the early to mid-1970s) could also enrol in the UDR made it a more attractive choice.

Was there any justification for the British government and security forces to act in this way? The nurturing of friendly forces was a well-trodden path adopted by Britain in other colonial/post-colonial situations in more far-flung places. Its army was suffering heavy casualties in its war with the IRA – 108 soldiers were killed in 1972 alone. It is undeniable that Britain would have had difficulty in fighting a war on two fronts – any government can govern only with the consent of a majority of the population. A war on two fronts would have meant that the British government had to rely on force alone to hold Northern Ireland – hardly ideal for a western democracy. Some might argue that turning a blind eye to, tolerating and, on occasion, encouraging loyalist violence, was the least-worst option from a British perspective.

The argument that the British government had no other option than to tolerate loyalist violence, however, carries with it a moral and legal implication that undermines the very notion of governance. If government policy towards loyalist paramilitaries was predicated on accepting that hundreds of Catholic civilians would die violent deaths, then the government could not fulfil that most fundamental responsibility to provide for the safety and well-being of its citizens. Instead, security policies were implemented that put at risk the safety and well-being of the Catholic community. This was immoral and illegal. It also helped to prolong the conflict, because the Catholic community remained aggrieved at the continuing failure to apply the rule of law impartially. The liberties of a democratic society are ultimately dependent on the maintenance of the rule of law.

The belief that the proscription of the UDA would result in much worse violence was not accepted by all civil servants. In an internal memo within the NIO, M. Bohill informed a colleague, Richard Davies, on 3 June 1982, that he had made changes to a prepared paper on the UDA. He advised that he had omitted the argument about proscription leading to mass defiance or that 'fringe' members would become more involved in terrorism. He stated emphatically: 'I simply do not believe it' (see Chapter 9).

British government policy towards loyalist paramilitaries, instead of being the least-worst option, was the preferred option for many within government and the security forces, given their convergence of aims and objectives – to defeat the IRA and maintain the union. Britain was never a neutral broker.

If it is accepted that the British government was unable to govern and apply the law impartially due to pressure from loyalist paramilitaries, one option would have been to call in the United Nations. In the wake of the 1975 murders of the Miami Showband members and two Gaelic Athletic Association fans at Altnamackin (see Chapter 6), *The Irish Times* editorialised:

> There are plenty of grounds for the widespread doubts which exist about Britain's will and ability to govern Northern Ireland effectively.

> It is obvious that the security forces are unable or unwilling to get under control the present wave of horrors ... If the extremists on both sides began ... a campaign of major violence, it is impossible to imagine how the security forces could withstand it, even if their loyalty and impartiality were in no doubt. And there *is* doubt about the position of the UDR and evidence which cannot be ignored and is believed by highly responsible people like Seamus Mallon, of collusion between the UDR and Loyalist extremists.

Quoting the Fianna Fáil spokesman, Ruairí Brugha, the editorial continued: 'If the British cannot cope, consideration should be given to seeking United Nations aid.' The editorial agreed that the United Kingdom should revisit an earlier Irish government proposal to invite in United Nations peacekeeping forces since 'this may at last be a serious policy option'. This is an implicit indictment of British security policies.[2]

In 1969 the Irish government had repeatedly urged its British counterpart to allow United Nations peacekeepers into Northern Ireland. Its appeals were rejected on the grounds that Northern Ireland was a domestic British issue.[3] It is clear that the UK government had no intention of inviting in UN forces. To do so would have been an admission that it was incapable of resolving the most serious and violent conflict in western Europe in the mid-1970s.[4] In deciding to take the path it did, the British government had no option but to prevaricate continually – to the European Commission and the European Court, to the Irish and US governments, to the SDLP, Alliance Party and Catholic Church – about the nature of loyalist organisations, particularly the UDA; about discrimination in internment; about the extent of sectarian murders; and about conviction rates for loyalists. Worse than that, the path chosen led to the directing of loyalist killings, as has been shown in the Brian Nelson case (see Chapter 10).

Over decades the British people were misled, just as they had been in respect of widespread human-rights violations committed by the British Army during the process of decolonisation in Malaya, Kenya, Cyprus and elsewhere. Most importantly, a massive fraud was perpetrated on the nationalist population.

Families and communities who bore the brunt of loyalist violence – whether in north Belfast or mid-Ulster – knew that it was UDA and not UFF death squads that were responsible for assassinations; they knew that the UVF was not on ceasefire in the mid-1970s, and that routine, ongoing collusion between members of the security forces and loyalist paramilitaries was not a republican myth.

The documents quoted throughout this book raise disturbing questions. Did the refusal by the British government over two decades to proscribe the UDA constitute a continuing breach of Article 2 of the European Convention on Human Rights? The Right to Life and the duty imposed on states to protect this right is a fundamental principle in domestic, European and international law. The UK government may have been guilty of a flagrant breach by formulating policies that put its citizens at risk and thus constituted misfeasance in public office on a hitherto unimaginable scale.

It is worth recalling senior NIO official N. R. Cowling's evaluation of the loyalist threat in July 1979: that they had perpetrated sectarian murder and violence in both Northern Ireland and the Republic of Ireland and had the capacity to do so again; that they had demonstrated their ability to bring normal life to a halt in the UWC strike of 1974; and that they were involved in criminal activities other than terrorism and were a considerable threat to the British government's authority and to law and order (see Chapter 8).

The British government's response to this warning was to ignore it and to carry on blithely as before in its policy of partiality towards loyalist paramilitaries. It would be another thirteen years before the UDA was, at last, proscribed. Britain was, undoubtedly, a state in denial.

# ENDNOTES

**FOREWORD**

1   Lord John Stevens presided over three external police inquiries in Northern Ireland into allegations of collusion. See Chapter 10 for further details of the Stevens inquiries.

2   De Silva, Rt Hon. Sir Desmond QC, *The Report of the Patrick Finucane Review* (The Stationery Office, London 2012), Volume II, p. 325. This report was the result of an inquiry into allegations of state involvement in the murder of Pat Finucane.

3   McKittrick, D., Kelters, S., Feeney, B., Thornton, C. and McVea, D., *Lost Lives: The Stories of the Men, Women and Children Who Died as a Result of the Northern Ireland Troubles* (Mainstream Publishing Company, Edinburgh 2007), p. 1552.

4   CAIN website, Sutton Index of Deaths, http://cain.ulst.ac.uk/sutton/tables/index.html (accessed 29 April 2016); Shirlow, Peter, *The End of Ulster Loyalism?* (Manchester University Press, Manchester 2012), p. 42.

5   The UVF was de-proscribed for a short period, between May 1974 and October 1975, but for the majority of its life it has been an illegal organisation.

6   Cohen, Stanley, *States of Denial: Knowing about Atrocities and Suffering* (Polity Press, Cambridge 2001).

7   Agent Stakeknife was a British agent who infiltrated the IRA. It is alleged that he was involved in a large number of murders in order to maintain his cover while providing information to the British security services.

8   Cadwallader, Anne, *Lethal Allies: British Collusion in Ireland* (Mercier Press, Cork 2013), p. 16.

9   Pat Finucane was a human-rights lawyer who was killed by the UDA on 12 February 1989 in front of his wife and three children at their home. The Stevens inquiries and, later, de Silva found there had been collusion in his death.

10  O'Callaghan, Eimear, *Belfast Days: A 1972 Teenage Diary* (Merrion Press, Newbridge 2014), p. 287.

I   FROM CONFLICT ORIGINS TO INTERNMENT AND DIRECT RULE

1   House of Commons debates, 16 January 2015, 42WS: http://www.
    publications.parliament.uk/pa/cm201415/cmhansrd/chan93.pdf (accessed
    1 April 2016).

2   For details of British postcolonial conflicts see Newsinger, John, *British
    Counter-Insurgency: From Palestine to Northern Ireland* (Palgrave, Bas-
    ingstoke 2002); Dorril, Stephen, *MI6: Fifty Years of Special Operations*
    (Fourth Estate, London 2000); Anderson, David, 'Policing and Com-
    munal Conflict: The Cyprus Emergency, 1954–60', in Anderson, D. and
    Killingray, D., *Policing and Decolonisation* (Routledge, New York 1992).

3   McGovern, Mark, 'State Violence and the Colonial Roots of Collusion
    in Northern Ireland', in *Race and Class*, Vol. 57, No. 2 (October–Decem-
    ber 2015), p. 11.

4   The Military Reaction Force was a secret undercover British Army unit
    established in 1971.

5   Q Patrols comprised members of both the British and Turkish-Cypriot
    security forces and at least one former member (who had been 'turned')
    of Ethniki Organosis Kyprion Agoniston (EOKA) – a Greek-Cypriot
    nationalist guerrilla organisation that fought a campaign for the end of
    British rule in Cyprus, for self-determination and for eventual union
    with Greece. For more on these see Cadwallader, *Lethal Allies*, p. 344.

6   NAUK (National Archives UK), DEFE13/921, Directions on Northern
    Ireland – Chain of Command, D. R. J. Stephens, AUS (GS), 17 March
    1972.

7   On 3 July 1970 the British Army carried out extensive house searches in
    the nationalist Falls Road area of Belfast for IRA members and arms. A
    military curfew was imposed in the area for a period of thirty-four hours
    with movement of people heavily restricted. The house searches lasted
    for two days and involved considerable destruction to many houses and
    their contents. During the searches illegal arms and explosives were
    found. However, the manner in which the searches were conducted
    broke any remaining goodwill between the nationalist community and
    the British Army. Four people were killed by the army during the period
    of the curfew, one of them deliberately run over by an army vehicle.

8   Bloody Sunday occurred on Sunday 30 January 1972. A Northern
    Ireland Civil Rights' Association march had been organised to protest
    against internment without trial. The march was prevented from
    entering the city centre by members of the British Army. After some
    stone-throwing by youths, soldiers of the Parachute Regiment moved
    into the Bogside area in armoured vehicles. During the next thirty

minutes, these soldiers shot dead thirteen unarmed men and boys and wounded fourteen others. A fourteenth person died later.

9     When an individual was arrested and taken away to an army barracks for interrogation by battalion intelligence officers without any crime having been committed, it was called screening.

10     National Archives of Ireland (NAI), Department of Foreign Affairs, 2003/17/406, A Guide to the Report of the European Commission of Human Rights: Ireland v UK, questioning on the written statement of Chief Constable Shillington to the Commission, p. 163.

11     Edward Carson was an Irish unionist politician, barrister and judge. He was leader of the Ulster Unionist Party from 1910 to 1921. The decision to dedicate the new bridge to Queen Elizabeth II upset hard-line unionists, including Ian Paisley, who wanted the bridge dedicated to Carson as a celebration of Protestant leadership and heritage.

12     Boulton, David, *The UVF 1966–73: An Anatomy of Loyalist Rebellion* (Torc Books, 1973), pp. 23–4.

13     O'Callaghan, Margaret and O'Donnell, Catherine, 'The Northern Ireland Government, the Paisleyite Movement and Ulster Unionism in 1966', in *Irish Political Studies*, Vol. 21, No. 2 (June 2006), p. 210.

14     O'Callaghan and O'Donnell, *Irish Political Studies*, Vol. 21, p. 210. The Loyal Orange Order was founded in 1795. It holds more than 2,000 marches each year in Northern Ireland, particularly around 12 July, when Orangemen celebrate the victory of King William III at the Battle of the Boyne in 1690. There are a number of contentious parades near Catholic areas, which have often led to violent confrontation.

15     *Ibid.*, p. 211.

16     *Ibid.*, p. 212.

17     *Ibid.*

18     *Ibid.*, p. 215.

19     *Ibid.*, p. 219; Robin Bailie's letter to Terence O'Neill, Public Records Office Northern Ireland (PRONI), PM 5/31/35, partly bears out Spence's claim, but this remains unproven. Bailie was a solicitor and a member of the Unionist Party who was elected an MP in 1969.

20     O'Callaghan and O'Donnell, *Irish Political Studies*, Vol. 21, p. 214.

21     Boulton, *The UVF 1966–73*, p. 36.

22     *Ibid.*, p. 92.

23     Boulton, *The UVF 1966–73*, p. 96. The Ulster Special Constabulary (USC), formed in 1920, was an auxiliary (official) paramilitary force made up of three units: A, B and C. The A Specials were full time, the B

Specials were part time and used on patrols and checkpoints, while the C Specials were mobilised only in emergencies. The A and C Specials were disbanded in 1925, but the B Specials were retained. They were an entirely Protestant force, viewed with distrust and fear by Catholics. They were disbanded and replaced by the Ulster Defence Regiment (UDR) in April 1970. Many former B Specials joined the UDR.

24  *The Irish Press,* 12 November 1970.

25  NAI, Department of Foreign Affairs, 2003/17/406, Report of the European Commission, 26 January 1976, p. 178.

26  NAUK, CJ4/1170, Letter from A. C. Thorpe, Western European Section, FCO to B. Scoltock, DS6, MoD, 12 November 1970.

27  *Ibid.*

28  Bew, Paul and Gillespie, Gordon, *Northern Ireland: A Chronology of the Troubles 1968–1999* (Gill & Macmillan, Dublin 1999), pp. 39–40.

29  Kincora, a boys' home in east Belfast, was at the centre of a child-sex-abuse ring involving staff (some of whom were later jailed), unionist politicians and MI5. William McGrath was a housemaster at the home. He was imprisoned for four years in 1981 for paedophile activities there. MI5 reportedly blackmailed prominent politicians and loyalists involved in the sex ring. In 2015 new allegations emerged claiming that some of the boys at Kincora had been trafficked to London. http://www.independent.ie/irish-news/child-sex-abuse-victim-claims-he-was-handpicked-trafficked-to-london-and-molested-by-very-powerful-people-31123562.html (accessed 16 April 2015).

30  Steven Dorril, writing in the February 1984 issue of *Lobster*, described John McKeague as the most important paramilitary figure in Northern Ireland at the beginning of the 1970s. He had been a ringleader in the overthrow of Prime Minister Terence O'Neill by planning a series of 'agent provocateur' bombings, e.g. the Silent Valley Reservoir (the intention being to blame these bombings on the Provisional IRA). The truth emerged when one of the conspirators, Thomas McDowell, was electrocuted setting a bomb at Ballyshannon, County Donegal, on 21 October 1969 (the first fatality of the Troubles in the Republic of Ireland). In the violence and upheaval of August 1969, McKeague was to the fore in orchestrating pressure on nationalists to move out of loyalist areas.

31  Charles Harding Smith was a former British soldier and the first leader of the UDA. He was later forced out of the organisation in an internal UDA power struggle and out of Northern Ireland. Tommy Herron was vice-chairman of the UDA and leader in east Belfast. He fell from favour and was killed in an internal feud in September 1973.

32 Dillon, Martin, *The Trigger Men* (Mainstream Publishing, Edinburgh 2004), p. 175.

33 *The Sunday Times*, 21 May 1972.

34 John White was later convicted of the double murder of Senator Paddy Wilson and Irene Andrews in 1973. Both suffered multiple stab wounds. In 2006 security correspondent Brian Rowan reported that White had been an RUC Special Branch agent for many years. http://www.belfasttelegraph.co.uk/incoming/loyalist-white-a-police-informer-28108844.html (accessed 16 April 2015).

35 Taylor, Peter, *Loyalists* (Bloomsbury Publishing, London 2000), p. 103.

36 *The Sunday Times*, 21 May 1972.

37 The first 'UK Representative' was appointed to Northern Ireland in August 1969 to represent the British government's views to the NI government, to report to the home secretary on the views of NI ministers and on the situation in NI, and to liaise with the general officer commanding (GOC) on matters of internal security. Howard Smith was appointed to the post in 1971. When direct rule was imposed in March 1972, Laneside, the house in Holywood, County Down, where the UK Representative resided, became formally Division 3 of the NIO. Smith remained for a short time as special adviser until he was replaced by his deputy, Frank Steele. Steele was then replaced by James Allan. In July 1975 Allan was replaced by Donald Middleton. In early 1976 the work of Laneside was taken over by a division of the NIO known as Public Affairs Branch (PAB) or Public Affairs Division (PAD).

38 Herbert was a graduate of Trinity College Dublin. He joined the Indian Civil Service in 1936, and in 1950 was recruited to MI5, becoming a security intelligence adviser at the Colonial Office in 1955.

39 NAUK, CJ4/462, Memo from UK Representative A. H. Hewins, Belfast to Philip Leyshon, J2 Division, Home Office, 11 August 1970.

40 Proinsias MacAirt was one of two men who would later meet with NIO officials at Laneside during the IRA ceasefire of 1975. The other was Jimmy Drumm, husband of IRA leader Máire Drumm.

41 *The United Irishman*, December 1969.

42 NAUK, CJ4/462, Memo from Hewins to Leyshon, 11 August 1970. It is unclear whether or not others were also interned at that time.

43 *Ibid.*, Draft reply to A. W. Hewins, undated.

44 *Ibid.*, Memo to Robin North, Home Office, from R. A. Burroughs, UK Representative, 9 September 1970.

45 *Ibid.*, Memo to Philip Leyshon from A. J. Langdon, J1 Division, Home Office, 4 November 1970.

46   *Ibid.*, Memo to C. Johnson, DS6, Ministry of Defence from Philip Leyshon, Home Office, 4 November 1970.

47   *Ibid.*, Memo to Mr Angel from G. W. (initials only), 7 December 1970.

48   Philip John Woodfield served in the Royal Artillery Regiment (1942–7) of the British Army and rose to the rank of captain. He went on to read English at King's College, London, and joined the Home Office in 1950, where he held a number of posts. He participated in what is believed to be the first meeting between the IRA and senior officials of the British government on 20 June 1972. He was promoted to deputy secretary in charge of NI Dept. of Home Office in 1972 and was then promoted to permanent under-secretary of state in 1981. He served for eight years from 1987 as the first staff commissioner for the Security and Intelligence Services (MI5 and MI6).

49   NAUK, CJ4/462, Memo to Philip Woodfield from R. A. Burroughs, 8 December 1970.

50   *Ibid.*, Memo to Philip Woodfield from D. R. E. Hopkins, J2 Division, Home Office, 9 December 1970.

51   *Ibid.*, Paper on internment prepared by Northern Ireland Department, undated.

52   McKittrick *et al.*, *Lost Lives*, p. 67.

53   NAUK, CJ4/462, Memo to Philip Woodfield from R. A. Burroughs, 9 March 1971.

54   *Ibid.*, (no file reference), Letter from [redacted name] Box No 500, Parliament Street, London to Robin North, Home Office, 16 March 1971 (copy on file). The file reference is not available but, as for all the other documents with reference numbers, there is a copy on file with PFC/JFF.

55   *Ibid.*, (no file reference), Paper on internment, 16 March 1971 (copy on file).

56   *Ibid.*, DEFE13/1394, Briefing paper to Private Secretary, Secretary of State for Defence, 1 April 1971.

57   *Ibid.*, CJ4/462, Paper on internment, undated.

58   *Ibid.*, (no file reference), Memo to Sir Stewart Crawford, DUS, FCO from W. K. K. White, West European Department, FCO, 3 August 1971 (copy on file).

59   *Ibid.*, (no file reference), Telegram to J. T. A. Howard-Drake, Home Office from Howard Smith, 8 August 1971 (copy on file).

60   *Ibid.*

61   *Ibid.*

62   'Brady' is Ruardhrí Ó Brádaigh (Brady) and 'Goulding' is Cathal Goulding, the then leaders of the Provisional and Official IRA respectively.

63   NAUK, (no file reference), Telegram to J. T. A. Howard-Drake, Home Office from Howard Smith, 8 August 1971 (copy on file).

64   McKittrick *et al.*, *Lost Lives*, pp. 79–90, 92–3, 95; see the Ballymurphy families' website www.ballymurphymassacre.com for full details.

65   Sir Anthony Farrer-Hockley had seen action in Palestine, Cyprus, Aden and Borneo ('Obituary', in *The Guardian*, 15 March 2006).

66   NAUK, (no file reference), Paper on Internment, W. K. K. White, West European Department, to Lord Bridges, 3 August 1971 (copy on file).

67   *Belfast Telegraph*, 12 August 1971.

68   NAUK, DEFE24/968, Memo from Brigadier J. M. H. Lewis, BGS (Int) DIS to Col. GS Mo3, 23 August 1971.

69   Bew and Gillespie, *Northern Ireland*, p. 109.

70   NAUK, DEFE24/824, MoD memo on 'Arrest Policy for Protestants', November 1972.

71   Generally known simply as the IRA and by the security forces as the Provisional IRA, this was the largest of the republican paramilitary groups. Following the split with the Official IRA in 1969, its military campaign continued virtually unbroken for more than two decades.

72   NAUK, DEFE24/824, MoD memos on the Arrest Policy that had been in place before the enactment of the Detention of Terrorists (NI) Order, 7 November 1972.

73   Frank Steele became deputy to UK Representative Howard Smith in 1971. Stephen Dorril describes Steele as 'a very large pipe-smoking Arabist, a veteran of Suez and the Sudan, who had recently been in Nairobi'. Dorril, Stephen, *MI6* (Fourth Estate, 2000), p. 739.

74   3, 8 and 39 British Army brigades covered the whole of Northern Ireland.

75   NAUK, FCO33/1486, Telegram from Frank Steele, MI6, to FCO, October 1971.

76   *Ibid.*, PREM15/1016, Memo to Christopher Roberts, No. 10 Downing Street from R. A. Custis, 29 November 1972.

77   *Ibid.*, DEFE24/746, Attitude towards vigilante groups (1971–74), Telex from GOC HQNI to AUS MoD, 19 October 1971.

78   *Ibid.*, Situation Report No. 38, 17 December 1971. Situation Reports were daily reports intended for senior civil servants, military and RUC officers and the secretary of state.

79   *Ibid.* Brian Faulkner was the sixth and last prime minister of Northern Ireland (March 1971 to March 1972). He was also the chief executive of the short-lived Northern Ireland Executive during the first five months of 1974.

80   Whelan, Kevin, *The Tree of Liberty: Radicalism, Catholicism and the Construction of Irish Identity 1760–1830* (The University of Notre Dame, South Bend 1997), p. 124.

81   NAUK, DEFE13/736, Minutes of meeting at Stormont Castle regarding Orange parade, 28 June 1970.

82   *Ibid.*, Northern Ireland Intelligence Reports, Minutes of meeting of 28 June 1970, Stormont Castle.

83   *Ibid.*

84   *Ibid.* (no file reference), Letter to Sir Philip Allen, Home Office, from Arthur Hockaday, MoD, 5 August 1971 (copy on file). In a document entitled 'Appreciation of the situation by CLF given to CGS [the chief of General Staff] on 9 September 1971' he refers to contingency plans for direct rule. He advised that the plan envisaged twenty army battalions 'organised on a four brigade basis'. Bearing in mind that seventeen battalions were fully engaged for the fourteen days following 9 August, he doubted that twenty battalions and two armoured reconnaissance regiments would be sufficient to maintain law and order in the initial stages of direct rule.

85   NAI, DFA 2003/17/406, Report of Commission of Human Rights, 26 January 1976, p. 195.

86   *Ibid.*, p. 181.

87   NAUK, FCO87/354, NIO meeting, 13 November 1974. The Irish government made a formal complaint against the UK to the European Commission of 16 December 1971 because of its use of extrajudicial powers of arrest, detention and internment in Northern Ireland. The complaint was about the scope and implementation of those measures and in particular the practice of psychological interrogation techniques and discrimination in its policy of internment.

88   Brigadier MS Bayley was Brigadier General Staff (BGS) Intelligence Northern Ireland.

89   NAUK, DEFE24/746, Note on Chiefs of Staff meeting, 5 June 1972.

90   *Ibid.* Captain Austin Ardill was awarded the Military Cross during the Second World War and later became a member of the UUP. He was opposed to the reforms of Terence O'Neill and became involved in the Ulster Vanguard movement, but when it broke away to form a separate political party Ardill chose to remain with the UUP. Billy Hull was the

leader of the Loyalist Association of Workers but also a senior member of the UDA.

91    Taylor, *Loyalists*, p. 103.

## 2    THE FIRST IRA CEASEFIRE AND THE REPERCUSSIONS OF ITS BREAKDOWN

1    NAUK, CJ4/266, Tuzo paper to Secretary of State for Northern Ireland, 9 July 1972.

2    Dorril, *MI6*, p. 739.

3    NAUK, PREM15/1009, Note of meeting with representatives of the Provisional IRA, 20 June 1972.

4    Bew and Gillespie, *Northern Ireland*, pp. 53–4. Special Category Status or political status provided prisoners with some of the privileges of prisoners of war, such as those specified in the Geneva Convention. This meant they did not have to wear prison uniforms or do prison work.

5    NAUK, PREM15/1010, Notes of meeting with IRA, 7 July 1972.

6    'Unhappy families', in *Private Eye*, No. 276, 14 July 1972.

7    *Ibid.*

8    *Ibid.*

9    *Ibid.*

10    McKittrick *et al.*, *Lost Lives*, pp. 212–17.

11    Harold Craufurd Tuzo was born in India in 1917, the son of a British Army officer. He studied jurisprudence at Oxford and served in the Second World War and in Borneo, before being appointed GOC Northern Ireland in 1971. He served there until February 1973.

12    NAUK, CJ4/266, Tuzo paper, 9 July 1972.

13    *Ibid.*

14    *Ibid.* The OV was a loyalist paramilitary group formed in the early 1970s, associated with the Orange Order and headed by Bob Marno, an ex-serviceman. At one time the OV was the second-largest loyalist paramilitary group after the UDA. It was also associated with the UVF, was involved in the Ulster Workers' Council (UWC) strike of 1974 and also supported the loyalist strike of 1977. The OV is believed to have ceased to exist during the 1980s.

15    NAUK, CJ4/266, Tuzo paper, 9 July 1972.

16    *Ibid.*

17    The MRF had two elements – soldiers seconded from their own regiments and young republicans whom the British Army had succeeded

in 'turning'. Its activities were at their height during 1972. On 12 May an MRF unit killed Patrick McVeigh and on 22 June – the day the forthcoming IRA ceasefire was announced – the same unit shot and seriously injured four men at a bus stop on the Glen Road. One of the activities of the MRF was to drive 'defectors' from nationalist areas into their own districts, so that individuals they believed to be members of the IRA could be pointed out. By 9 July the MRF had killed at least one man and wounded nine others, none of whom had any connection to the IRA. The unit had a short lifespan because of its indiscipline and was disbanded after the debacle of the Four Square Laundry affair in October 1972. Four Square Laundry was a bogus company run by the MRF, which allowed the force to collect clothing and forensically test it for lead residue and explosive traces before sending it to a legitimate laundry for cleaning. It was then returned to its owners. It also allowed the operators to observe people as they went on their rounds in nationalist housing estates. The IRA found out about this bogus laundry service from double agents Kevin McKee and Seamus Wright, who were members of the MRF. The IRA shot and killed one of its operatives and, on the same day, abducted McKee and Wright, who were two of the 'disappeared'. Their bodies have recently been recovered. The MRF was replaced with a much more disciplined and coordinated unit called the Special Reconnaissance Unit. Urwin, Margaret, *Counter-Gangs: A History of Undercover Military Units in Northern Ireland 1971–1976* (Spinwatch, Justice for the Forgotten and The Pat Finucane Centre, 2013), available at http://www.spinwatch.org/index.php/issues/northern-ireland/item/5448-counter-gangs-a-history-of-undercover-military-units-in-northern-ireland-1971-1976, pp. 6–7.

18    NAUK, CJ4/266, Tuzo paper, 9 July 1972.

19    McKittrick *et al., Lost Lives*, p. 1553.

20    Barron, Justice Henry, *Interim Report on the Report of the Independent Commission of Inquiry into the Dublin bombings of 1972 and 1973* (Joint Oireachtas Committee on Justice, Equality, Defence and Women's Rights, Dublin 2004), p. 131; Barron, Justice Henry, *Interim Report on the Report of the Independent Commission of Inquiry into the Bombing of Kay's Tavern, Dundalk* (Joint Oireachtas Committee on Justice, Equality, Defence and Women's Rights, Dublin 2006), p. 143.

21    McKittrick *et al., Lost Lives*, p. 1553.

22    Newsinger, *British Counter-Insurgency*, p. 164.

23    The IPU, based at British Army HQNI in Lisburn, was responsible for the dissemination of information and propaganda; it included the SyOps (Psychological Operations) section, the *raison d'être* of which

was to disseminate false information for propaganda purposes. It was very influential in terms of policy.

24  NAUK, CJ4/3291, Report of May 1972, Information Policy and work in NI: briefs for incoming secretary of state, February and October 1974.

25  *Ibid.*

26  *Ibid.*, Report of July 1972: briefs for incoming secretary of state, February and October 1974.

27  Wood, Ian, *Crimes of Loyalty: A History of the UDA* (Edinburgh University Press, Edinburgh 2006), p. 8.

28  Moloney, Ed and Mitchell, Bob, 'Northern Ireland, 1972: A British Army-loyalist paramilitary alliance', in *The Irish Times*, 19 January 2013.

29  NAUK, CJ4/589, Diary of meetings in the early 1970s, 1972.

30  *Ibid.*, Minutes of Joint Security Meeting at Stormont Castle, 20 June 1972.

31  The peace lines were barricades set up to separate Catholic and Protestant neighbourhoods in Belfast. The first of these were erected in 1969 on the outbreak of the Troubles and although they were originally meant to be temporary, many still exist to this day.

32  *Ibid.*, PREM15/1010, Situation Report 3–4 July 1972.

33  *Ibid.*, CJ4/589, Diary of Historical Events, 1972.

34  *Ibid.*, PREM15/1010, Note of meeting, 4 July 1972.

35  *Ibid.*, SitRep, week ending 5 July 1972.

36  PRONI, CAB/9/G/27/6/3, Conclusions of meeting at Stormont Castle, 10 July 1972.

37  *Ibid.*

38  *Ibid.*

39  *Ibid.*

40  NAUK, PREM15/1010, Letter from Sir William Nield, Permanent Under-Secretary, NIO, to Sir Burke Trend, Cabinet Office, 10 July 1972.

41  The Irish government's case against the UK concerning discrimination in internment and use of interrogation.

42  NAUK, PREM15/1010, Meetings in House of Commons, July 1972.

43  *Ibid.*

44  Anthony Royle (later Lord Fanshawe) was a former member of the Life Guards and the SAS.

45  NAI, TSCH 2003/16/465, Letter from Donal O'Sullivan, Irish

Ambassador, London, to Assistant Secretary, Department of Foreign Affairs, 13 July 1972.

46 NAUK, PREM15/1010, Note for the record, 20 July 1972.

47 *Ibid.*

48 *Ibid.*

49 *Ibid.*

50 PRONI, CAB/9/G/27/6/3, Conclusions of meeting at Stormont Castle, 10 July 1972.

51 *The Irish News*, 22 May 1973, Testimony of Mrs Sarah McClenaghan and guilty plea of Trevor Hinton.

52 *Ibid.*

53 McKittrick *et al., Lost Lives*, pp. 217–18.

54 *Ibid.*, pp. 209–10.

55 *Ibid.*, p. 209.

56 NAUK, PREM15/1010, Note for the record, 20 July 1972.

57 *Ibid.*, CJ4/3291, Information Policy and work in NI: briefs for incoming secretary of state, February and October 1974, Report of July 1972.

58 Historical Enquiries Team (HET) Review Summary Report (RSR) concerning the death of John James McGerty. The HET was a Police Service of Northern Ireland (PSNI) unit established in 2005 to review all conflict-related deaths that took place in Northern Ireland. It was answerable to the chief constable of the PSNI and closed in 2014. Readers will be unable to access this source document as HET reports were private reports compiled for individual families. The families included in this book have given permission for them to be used.

59 HET RSR concerning the death of John James McGerty.

60 *Ibid.*, Memo to PM from Sir Burke Trend, 26 July 1972.

61 *Ibid.*, Instructions to Army from Chief of the Defence Staff, 27 July 1972.

62 *Ibid.*, PREM15/1011, Army Operations in NI, 26 July 1972.

63 http://www.cain.ulst.ac.uk/othelem/chron/ch72.htm#31772 (30 March 2016).

64 McKittrick *et al., Lost Lives,* p. 240.

65 NAUK, PREM15/1011, Memo to PM from Sir Burke Trend, 31 July 1972.

66 *Ibid.*, CJ4/3291, Information Policy and work in NI: briefs for incoming secretary of state, February and October 1974, Report of August 1972.

67    Senior Foreign Office diplomat James Nicholas Allan and MI6 officer Frank Steele (and later Michael Oatley) operated from Laneside, a house in Holywood, County Down, in the mid-1970s, holding meetings with loyalists and republicans. Allan's title was counsellor at NIO 1973–5.

68    NAUK, PREM15/1012, Notes on meeting with SDLP at Laneside, 7 August 1972.

69    *Ibid.*, (no file reference), Memo to Lt Col J. L. Pownall from J. F. Howe, Civil Adviser, HQNI, 31 July 1972 (copy on file).

70    *Ibid.*

71    *Ibid.*, DEFE24/822, Inventory of missing weapons 1972–73.

72    *Ibid.*, (no file reference), Memo to Lt Col J. L. Pownall from J. F. Howe, Civil Adviser, HQNI, 31 July 1972 (copy on file).

73    These road checks seem to have been of a temporary nature. UDA members, patrolling certain streets, set up a temporary road check, stopping vehicles at that point for a short period of time, before moving on and doing the same elsewhere.

74    NAUK, CJ4/838, Memo on UDA Road Checks, 22 August 1972.

75    *Ibid.*

76    NAUK, PREM15/1012, Situation Report, 20–21 August 1972.

77    *Ibid.*

78    *Ibid.*, Briefing paper on UDA.

## 3    ARMING THE LOYALISTS

1    Wood, *Crimes of Loyalty*, p. 113 – interview with Tyrie. Andy Tyrie took over the leadership of the UDA after the killing of Tommy Herron in 1973 and continued until 1988, when an attempt on his life forced him to resign.

2    NAUK, DEFE24/822, List of weapons thefts, October 1970–August 1973.

3    *Ibid.*, Letter to GOC from J. F. Howe, Civil Adviser to GOC NI, 25 September 1972.

4    *Ibid.*, Memo from I. B. C. McLeod, DS10, to Under-Secretary of State (Army), 1 February 1973.

5    *Ibid.*, Minute on TAVR Centre raid by Col H. S. L. Dalzell-Payne, 23 October 1972.

6    *Ibid.*, Minute on UDR Armoury raid by Col C. R. Huxtable, 24 October 1973.

7    The British Army was using the term 'collusion' from at least 1972.

8     NAUK, DEFE24/835, Memo to BGS (Int.) from A. W. Stephens, Head of DS10. Stephens refers to the questions which were bound to follow once the document 'Subversion in the UDR' reached No. 10 [Downing Street], 16 August 1973.

9     *Ibid.*, 'Subversion in the UDR' document, prepared by Int. and Sy, August 1973.

10    *Ibid.*

11    *The Irish News*, 15 May 2006.

12    HET RSR concerning the death of Patrick James Loughrey.

13    On 9 August 1973 UVF gunmen opened fire from a bridge over the M2 motorway at a van carrying workmen back to County Donegal from a building site near Glengormley. Sixteen-year-old Henry Cunningham was killed and his brother was injured. The men had been travelling the same route for three months and it is thought the van was targeted by the UVF because it carried southern registration plates and the killers presumed the workmen were Catholics. Henry was in fact a Presbyterian. In 2008 a HET report concluded that two SMGs were used in the attack; one was a homemade gun and another was a second Sterling SMG, which had also been stolen from the TAVR Centre in Lurgan on 23 October 1972. This UDR weapon was also used in the double killing of two Catholic workmen, Terence McCafferty and James McCloskey, in January 1974. The homemade SMG was used in an attempted killing in 1973. Both weapons were recovered by the RUC in separate incidents in 1974. The HET has revealed that, despite being linked to a number of unsolved serious crimes, both weapons were destroyed by the RUC – in 1976 and 1978. Readers will be unable to access this source document as HET reports were private reports compiled for individual families. The families included in this book have given permission for them to be used.

14    NAUK, CJ4/145, Minutes of Meeting with UDA at Stormont Castle, 17 October 1972.

15    *Ibid.*

16    *Ibid.*

17    *Ibid.*

18    *Ibid.*

19    European Court of Human Rights, Case of Ireland v United Kingdom, Report of 18 January 1978. The Order defined 'terrorism' as the use of violence for political ends including any use of violence for the purpose of putting the public or any section of the public in fear.

20    Dickson, Brice, 'The Detention of Suspected Terrorists in Northern Ireland and Great Britain', *University of Richmond Law Review*, Vol. 43,

No. 3 (March 2009). Brice Dickson is Professor of International and Comparative Law at the School of Law, Queen's University, Belfast.

21    NAUK, DEFE24/824, Memo on 'Arrest Policy', November 1972.

22    *Ibid.*, FCO87/81, Memo from Platt to Christopher Roberts, 10 Downing Street, 18 October 1972.

23    *Ibid.*

24    NAUK, CJ4/1276, Extract from 3rd Draft of counter-memorial prepared by FCO, 8 October 1976; also see Chapter 2, note 42.

25    *Ibid.*, DEFE24/824, MoD memos, November 1972.

26    NAUK, DEFE24/824, MoD memos, November 1972. Orbat means the identification, strength, common structure and disposition of the personnel, units and equipment of any military force, while Provos is a common abbreviation for the Provisional IRA.

27    *Ibid.*

28    DS10 was a division within the MoD in the 1970s responsible for providing policy advice to ministers and military staff concerning the army's involvement in Northern Ireland and for playing a liaison role between the MoD and FCO: http://powerbase.info/index.php/Defence_Secretariat_10 (accessed 5 July 2015).

29    NAUK, DEFE24/824, Loose Minute to R. C. Kent, DUS (Army) from A. W. Stephens, DS10, MoD, 8 December 1972.

30    *Ibid.*, Civil Adviser's paper with memo to R. C. Kent DUS (Army) from A. W. Stephens, Head of DS10, MoD, 8 December 1972. An ICO was a legal document signed by the secretary of state which ordered the internment of an individual.

31    NAUK, CJ4/838, Briefing for meeting with Taoiseach, Jack Lynch, 23 November 1972.

32    *Ibid.*, Security force policy towards the UDA, 6 November 1972. The Catholic Ex-Servicemen's Association was set up in 1971, following the introduction of internment, with the stated aim of protecting Catholic areas. Its founding member was Phil Curran, who, in common with other members, had previous military training. The CESA (or CEA) was paramilitary in nature but unarmed and, when it was at its most active in 1972, it was claimed that the membership was 8,000: http://cain.ulst.ac.uk/othelem/organ/corgan.htm#cea (accessed 14 July 2015).

33    NAUK, CJ4/838, Security force policy towards the UDA, 6 November 1972.

34    *Ibid.*, Briefing paper on the UDA and other paramilitary organisations, 23 November 1972.

35   *Ibid.*

36   *Ibid.*

37   The Northern Ireland Advisory Commission comprised influential people from both communities, who discussed legislation and were kept informed of the security situation by the secretary of state.

38   NAI, TAOIS, 2003/16/467, Note of a meeting, 13 October 1972.

39   Hansard, House of Lords, Vol. 337, Columns 233–6, 5 December 1972.

40   *Ibid.*

41   *Ibid.*

42   *Ibid.*

43   *Ibid.*

44   NAUK, CJ4/838, Briefing note for meeting with Taoiseach Jack Lynch, 23 November 1972.

45   McKittrick *et al., Lost lives*, pp. 139–312.

46   *The Daily Telegraph*, 30 January 1973.

47   *Ibid.*, 31 January 1973.

48   A young Catholic man, Patrick Connolly, had been killed in Portadown the previous October by another British Army-issue grenade. HET RSR concerning the death of Patrick Connolly. Readers will be unable to access this source document as HET reports were private documents compiled for individual families. The families included in this book have given permission for them to be used.

49   McKittrick *et al., Lost Lives*, pp. 320–4.

50   The names of the two men arrested are not disclosed in the available sources.

51   Anderson, Don, *14 May Days: The Inside Story of the Loyalist Strike of 1974* (Gill & Macmillan, Dublin 1994), p. 3.

52   McKittrick *et al., Lost Lives*, p. 329.

53   NAUK, PREM15/1689, Official Weekly Intelligence Report, 9 February 1973.

54   The Red Hand Commando was founded by John McKeague in 1972. Later that year it came under the control of the UVF.

55   NAUK, PREM15/1669, Situation in NI, part 31, 1 January–13 February 1973.

56   PRONI, CAB/9/J/86/2, Notes of meeting of Northern Ireland Advisory Commission, transcribed 8 February 1973.

57   *Ibid.*

58    *Ibid.*

59    *Ibid.*

60    NAUK, CJ4/3291, Information Policy and work: briefs for incoming secretary of state, February and October 1974, report of February 1973.

61    *Ibid.*

62    Paul Rose was chairman of the 'Campaign for Democracy in Ulster', which was established in 1965 by a group of British Labour MPs. It was especially active in pressing for reforms during the late 1960s, and investigated allegations of religious discrimination in Northern Ireland.

63    Hansard, House of Commons, Vol. 850, Columns 636–8, 8 February 1973.

64    NAUK, FCO87/227, Memo to K. C. Thom, British Embassy, Dublin from Kelvin White, FCO, 7 February 1973. White, when giving evidence at the Bloody Sunday Inquiry, said it was an old joke in the department that the 'no-go' areas would not survive if Guinness wagons supplying the pubs were refused entry: webarchive.nationalarchives. gov.uk/20101103103930/http://report.bloody-sunday-inquiry.org/ transcripts/Archive/Ts269.htm - Tuesday, 3 December 2002, p.97, lines 20-25 (accessed 14 August 2016).

65    *Jeu d'esprit*: According to the Collins Dictionary this is 'a light-hearted display of wit or cleverness'.

66    NAUK, FCO87/227, Memo to K. C. Thom, British Embassy from Kelvin White, FCO, 7 February 1973.

67    Barron, *Interim Report on the Report of the Independent Commission of Inquiry into the Dublin Bombings of 1972 and 1973*, pp. 35–129.

68    *Ibid.*, p. 137.

69    *Belfast Newsletter*, 30 April 1973.

70    *The Glasgow Herald*, 15 June 1973.

71    Jean Moore was head of the UDA's women's department. She was a sister of Ingram 'Jock' Beckitt, one of the founder members of the UDA, who was later killed as the result of an internal dispute in the organisation.

72    Dillon, *The Trigger Men*, p. 187.

73    *Ibid.*, p. 189–90; *The Troubles*, No. 21, (May–June 1973).

74    NAUK, DEFE24/969, Letter to Sir Michael Carver, MoD, from Sir Frank King, HQNI, 11 July 1973.

75    *Ibid.*, CJ4/523, Joint Information Policy Committee meetings, 13 June 1973.

76   McKittrick *et al., Lost Lives*, p. 249.

77   NAUK, DEFE24/969, IPU meeting, 19 June 1973.

78   *Ibid.*, CJ4/523, 27 June 1973.

79   *Ibid.*, (no file reference), Memo to CGS from Lt Col D. J. Ramsbotham, MoD, 26 July 1973 (copy on file). Following the publication of a White Paper by the British Government in March 1973 on the establishment of a Northern Ireland Assembly, elections were held on 28 June when anti-Agreement unionists won twenty-eight seats while pro-Agreement unionists won twenty-six. The SDLP won nineteen seats and the Northern Ireland Labour Party just one. An Executive was to be formed and, crucially, a Council of Ireland. All the parties, including the Irish government, met in Sunningdale, Berkshire, England in December 1973, where agreement was reached on the establishment of an Executive, a Council of Ireland, RUC reform and the phasing out of internment. Officials feared that Paisley and Craig would attempt to prevent it working effectively and, of course, this is what happened in 1974.

80   NAUK, CJ4/523, 21 August 1973.

81   Wood, *Crimes of Loyalty*, p. 22.

82   *Ibid.*

83   NAUK, CJ4/834, Descriptions of various 'Protestant extremist organisations', 1973. Heavy squads, in this context, were those members of the UDA involved in carrying out terrorist attacks. The Young Citizen Volunteers was the youth movement attached to the UVF.

84   *Ibid.* HMP (Her Majesty's Prison) the Maze was formerly Long Kesh Detention Centre, but when 'criminalisation' was introduced in March 1976 the name was changed.

85   Robin Jackson was the most prolific killer during the entire period of the conflict. It is believed that he was responsible for up to 100 deaths. For detailed information on Jackson, see Cadwallader, *Lethal Allies*.

86   NAUK, CJ4/523, IPU meeting, 13 November 1973.

87   US State Paper, Telegram to secretary of state, Washington, from US Consul, Belfast, 13 November 1973, http://www.wikileaks.org/plusd/cables/1973 BELFAS00164 _b.html (accessed 12 August 2015).

88   Public Library of US Diplomacy, Cable from Consul, Belfast, to secretary of state, Washington, 15 November 1973, https://www.wikileaks.org/plusd/cables/1973BELFAS00164_b.html (accessed 9 February 2015).

## 4 IRELAND V UNITED KINGDOM (EUROPEAN COMMISSION OF HUMAN RIGHTS)

1 NAI, Department of Foreign Affairs, 2003/17/406, A Guide to the Report of the European Commission of Human Rights, Commission hearings, Philip Woodfield, p. 48.

2 The first judgement to be handed down by the European Court of Human Rights (ECtHR) was Lawless v Ireland in 1960. The case of Ireland v United Kingdom was one of the first inter-state cases to be brought to the European Commission and was the first inter-state case to be adjudicated by the ECtHR.

3 The ECHR was operational from 1953 until 1998, when the European human-rights system was restructured under Protocol 11.

4 Usually the applicant to the original complaint brought it to the ECHR.

5 The commission held that there was no breach of Article 1, that the application in respect of Article 2 was inadmissible, but that the UK had breached Article 3 and that the treatment of the 'Hooded Men' constituted torture. (When internment was introduced in August 1971, the British Army took fourteen men to a secret location – Ballykelly, County Derry – where they were subjected to horrific interrogations.) The ECtHR subsequently held that the treatment amounted to inhuman and degrading treatment, but not torture. This aspect of the ROI v UK 1978 ECtHR decision is now being challenged in light of new material relevant to the case uncovered by the PFC/JFF and RTÉ Investigations Department.

6 In relation to Article 5, the commission held that the use of detention and internment without trial was justified under Article 15 as it occurred during a time of 'public emergency'. The commission held that it could not consider or determine whether Article 6 in relation to the internment/detention policy of the UK government was relevant to the applicant's complaints, and/or whether it could be substantiated. The UK government argued that Article 6 was not relevant as those interned were not charged with a criminal offence and therefore could not be said to be deprived of their right to a fair trial. Further, if it was relevant, derogation from Article 6 would be justified under Article 15 as it occurred during a time of 'public emergency'.

7 Article 14 is not a stand-alone right, but is a right that is protected and enforced in conjunction with other convention rights, in this case Articles 5 and 6. Article 14 states: 'The enjoyment of the rights and freedoms set forth in [the] Convention shall be secured without discrimination on any ground such as sex, race, colour, language, religion, political or other opinion, national or social origin, association with a national minority, property, birth or other status.'

8    NAI, Department of Foreign Affairs, 2003/17/406, Report of the European Commission of Human Rights.

9    Case of Ireland v United Kingdom, Application No. 5310/71, Judgment, Strasbourg, 18 January 1978, http://hudoc.echr.coe.int/eng?.i=001575 06#{%22fulltext%22:[%22ireland%20v%20united%20kingdom%22], %22itemid%22:[%22001-57506%22]} (accessed 25 April 2016), p. 79, paragraph 232.

10   NAI, Department of Foreign Affairs, 2003/17/406, A Guide to the Report of the European Commission of Human Rights, Commission hearings, Commission findings.

11   *Ibid.*, Commission hearings, General Tuzo, 20 February 1975, p. 103.

12   *Ibid.*

13   *Ibid.*, Commission hearings, Chief Constable Shillington, p. 163.

14   *Ibid.*

15   *Ibid.*, Commission hearings, Philip Woodfield, p. 48.

16   *Ibid.*, p. 56.

17   *Ibid.*

18   *Ibid.*

19   NAUK, CJ4/596, Memo to Sir Frank Cooper from D. J. Trevelyan, 22 October 1974.

20   *Ibid.*

21   McKittrick *et al.*, *Lost Lives*, pp. 122–5.

22   *Ibid.*, p. 133.

23   HET RSR concerning the deaths of the victims of the McGurk's Bar Bombing on 4 December 1971. Readers will be unable to access this source document as HET reports were private reports compiled for individual families. The families included in this book have given permission for them to be used.

24   *Ibid.* For further reading on McGurk's Bar, see MacAirt, Ciarán, *The McGurk's Bar Bombing* (Frontline Noir Publishing, Edinburgh 2012).

25   This should read 1973, not 1972.

26   NAUK, (no file reference), Note of a meeting in the NIO on 13 November 1974 (copy on file).

27   NAI, Department of Foreign Affairs, 2003/17/406, Report of the European Commission of Human Rights: Ireland v UK, 25 January 1976, pp. 188–9. The PFC has supported the McGurk's families and has had access to many declassified documents regarding the 'own goal' theory. No RUC or MoD documents supplied to the more recent official investigations contained this particular reference to a hotel.

28    *Ibid.*, p. 193.

29    McKittrick *et al.*, *Lost Lives*, pp. 139–322.

30    NAI, Department of Foreign Affairs, 2003/17/406, A Guide to the Report of the European Commission of Human Rights: Ireland v UK, 25 January 1976, Memo prepared by NIO.

31    NAUK, PREM15/1016, Letter to Christopher Roberts, No. 10 Downing Street, from R. A. Custis, MoD, 29 November 1972.

32    NAI, Department of Foreign Affairs, 2003/17/406, A Guide to the Report of the European Commission of Human Rights: Ireland v UK, 25 January 1976, Memo prepared by NIO.

33    *Ibid.*, Report of the European Commission of Human Rights: Ireland v UK, 25 January 1976, pp. 131–2.

34    *Ibid.*

35    *Ibid.*, pp. 217–18.

36    Report of the European Court of Human Rights: Ireland v United Kingdom, 18 January 1978, http://hudoc.echr.coe.int/eng?.i=001575 06#{%22fulltext%22:[%22ireland%20v%20united%20kingdom%22]} (accessed 25 April 2016), p. 78, paragraph 228 and p. 79, paragraph 231.

37    NAUK, (no file reference), Draft letter and paper to Frank Cooper from Bill Webster, 15 May 1975 (copy on file).

38    Report of the European Court of Human Rights: Ireland v United Kingdom, 18 January 1978, http://hudoc.echr.coe.int/eng?.i=001575 06#{%22fulltext%22:[%22ireland%20v%20united%20kingdom%22]} (accessed 25 April 2016), pp. 127–8.

39    The terror inflicted on Catholics in 1968–9 is an often-ignored aspect of the discussion around loyalist violence. According to the official inquiry into 'Violence and Civil Disturbances in Northern Ireland in 1969', the Scarman Tribunal, at least 1,505 Catholic families were displaced in Belfast in July, August and September 1969 (p. 248, Table 5). Over 10,000 people within the Catholic community (5.3 per cent of all Catholic households in Belfast) were left homeless; 315 families within the Protestant Unionist Community (PUL) were displaced in the same period. These were conservative estimates since Scarman, in part, relied on statistics supplied by the RUC, which was perceived as a dubious source by nationalists. Ten people died that summer, eight Catholics and two Protestants.

40    Report of the European Court of Human Rights: Ireland v United Kingdom, Separate opinion of Judge Philip O'Donoghue, http://hudoc. echr.coe.int/eng?.i=00157506#{%22fulltext%22:[%22ireland%20v%20 united%20kingdom%22]} (accessed 25 April 2016), p. 40.

41    For more on this see Chapter 5.

42   Report of the European Court of Human Rights: Ireland v United Kingdom, http://hudoc.echr.coe.int/eng?.i=00157506#{%22fulltext%22:[%22ireland%20v%20united%20kingdom%22]}, p. 21, paragraph 66.

43   *Ibid.*, p. 22, paragraph 66.

44   NAUK, CJ4/461, Memo to P. R. N. Fifoot, Legal Counsellor at FCO, leading counsel for British Government at Stavanger hearings from A. H. (Wally) Hammond, Home Office, 25 January 1973.

45   *Ibid.*, CJ4/1276, Memo to Henry Steele, OBE, Legal Advisers, FCO from Anthony Lester, QC, 28 September 1976.

## 5   LOYALISTS TORPEDO THE NORTHERN IRELAND POWER-SHARING EXECUTIVE

1   *The Irish Times*, 18 May 1974.

2   Sinn Féin had split in 1969, at the beginning of the northern conflict, into Official Sinn Féin and Provisional Sinn Féin. The Official IRA and Provisional IRA were regarded as the armed wings of the parties. The reference here is to Provisional Sinn Féin, which soon became the dominant party.

3   NAUK, CJ4/643, Memo from J. F. Halliday, NIO, to D. Trevelyan, 6 March 1974.

4   *Ibid.*, De-proscription of unlawful organisations, paper on de-proscription described as a 'think-piece', February 1974.

5   *Ibid.*

6   *Ibid.*

7   *Ibid.* Emphasis added.

8   *Ibid.*, CJ4/862, Proposed de-proscription of Provisional Sinn Féin and UVF: advice by officials to ministers, 21 March 1974.

9   *Ibid.*

10  *Ibid.*

11  Hansard, House of Commons debates, Vol. 871, Columns 1475–6, 4 April 1974.

12  Official Sinn Féin used the term 'Republican Clubs', in Northern Ireland to avoid a proscription on Sinn Féin imposed in 1964.

13  Hansard, House of Commons debates, Vol. 871, Columns 1475–6, 4 April 1974.

14  NAUK, CJ4/1919, Provisional Sinn Féin and UVF: ending of proscription; exchanges between Ministers and officials, Meeting with Hugh Smyth, *c.* 15 May 1974.

15    Hugh Smyth was a UVF spokesman who was elected as an Independent Unionist councillor in June 1973. He was awarded an OBE in 1996.

16    NAUK, CJ4/1919, Briefing, 10 May 1974.

17    *Ibid.*

18    Hansard, House of Commons debates, Vol. 873, Columns 1240–1, 14 May 1974.

19    *Ibid.*, House of Lords debates, Vol. 351, Columns 1092–5, 15 May 1974.

20    NAUK, CJ4/862, Memo to Lord Donaldson from NIO official, 14 May 1974.

21    DOW was founded by Lieutenant Colonel Edward James Augustus Howard Brush (known as Peter). He was born in Fermoy, County Cork in 1901. Brush enjoyed a long military career. At the request of the county grand master of the Orange Order in County Down, he had founded the paramilitary organisation DOW in 1972. It was, in Brush's own words: 'a military organisation which we set up in this county in 1972 to be ready in case the political situation, or the upheaval and general murder and arson which could well follow the withdrawal of the British Army from this Province, caused us to mobilise men of good will to maintain law and order, and to protect those who required protection' (Imperial War Museum, collections, 3525 85/8/1, Private papers of Lt Col E. J. A. H. (Peter) Brush). Brush was recruiting from 1971 onwards, helped by a large number of men from all over County Down, and he eventually formed five battalions of volunteers. DOW played an active role in support of the UWC strike in May 1974.

22    The USCA was an association of former members of the USC or 'B Specials'. The group was formed around 1970 following the disbanding of the USC. It claimed to have a membership of 10,000 in 1970. There were claims of links between the USCA and loyalist paramilitary groups. The USCA assisted in roadblocks during the 1974 UWC strike.

23    The UAC was an umbrella group of loyalist paramilitaries set up in 1973. It was headed by Andy Tyrie, who at the time was commander of the UDA. The UAC covered the following groups: UDA, OV, DOW, USCA, Ulster Volunteer Service Corps and RHC. Its main aim was to set up a loyalist army of 20,000 men to take control of Northern Ireland if needed. The UAC was replaced by the Ulster Loyalist Central Coordinating Committee after the loyalist strike in 1974.

24    NAUK, CJ4/2038, Minutes of meeting of representatives of the United Ulster Workers' Council with secretary of state at Stormont Castle, 8 April 1974.

25   Anderson, *14 May Days*, pp. 29 and 33.

26   James Allan was a counsellor at the NIO, specifically Laneside, from 1973 until 1975. He was on secondment from the FCO.

27   Anderson, *14 May Days*, p. 33.

28   NAUK, CJ4/862, Minutes of meeting with UVF leaders, 15 May 1974.

29   Taylor, *Loyalists*, p. 124.

30   NAUK, CJ4/862, Minutes of meeting with UVF leaders, 15 May 1974.

31   McKittrick *et al., Lost Lives* pp. 414–46.

32   When the man who was charged with the Devlin killings appeared in court the RUC deliberately suppressed the crucial information that he was also a member of the UDR. HET RSR concerning the deaths of James and Gertrude Devlin. Readers will be unable to access this source document as HET reports were private reports compiled for individual families. The families included in this book have given permission for them to be used.

33   NAUK, CJ4/1919, Meeting with Hugh Smyth, *c.* 15 May 1974.

34   NAUK, CJ4/2038, Memo on loyalist strike to NIO officials from J. N. Allan, 17 May 1974.

35   JFF interview with Colin Wallace, 8 September 2000. The interview was private and is not available to the reader.

36   Affidavit of former RUC Sergeant John Weir, January 1999, https://wikispooks.com/wiki/Document:John_Weir_Affidavit (accessed 8 April 2016); Cadwallader, *Lethal Allies*, pp. 217–32. The Glenanne Gang was a paramilitary group made up of members from the UVF, RUC and UDR, which operated from James Mitchell's farm in Glenanne, County Armagh, in the 1970s and carried out about 120 murders on both sides of the border.

37   http://cain.ulst.ac.uk/events/dublin/chron.htm (accessed on 27 February 2015).

38   *The Irish Times*, 18 May 1974.

39   Barron, Justice Henry, *Interim Report on the Report of the Independent Commission of Inquiry into the Dublin and Monaghan Bombings* (Joint Oireachtas Committee on Justice, Equality, Defence and Women's Rights, Dublin, December 2003).

40   *Ibid.*, p. 209. John Weir served as an RUC officer from 1970 to 1978. He was convicted of the murder of William Strathern in 1980 and served twelve years in prison. He was a member of the Armagh Special Patrol Group of the RUC from 1973 to 1975 and has provided information on the Glenanne Gang.

41  *Ibid.*, p. 74. When this memo was written Marchant was actually interned and therefore available for interview.

42  NAUK, CJ4/2038, Memo to Philip Woodfield from James Allan, 23 May 1974.

43  Michael Oatley replaced Frank Steele as MI6 officer in Northern Ireland.

44  NAUK, CJ4/1147, Notes of meeting with UVF, 27 May 1974.

45  *Ibid.*

46  *Ibid.*, CJ4/2038, Notes of a security meeting at Stormont Castle during the UWC strike, 23 May 1974.

47  *Ibid.*

48  *Ibid.*

49  NAI, TAOIS 2005/7/630, Internal Taoiseach's Department memo regarding the SDLP, May 1974.

50  NAUK, CJ4/2038, Telegram to FCO from British Embassy, 23 May 1974.

51  NAUK, CJ4/1147, Notes of meeting with UVF on 29 May 1974. Marian and Dolours Price were sentenced for their part in the 1973 bombing of the Old Bailey, London. They went on hunger strike and were force fed as they tried to compel the authorities to repatriate them back to Northern Ireland. They were eventually transferred to Armagh Women's Prison. Dolours died in 2013, aged sixty-one.

52  NAUK, (no file ref), Memo to secretary of state from A. Huckle, Private Secretary, transcribed 31 May 1974 (copy on file).

53  *Ibid.* In the aftermath of its de-proscription, on 22 June 1974, the UVF launched a new political party in Belfast. Members of the executive of the new party said it would be called the Volunteer Political Party and would be solely identified with the UVF. It had a very short life, however. Its chairman, Ken Gibson, stood as a candidate for west Belfast in the October 1974 Westminster election but polled only 2,690 votes. The party was dissolved soon afterwards.

54  JFF interviews with Brendan Hughes in Belfast, 8 January and 7 February 2003. These interviews were private and are not available to the reader.

55  JFF interview with Colin Wallace, 19 April 2002. The interview was private and is not available to the reader.

56  *Ibid.*

57  *Ibid.* In August 1969 loyalist mobs attacked nationalist areas, particularly in Belfast. Scores of houses, as well as businesses and factories, were burned out. Thousands of mostly Catholic families were forced from

their homes. In some areas, the RUC helped the loyalists and failed to protect Catholic areas. Many view these events as a pogrom against the Catholic community.

58   Hansard, House of Commons debates, Vol. 873, Columns 891–7, 13 May 1974.

59   *Ibid.*

60   NAUK, CJ4/3291, Information Policy and work: briefs for secretary of state, February and October 1974, Report of May 1974.

61   *The Guardian*, 14 May 1974.

62   *The Daily Telegraph*, 14 May 1974.

63   *The Irish Times*, 14 May 1974.

64   *The Irish Press*, 14 May 1974.

65   *Ibid.* Dr Garret FitzGerald was an Irish politician who served as Taoiseach from July 1981 to February 1982 and again from December 1982 to March 1987. In the period 1973–7 he was minister for foreign affairs.

66   NAUK, CJ4/645, Handwritten note with tabloid pamphlet.

67   *Ibid.*, Memo to R. C. Cox, NIO, from P. R. N. Fifoot, Legal Counsellor at FCO, 16 May 1974.

68   *Ibid.*, Memo to R. C. Cox, NIO, from John Simeon, Republic of Ireland Department of FCO, 17 May 1974.

69   Amazon biography of Gary Hicks. http://www.amazon.com/Gary-Hicks/e/B0034Q14WK (accessed 24 July 2015).

70   NAUK, CJ4/645, Letter to Sir Tom Bridges, 10 Downing Street, from D. J. Trevelyan, NIO, 14 May 1974. Emphasis added.

71   Fisk, Robert, *The Point of No Return* (André Deutsch, London 1975), pp. 79–81.

72   *Ibid.*, p. 80.

73   NAUK, FCO87/440, Brief from G. W. Harding for Cabinet Official Committee on Northern Ireland meeting, 4 July 1975.

74   Frank Cooper served as PUS at the NIO (1973–6) under William Whitelaw and Merlyn Rees. A former Spitfire pilot in the Second World War, he was prominently involved in the talks with Sinn Féin that led to the IRA ceasefire in 1975. He returned to the MoD in 1976. See 'Obituary', *The Telegraph*, 30 January 2002.

75   NAUK, FCO87/342, Meeting at Stormont Castle, 7 August 1974.

76   The Ulster Service Corps joined the umbrella group of the UAC in early 1974. Its areas of operation were Counties Fermanagh and Tyrone.

77 NAUK, FCO87/342, Meeting at Stormont Castle between the secretary of state and UWC Coordinating Committee, 7 August 1974.

78 *The Irish Times*, 8 August 1974.

79 NAUK, FCO87/342, Meeting at Stormont Castle, 7 August 1974.

80 *The Irish Times*, 3 September 1974.

81 *Ibid.*

82 NAUK, CJ4/1300, Draft minute to Mr Chesterton from T. C. Barker, January 1976.

83 *The Irish Times*, 27 September 1974.

84 NAUK, CJ4/1300, Minutes of meeting with UWC Coordinating Committee, 19 December 1974.

## 6 THE NEW IRA CEASEFIRE AND THE LOYALIST BACKLASH

1 NAUK, (no file ref), Paper on sectarian murders by Frank Cooper, 15 May 1975 (copy on file).

2 University College Dublin (UCD) Archives, Garret FitzGerald Northern Ireland papers, P215/118, Memo to Minister for Foreign Affairs from Seán Donlon, 20 January 1975.

3 NAUK, CJ4/2928, IRA ceasefire: records of meetings between NIO officials and Provisional Sinn Féin, Jan–Sept. 1975.

4 CAIN website, chronology of the conflict, http://cain.ulst.ac.uk/othelem/chron/ch75.htm#10275 (accessed 21 October 2015).

5 Taylor, Peter, *Provos: The IRA and Sinn Féin* (Bloomsbury Publishing, London 1997), p. 187.

6 McKittrick *et al.*, *Lost Lives*, pp. 515–17.

7 NAUK, CJ4/3734, Loyalist paramilitary organisations, Meetings with NIO officials, Laneside, 1975.

8 *Ibid.*

9 McKittrick *et al.*, *Lost Lives*, pp. 488–511.

10 NAUK, CJ4/3734, Loyalist paramilitary organisations, Meetings with NIO officials, Laneside, 1975.

11 UCD Archives, Garret FitzGerald Northern Ireland papers, P215/118, Telegram to Seán Donlon from Irish Ambassador, London, 20 January 1975.

12 NAUK, CJ4/3734, Minutes of meeting with Andy Tyrie, 10 February 1975.

13 *Ibid.*

14   *Ibid.*, Meeting with UDA, 11 February 1975.

15   *Ibid.*

16   McKittrick *et al., Lost Lives*, pp. 513–17.

17   NAUK, CJ4/3734, Minutes of meeting with UDA, 13 February 1975.

18   *Ibid.*

19   *Ibid.*, CJ4/969, Letter to Sir Michael Carver, MoD, Whitehall from Sir Frank King, HQNI, 11 July 1973; the 'sic' is included here because this was a disrespectful and sexist way to describe a twenty-nine-year-old woman.

20   *Ibid.*, CJ4/838, Minutes of meeting with UDA, 27 February 1975.

21   *Ibid.*

22   *Ibid.*, Situation Reports, March 1975.

23   Vehicle checkpoints were permanent at border crossings, but during the Troubles mobile checkpoints were also set up randomly by the British Army, including the UDR, where motorists were stopped and asked to produce their licences.

24   NAUK, CJ4/838, Situation reports, March 1975.

25   *Ibid.*, CJ4/3734, Meeting with Andy Tyrie, 10 March 1975.

26   *Ibid.*, Minutes of meeting with Andy Tyrie and bodyguard, 21 March 1975.

27   David Burnside was press officer for Bill Craig's Vanguard Party. When Vanguard collapsed, Burnside joined the UUP and was MP for south Antrim from 2001 to 2005. He also served in the UDR and later became head of public relations at British Airways when the airline was engaged in lengthy legal action over alleged 'dirty tricks' against Virgin Airlines. See http://powerbase.info/index.php/David_Burnside (accessed 18 August 2015).

28   NAUK, CJ4/3734, Minutes of meeting with Andy Tyrie and bodyguard, 21 March 1975.

29   *Ibid.*, Letter from J. N. Allan to unknown recipient, copied to PUS, Peter England and J. B. Bourn, 24 March 1975.

30   *Ibid.*

31   *Ibid.*, Note of a meeting with Andy Tyrie and John Orchin, 23 May 1975.

32   *Ibid.*, (no file ref), 'Preliminary analysis of RUC statistics of persons charged during 1975 (up to 14 September) with terrorist type offences', K. J. Jordan, 17 September 1975 (copy on file).

     *Ibid.*, CJ4/3734, Minutes of meeting with Andy Tyrie and Orchin, 23 May 1975.

34    Moore, Chris, *The Kincora Scandal: Political Cover-up and Intrigue in Northern Ireland* (Marino, Dublin 1996), p. 86.

35    *Ibid.*, p. 144.

36    UCD Archives, Garret FitzGerald Northern Ireland papers, P215/94, Notes of meeting between John McColgan and Ken Gibson, UVF, 15 January 1975.

37    The origin of this feud was in the UWC strike in May 1974. It began with a row about whether a particular bar should remain open. On 18 May UVF member Joseph Shaw was shot dead by the UDA. The feud rumbled on for years, into 1977. Ten men in total from both organisations lost their lives as a result.

38    UCD Archives, Garret FitzGerald Northern Ireland papers, P215/94, Notes of meeting between John McColgan and Andy Tyrie, Glen Barr and Herbie McMorrow, UDA, on 21 May, 23 May 1975.

39    Romper rooms were places where Catholics, having been abducted, were sometimes taken in the early 1970s by UDA gangs. There they were interrogated, tortured and eventually killed. These rooms were located in UDA pubs, drinking clubs or, sometimes, private houses. David Payne is believed to have invented these notorious romper rooms. Catholics were interrogated, tortured and killed in this way by the Baker/McCreery gang.

40    UCD Archives, Notes of meeting between John McColgan and John McKeague, RHC, 22 July 1975.

41    *Ibid.*, Notes of meeting between John McColgan and Glen Barr, 22 July 1975.

42    McKittrick *et al.*, *Lost Lives*, p. 1553.

43    NAUK, CJ4/838, Policy towards UDA, report of Radio Ulster News Summary, 30 April 1975.

44    *Ibid.*, Internal NIO memo to Bill Webster from Douglas Janes, 1 May 1975.

45    *Ibid.*

46    *Ibid.*

47    *Ibid.*

48    Taylor, *Provos*, p. 187. One such killing was the case of eighteen-year-old Joey Clarke. He was shot in his family home when a gunman fired through the glass of the front door at approximately 6 p.m. on 12 March 1975. His brother pursued one of the gunmen to a waiting car; the gunman was so obese that he was unable to run to the getaway car and had difficulties entering the vehicle to escape with three accomplices.

Just four weeks later a known UVF gunman fitting the description of the shooter in the Clarke case was arrested in a vehicle with another UVF member. The obese gunman was picked out at a subsequent identity parade by both Joey's mother and a neighbour who had witnessed the shooting. Other witnesses were not called to the identity parade. Notwithstanding this and other significant investigative failures, the man was initially charged with Joey's murder. The Clarke family only recently discovered through the HET that the charges were subsequently dropped, in part because a senior RUC officer in the case sought to actively downplay the evidence of the eyewitnesses. The family and the PFC have good reason to surmise that the suspect had an agent–handler relationship with RUC Special Branch at the time. He is since deceased.

49   NAUK, CJ4/830, Minutes of meeting between Cardinal Conway and Roland Moyle MP, 9 April 1975.

50   *Ibid.*

51   *Ibid.*, Note to Bill Webster from R. C. Masefield, NIO, 3 April 1975.

52   McKittrick *et al., Lost Lives*, pp. 139–40, 152, 165, 176, 178.

53   NAUK, CJ4/830, Memo on sectarian murders to Roland Moyle from Bill Webster, 16 May 1975.

54   *Ibid.*

55   *Ibid.*, Memo to Bill Webster from J. N. Allan, 14 May 1975.

56   *Ibid.*

57   *Ibid.*, CJ4/829, Letter to G. W. Harding, FCO, from John K. Hickman, British Embassy, Dublin, 7 July 1975.

58   *Ibid.*, (no file ref), Briefing paper from NIO to J. Hickman, British Embassy, Dublin, May 1975 (copy on file).

59   *Ibid.*

60   NAUK (no file reference), Paper entitled 'Charges and convictions', 28 April 1975 (copy on file).

61   London School of Economics, Papers of Merlyn Rees, 5/12/39, Minutes of meeting between Rees and Garret FitzGerald, 15 May 1975 (made available to Judge Henry Barron, Independent Commission of Inquiry into the Dublin and Monaghan Bombings).

62   NAUK, CJ4/1156, Sectarian assassinations 1975–6, Paper on sectarian murder, 29 July 1975.

63   *Ibid.*, CJ4/830, Letter to Robin Masefield, NIO Laneside, from A. G. L. Turner, FCO, 16 April 1975.

64   *Ibid.*

65 *Ibid.*, (no file ref), Paper on sectarian murders by Frank Cooper, 15 May 1975 (copy on file).

66 *Ibid.*

67 *Ibid.*

68 *Ibid.*, Notes of meeting of secretary of state with several NIO officials, transcribed 29 May 1975.

69 *Ibid.*, Letter to Frank Cooper from Major General D. T. Young, HQNI, 5 June 1975.

70 *Ibid.*

71 NAUK, (no file ref), Notes on points raised in CLF's letter of 5 June 1975. The Protestant Action Force was used as a pseudonym for some attacks by the UVF.

72 *Ibid.*, CJ4/1156, Guidance to overseas posts on sectarian assassinations in Northern Ireland, prepared by A. G. L Turner, 22 August 1975.

73 *Ibid.*

74 *Ibid.*

75 Sir David House replaced Sir Frank King as GOC Northern Ireland on 1 August 1975. He had served in Italy during the Second World War and had afterwards served in Penang and, later, Berlin.

76 NAUK, CJ4/1228, Letter to GOC Sir David House from Frank Cooper, NIO, 12 December 1975.

77 UCD Archives, Garret FitzGerald Northern Ireland papers, P215/94, Notes of meeting between John McColgan and J. N. Allan, transcribed 18 April 1975.

78 *Ibid.*, Notes of meeting between John McColgan and J. N. Allan, 14 July 1975.

79 *Ibid.*, Notes of meeting between John McColgan and Donald Middleton, 25 July 1975.

80 *Ibid.*, Notes of meeting between John McColgan and Donald Middleton, transcribed 12 September 1975.

81 Travers, Stephen and Fetherstonhaugh, Neil, *The Miami Showband Massacre* (Hachette Ireland, Dublin 2008); Cadwallader, *Lethal Allies*, pp. 99–108.

82 HET RSR concerning the deaths of Seán Farmer and Colm McCartney.

83 According to the HET, the RUC believed two UDR officers were involved in the Altnamackin killings.

84 NAUK, CJ4/1920, Notes of meeting of 4 August at Stormont Castle by D. Chesterton, transcribed 5 August 1975.

85   *Ibid.*

86   *Ibid.*

87   UCD Archives, Garret FitzGerald Northern Ireland papers, P215/94, Notes on meeting between John McColgan and Bill Craig, Vanguard Party, transcribed 8 August 1975.

88   *Ibid.*

89   NAUK, (no file ref.), Memo to Peter England from Bill Webster, 26 August 1975 (copy on file).

90   *Ibid.*

91   *Ibid.*, Memo to Peter England from J. B. Bourn, 23 June 1975.

92   *Ibid.*

93   *Ibid.*, CJ4/1919, Memo to Bill Webster from D. J. Wyatt, 17 September 1975.

94   The four UVF men killed in the premature explosion were Mark Dodd, Aubrey Reid, Samuel Swanson and Andrew Freeman. They were the likely killers of Christopher Phelan at Baronrath Bridge, County Kildare, on 21 June 1975. Swanson's fingerprints were found on a dagger recovered near the scene, and the bomb at Farrenlester had a similar timing device to that used in the bomb that exploded on the railway line at Baronrath.

95   NAUK, CJ4/1920, Text of speech by secretary of state, Merlyn Rees in House of Commons, 4 November 1975.

96   The VPP emerged in June 1974 as the 'political wing of the Ulster Volunteer Force'. The chairman of the VPP, Ken Gibson, stood as a candidate for west Belfast in the October 1974 Westminster election, but polled only 2,690 votes. The VPP was dissolved soon after the election. The VPP is considered the precursor of the Ulster Democratic Party.

97   NAUK, CJ4/1920, Text of speech by secretary of state, Merlyn Rees in House of Commons, 4 November 1975.

98   *Ibid.*, CJ4/2262, Notes of a meeting in secretary of state's room in House of Commons, 22 October 1975.

99   *Ibid.*

100  Barron, *Interim Report on the Report of the Bombing of Kay's Tavern, Dundalk.*

101  NAUK, CJ4/1228, Minutes of security meeting, 1 December 1975.

102  *Ibid.*, CJ4/3731, Memo to Donald Middleton from Frank Cooper, 19 November 1975.

103 *Ibid.*

104 UCD Archives, Garret FitzGerald Northern Ireland papers, P215/94, Notes on a meeting between John McColgan and Rev. William Arlow, 11 December 1975.

105 *Ibid.*

106 *Ibid.*

107 'Fearless "Canon of Peace" believed in power of talk' – Obituary for Canon William Arlow, in *The Irish Times*, 5 August 2006.

108 UCD Archives, Garret FitzGerald Northern Ireland papers, P215/94, Report for the Minister for Foreign Affairs from Seán Donlon, 10 April 1975.

109 *Ibid.*

110 This should read 'pre-1973', before the internment of loyalist paramilitaries.

111 UCD Archives, Garret FitzGerald Northern Ireland papers, P215/94, Report for the Minister for Foreign Affairs from Seán Donlon, 10 April 1975.

## 7   DISCRIMINATION IN 'SCREENING' AND THE POWER OF PROPAGANDA

1 NAUK, (no file ref), A Guide to Paramilitary and Associated Organisations, 2 September 1976 (copy on file).

2 Screening was eventually ruled illegal in a test case taken by Clara Reilly, Association for Legal Justice, Belfast, following her arrest on 20 February 1980. A year later, the High Court, Belfast, ruled in her favour and the practice was discontinued.

3 3 Brigade covered Counties Armagh and Down; 8 Brigade included Counties Derry, Fermanagh and Tyrone; 39 Brigade covered Belfast and County Antrim.

4 NAUK, (no file ref), Situation reports, January–March 1976 (copy on file); these details are taken directly from British documents which use religious terms.

5 *Ibid.*, September 1975–March 1976 (copy on file).

6 The practice of screening a much higher percentage of Catholics was discriminatory because loyalists were responsible for nearly half the killings at that particular time. It doesn't mean that those who were killed had been screened. Screening greatly increased the isolation of the nationalist community and reduced its confidence in the rule of law.

7 The Samaritans are a registered charity aimed at providing emotional

support to anyone in distress, struggling to cope or at risk of suicide throughout Ireland and the UK, often through its telephone helpline.

8    NAUK, (no file ref), A Guide to Paramilitary and Associated Organisations, 2 September 1976 (copy on file). Emphasis added.

9    *Ibid.*

10   De Silva, *The Report of the Patrick Finucane Review* p. 38, paragraph 1.70.

11   NAUK, CJ4/3963, Telegram to British embassy, Washington from Foreign Secretary, Lord Carrington, 4 November 1980.

12   *Ibid.*, (no file ref), *A Guide to Paramilitary and Associated Organisations,* 2 September 1976.

13   JFF interview with Colin Wallace, 8 September 2000.

14   The Castleblayney bombing occurred on 7 March 1976. A no-warning car bomb exploded outside the Three Star Inn on Main Street, killing one man, Patrick Mone. Several other civilians were injured.

15   JFF interview with John Weir, Paris, 14–15 February 2001; William McCaughey on BBC *Spotlight* programme, 25 May 2004.

16   Cadwallader, *Lethal Allies*, pp. 164–5 (for detailed information on the mid-Ulster UVF, see *Lethal Allies*).

17   UCD Archives, Garret FitzGerald Northern Ireland papers, P215/159, Handwritten note on an unrelated letter to the Minister for Foreign Affairs from Seán Donlon, Assistant Secretary, 18 August 1975. 'The Murder Triangle' was the name given to a notorious area of Northern Ireland within which many sectarian murders of Catholics took place in the early to mid-1970s. The two priests who gave the area this name were Raymond Murray and Denis Faul. The points of the triangle were Portadown, County Armagh; Aughnacloy, in south County Tyrone; and Pomeroy, in mid-County Tyrone.

18   UCD Archives, Garret FitzGerald Northern Ireland papers, P215/162, Telegram to Seán Donlon, DFA from Donal O'Sullivan, Irish ambassador, London, 20 August 1975.

19   Barron, Interim Report on the *Report of the bombing of Kay's Tavern, Dundalk,* pp. 119–20.

20   NAUK, CJ4/741, Political situation in Northern Ireland, Dr Garret FitzGerald raised concerns; FCO87/423, Relations between Republic of Ireland and UK, Letter to G. W. Harding from J. D. W. Janes, 29 August 1975.

21   Dillon, Martin, *The Shankill Butchers: A Case Study of Mass Murder* (Arrow Books, London 1990).

22  *The Detail*, 31 July 2011, article by Barry McCaffrey. *The Detail* is an investigative news and analysis website based in Belfast: www.thedetail.tv.

23  The Pat Finucane Centre, *The Hidden History of the UDR: The Secret Files Revealed* (pamphlet, August 2014), p. 23.

24  *Ibid.*

25  NAUK, DEFE70/599, UDR: Criminal and security investigations of 10 UDR, February–December 1978.

26  Dillon, *The Shankill Butchers*, p. 258.

27  *The Irish News* and *Belfast Telegraph*, 22 February 1979.

28  MacAirt, *The McGurk's Bar Bombing*, p. 95.

29  *Ibid.*, pp. 95–6; HET Review Summary Report (RSR); Police Ombudsman for Northern Ireland (PONI) report, http://www.PONI/files/8b/8b634ea-7575-4015-b9bf-1548536a9f2f.pdf (accessed 9 April 2016).

30  MacAirt, *The McGurk's Bar Bombing*, p. 204.

31  *Ibid.*, p. 205.

32  NAUK, WO305/4199, Watchkeeper's log, 14 May 1972.

33  HET RSR concerning the death of George Potsworth. Readers will be unable to access this source document as HET reports were private reports compiled for individual families. The families included in this book have given permission for them to be used.

34  HET RSR concerning the death of Francis McCaughey. Readers will be unable to access this source document as HET reports were private reports compiled for individual families. The families included in this book have given permission for them to be used. For more on this killing see Cadwallader, *Lethal Allies*, pp. 48–50.

35  McKittrick *et al.*, *Lost Lives*, p. 400.

36  HET RSR concerning the death of Martin Crossen. Readers will be unable to access this source document as HET reports were private reports compiled for individual families. The families included in this book have given permission for them to be used.

37  *Ibid.*

38  *Ibid.*

39  *Ibid.*

40  NAUK, (no file ref), Note of a security meeting at Stormont Castle, 5 July 1976 (copy on file).

41  *Ibid.*

42  McKittrick *et al.*, *Lost Lives*, p. 666.

8   CIVIL WAR? THE 'OFFICIAL' ARRIVAL OF THE SAS AND 'ULSTERISATION'

1   NAUK, CJ4/3107, Note for the Record, P. W. J. Buxton, 6 July 1979.

2   Cadwallader, *Lethal Allies*, p. 159.

3   Chequers is the country residence of the British prime minister.

4   NAUK, PREM16/959, Notes of a meeting at Chequers, 11 January 1976.

5   NAUK, (no file ref), Minutes of meeting with UDA leaders on 19 January 1976 (copy on file).

6   After the collapse of the NI Assembly in May 1974, the British government published a White Paper which set out government plans to hold elections to a Constitutional Convention, which would look for an agreed political settlement to the Northern Ireland conflict. Elections took place on 1 May 1975. However, as the UUUC opposed power-sharing, the chance of the convention reaching agreement on a constitutional settlement was remote from the outset. The convention collapsed in the autumn. Merlyn Rees announced its reconvening on 12 January 1976, but it collapsed in uproar on 3 March 1976, as the UUUC would not agree on SDLP involvement in any future cabinet.

7   NAUK, (no file ref), Minutes of meeting with UDA leaders on 19 January 1976 (copy on file).

8   *Ibid.*

9   *Ibid.*

10  Curtis, Liz, *Ireland: The Propaganda War* (Pluto Press, London 1984), pp. 68–9.

11  Bourke, Richard, *Peace in Ireland: The War of Ideas* (Pimlico, 2003), p. 164.

12  NAUK, CJ4/2521, GOC's Security Review, 1 September 1976.

13  *Ibid.*

14  *Ibid.*

15  *Ibid.*

16  *Ibid.*, Memo to PUS from A. W. Stephens, 18 February 1977.

17  *Ibid.*

18  *Ibid.*, Report of Contingency Study of Preventive Custody.

19  Internment was phased out during the latter half of 1975 and all detainees had been released by December. This was done for a number of reasons: it was generally considered a political failure, which had actually greatly increased support for the IRA; the case before the

ECHR had a discouraging effect on its continuation; and it may have been part of the agreement the British made with the IRA in January 1975, which resulted in the renewal of their ceasefire on 9 February.

20   These declassified documents suggest that some elements of the British Army had a much more positive view of the original internment operation than was publicly admitted. Internment is described as 'a major mistake' in the official MoD analysis of Operation Banner – the operational name for the period 1969–2006. In response to the study, however, the GOC took issue with the 'unqualified contention that there is wide measure of acceptance that [detention] was counter-productive. Such a contention, arising from so much repetition over the past two years, appears to have become a matter of Holy Writ' (NAUK, CJ4/2521). Lieutenant Colonel McLarney at HQNI made the same point when he suggested that 'the contention that detention was counterproductive is unproven'. He went on to argue that 'a necessary precondition to introducing any form of detention would be the preparation of public opinion' (NAUK, CJ4/2521, Letter from Lt Col McLarney to A. W. Stephens, 17 January 1977).

21   NAUK, CJ4/2521, Report of Contingency Study, Part II.

22   *Ibid.*

23   *Ibid.*, Part V.

24   *Ibid.*

25   *Ibid.*

26   *Ibid.*

27   McKittrick *et al.*, *Lost Lives*, Table 2, p. 1553.

28   Taylor, Peter, *Brits: The War against the IRA* (Bloomsbury, London 2002), p. 201.

29   NAUK, CJ4/3731, Report on RUC investigation into PSF/PIRA, 19 October 1978.

30   *Ibid.*

31   *Ibid.*

32   *Ibid.*

33   *Ibid.*

34   *Ibid.*, Memo to PUS from Douglas Janes, 29 April 1977.

35   *Ibid.*

36   http://cain.ulst.ac.uk/events/uuac/sum.htm (accessed 28 January 2015).

37   McKittrick *et al.*, *Lost Lives*, p. 1553.

38   NAUK, CJ4/3731, Sinn Féin Report by P. W. J. Buxton, October 1978.

39   McKittrick *et al.*, *Lost Lives*, p. 1553.

40   NAUK, CJ4/3107, Note for the Record, P. W. J. Buxton, 6 July 1979.

41   *Ibid.*, Memo from Miss Stewart, 5 September 1979.

42   The United Ulster Unionist Council was established in January 1974. It sought to bring together unionists opposed to the Sunningdale Agreement.

43   NAUK, CJ4/3963, Paper on loyalist paramilitary organisations, July 1979.

44   *Ibid.*

45   *Ibid.*

## 9   UDA MURDERS OF HIGH-PROFILE REPUBLICANS

1   NAUK, CJ4/4198, Letter to Congressman Hamilton Fish from the British Ambassador to the US, Nicholas Henderson, 24 May 1982.

2   The H-Blocks crisis developed after the introduction of 'Ulsterisation' and 'criminalisation' in March 1976. Republican prisoners refused to wear a prison uniform, and so began the 'blanket protest'. In 1978, after a number of attacks on prisoners who left their cells to 'slop out', the dispute escalated into the 'dirty protest' when prisoners refused to leave their cells and covered their cell walls with excrement. In 1980 seven prisoners participated in the first hunger strike, which ended, without resolution, after fifty-three days.

3   Routledge, Paul, *Public Servant, Secret Agent: The Elusive Life and Violent Death of Airey Neave* (Fourth Estate, London 2002), pp. 313 and 336–7.

4   Hansard, House of Commons debates, Vol. 971, Columns 741–70, 25 July 1979.

5   Paul Routledge quotes the magazines *Hibernia, Magill*, and *Lobster* as supporters of this theory, as well as Raymond Murray (author of *The SAS in Ireland*) and the IRSP itself. Routledge appears to give credence to the theory too. Routledge, *Public Servant, Secret Agent*, pp. 340–1.

6   *Ibid.*, p. 346.

7   HET RSR concerning the death of Rodney McCormick. Readers will be unable to access this source document as HET reports were private reports compiled for individual families. The families included in this book have given permission for them to be used.

8   Dillon, Martin, *The Dirty War* (Routledge, 1990), pp. 276–7.

9   PRONI, CRCT/3/2/3/506, R v McClelland, McConnell and McConnell, Bill No. 496/81.

10   *Ibid.*, R v McClelland, McConnell and McConnell, Statement of Constable [name redacted].

11   *Ibid.*

12   *Ibid.*

13   HET RSR concerning the death of Rodney McCormick.

14   Letter to the Pat Finucane Centre, from Northern Ireland Inquiries, MoD [Ministry of Defence], Whitehall, London, 15 January 2016.

15   Letter to the Pat Finucane Centre, from Northern Ireland Prison Service, 4 April 2016.

16   PRONI, CRCR/3/2/3/506, R v McClelland, McConnell and McConnell.

17   According to Paul Routledge, Sergeant Tom Aiken had just returned from a tour of duty in Hong Kong. Routledge, *Public Servant, Secret Agent*, p. 342.

18   Gerry Adams was associated with the provisional republican movement from its foundation. He was interned without trial in 1972. In July 1972 he was released to participate in secret talks in London. After his rearrest he tried to escape and was imprisoned. He was released in 1976. He has been president of Sinn Féin since 1983. In 1984 he was shot and seriously wounded by the UDA. With John Hume of the SDLP he initiated the peace process, which brought an end to the conflict, and was one of the architects of the Good Friday Agreement. In 2011 he resigned his seat in the British Parliament and was subsequently elected to the Dáil (Irish Parliament) in the general election of February 2011. He is the Teachta Dála for Louth and East Meath.

19   Dillon, *The Dirty War*, p. 278.

20   *East Antrim Times*, 19 March 1982.

21   PRONI, CRCT/3/2/3/506, R v McClelland, McConnell and McConnell, Bill No. 496/81.

22   *Ibid.*

23   *East Antrim Times*, 19 March 1982.

24   Wood, *Crimes of Loyalty*, p. 117; Routledge, *Public Servant, Secret Agent*, p. 343.

25   *Ibid.*

26   Rolston, Bill, *Children of the Revolution: The Lives of Sons and Daughters of Activists in Northern Ireland* (Guildhall Press, Derry 2011), pp. 101–8.

27   Routledge, *Public Servant, Secret Agent*, p. 345.

28   *Ibid.*

29   *Ibid.*

30   *The Irish News*, 30 October 1980.

31   The political affairs division (or the political affairs branch) replaced Laneside in the mid–late 1970s.

32   NAUK, CJ4/3963, Memo to Tim H. Gee from Stephen J. Leach, Political Affairs Division, 7 November 1980.

33   *Ibid.*

34   *Ibid.* The first of two IRA hunger strikes began on 27 October 1980 when seven IRA members in Long Kesh/Maze refused food.

35   *Ibid.*

36   NAUK, CJ4/3963, Telegram to British Embassy, Washington, from Foreign Secretary, Lord Carrington, 4 November 1980.

37   *Ibid.*

38   *Ibid.*

39   Alexander Haig was a US Army general who served as the US secretary of state under President Ronald Reagan. What is being referred to here is the 'Third Force' established by Dr Ian Paisley in April 1981.

40   NAUK, CJ4/4198, Letter to Congressman Hamilton Fish from the British Ambassador to the US, Nicholas Henderson, 24 May 1982.

41   *Ibid.*

42   *Ibid.*, Handwritten note to Richard Davies, Law and Order Division, from M. Bohill, PAB, 3 June 1982.

43   Jonathan Margetts worked for twenty-five years in the NIO from its inception until 2007. He was awarded an OBE in 2006 'for his part in bringing peace and stability to Northern Ireland'. He worked under every secretary of state.

44   NAUK, CJ4/4198, Memo to secretary of state's private secretary from C. Davenport, Stormont House, 2 December 1980.

45   *Ibid.*

46   *Ibid.*, Memo to secretary of state's private secretary, from C. Davenport, 28 January 1981.

47   *Ibid.*

48   *Ibid.*, CJ4/3575 and CJ4/3107, Letter to Secretary, ECtHR, Strasbourg from John Cousins, Alliance Party, 4 November 1980.

49   *Ibid.*

50   Humphrey Atkins was appointed secretary of state for Northern Ireland by Margaret Thatcher when she came to power in May 1979. He served in the post until September 1981.

51  NAUK, CJ4/3575 and CJ4/3107, Letter to secretary of state from John Cousins, Alliance Party, 5 November 1980.

52  *Ibid.*, CJ4/3107, Memo to Miss Elliot from A. C. Stott on the UDA, 6 November 1980.

53  *Ibid.*

54  *Ibid.*

55  *Ibid.*, Memo to C. Davenport from J. M. Burns, 10 November 1980.

56  *Ibid.*, CJ4/3575, Paper on proscription of UDA, November 1980.

57  *Ibid.*

58  *Ibid.*

59  *Ibid.*

60  *Ibid.*, CJ4/3963, Memo to D. Chesterton from J. A. Daniell, 10 November 1980.

61  *Ibid.*

62  *Ibid.*

63  Roy Mason served as secretary of state for Northern Ireland from 10 September 1976 to 4 May 1979.

64  NAUK, CJ4/2841, UDA: Meetings and contacts with UDA leadership 1976–1979.

65  NAUK, CJ4/4198, Memo to Tim H. Gee from Julie Ireland, Public Affairs Division, 22 January 1981. John McMichael became deputy commander of the UDA in the 1980s. He had been leader of its south Belfast brigade since the 1970s. He is believed to have been responsible for directing the attacks on republicans in 1980–1. He was killed by an IRA booby-trap car bomb outside his home in December 1987.

66  *Ibid.*, FCO87/1207, Telegram to FCO from Sir Leonard Figg, British ambassador, Dublin, 2 February 1981.

67  Robert McConnell later joined the UUP and was appointed to the position of chairman of west Belfast Ulster Unionist Association. He was released from jail on 13 December 1996.

68  NAUK, FCO87/1207, Newspaper cutting, *The Irish News*, 11 March 1982.

69  *Ibid.*

70  *Ibid.*, CJ4/4198, Memo from DFE (Frances) Elliot, Law and Order Division, NIO, 18 February 1981.

71  *Ibid.*, Newspaper cutting, *New York Daily News*, 19 December 1980.

72  *Ibid.*

73   *Ibid.*

74   *Ibid.*

75   *Ibid.*

76   *Hidden Hand: The Forgotten Massacre*, produced by Yorkshire Television, broadcast on Channel 4, 6 July 1993.

77   NAUK, CJ4/4198, Memo from Miss D. F. E. Elliot, Law and Order Division, NIO, 18 February 1981.

78   According to the de Silva report into Pat Finucane's murder, MI5 initiated a propaganda offensive against certain lawyers in the 1980s, including Pat Finucane. The aim of the propaganda was to smear them as members of or sympathisers with the IRA; de Silva, *The Report of the Patrick Finucane Review*, Volume I, p. 298, para 15.32.

79   McKittrick *et al.*, *Lost Lives*, p. 815.

80   NAUK, CJ4/4198, Statement of the Hon. Mr Justice Murray after the conviction of Stanley Millar Smith for the murder of Alexander Reid, 4 February 1981.

81   *Ibid.*, Memo to secretary of state's private secretary from J. M. Burns, 5 February 1981.

82   *Ibid.*

83   D. J. (David) Wyatt was assistant secretary at the NIO. A *Lobster* article in April 1984 made the following claim: 'The Counter Intelligence branch of the Secret Service, MI5, is now believed to be running the show in Northern Ireland after the removal of MI6's top man in Ulster, David Wyatt. Mr Wyatt, a casualty of the internal row in the intelligence services, was replaced by an MI5 officer. Described by one source as being a "link with the foreign office", he was trusted by the foreign office mandarins even more than security overlord Sir Maurice Oldfield, appointed by Mrs Thatcher in 1979.' 'Kincoragate – Loose Ends', in *The Lobster*, No. 4, April 1984, http://www.8bitmode.com/rogerdog/lobster/lobster04.pdf (accessed 12 April 2016).

84   NAUK, CJ4/4198, Memo to PUS from D. J. Wyatt, 12 February 1981.

85   *Ibid.*, Memo to J. F. Halliday, Home Office, from M. W. Hopkins, NIO, 11 March 1981.

86   Ross, F. Stuart, *Smashing H-Block: The Rise and Fall of the Popular Campaign against Criminalization, 1976–1982* (Liverpool University Press, Liverpool 2011), p. 149, paperback edition; McKittrick *et al.*, *Lost Lives*, p. 862.

## IO   RUC RAIDS ON UDA HEADQUARTERS EMBARRASS THE BRITISH GOVERNMENT

1   NAUK, CJ4/4198, Memo to George Fergusson from C. Davenport, 22 September 1981.

2   The IRA/INLA hunger strike (second hunger strike) of 1981 was the culmination of the H-Blocks crisis, with ten republicans – seven IRA men and three INLA men – dying over a period of three months between May and August.

3   NAUK, CJ4/4198, Situation Report, 26–27 May 1981, Eric Dalzell, Duty Officer; *The Irish Times*, 28 May 1981.

4   Stephen Boys-Smith later became the British joint secretary of the Independent Monitoring Commission with the joint Irish secretary, Michael Mellett.

5   NAUK, CJ4/4198, Memo to P. W. J. Buxton from Stephen Boys-Smith, 2 June 1981.

6   NAUK, CJ4/4225, Memo to D. J. Wyatt from David Blatherwick, 22 April 1981.

7   *Ibid.*, CJ4/4198, Memo to P. W. J. Buxton from Stephen Boys-Smith, 2 June 1981.

8   John Blelloch is alleged to have been an MI5 agent. http://www.bobby sandstrust.com/archives/1069 (accessed 12 April 2016).

9   NAUK, CJ4/4198, Memo to Deputy Secretary NIO Sir John Blelloch from P. W. J. Buxton, 3 June 1981.

10   *Ibid.*, Memo to Secretary of State's Private Secretary from P. W. J. Buxton, 3 June 1981.

11   *Ibid.*

12   *Ibid.*

13   *Ibid.*

14   *Ibid.*

15   *Ibid.*

16   *Ibid.*

17   *Ibid.*

18   NAUK, CJ4/3963, Memo to Sir John Blelloch from Stephen Boys-Smith, NIO, 5 June 1981.

19   De Silva, *The Report of the Patrick Finucane Review*, p. 11, paragraph 49.

20   BBC *Panorama* programme: 'Britain's Secret Terror Deals', 28 May 2015. Lord John Stevens presided over three external police inquiries in Northern Ireland into allegations of collusion between the British

Army, the RUC and loyalist paramilitaries. While Stevens declared in 1990 that collusion was 'neither widespread nor institutionalised', by April 2003 he acknowledged that he had uncovered collusion at a level 'way beyond' his 1990 view. Stevens concluded that there was collusion in the murders of Patrick Finucane and Brian Adam Lambert and that they could have been prevented. https://madden-finucane.com/files/2016/01/2003-04-17_stevens_report.pdf (accessed 3 March 2016).

21   The Anglo-Irish Agreement was a treaty between the UK and Ireland, which was signed in November 1985. It gave the Irish government an advisory role in Northern Ireland affairs for the first time while confirming that there would be no change in the constitutional status of Northern Ireland unless a majority of its people agreed to join the republic. It was bitterly opposed by unionists.

22   De Silva, *The Report of the Patrick Finucane Review*, Vol. II, documents, p. 327.

23   NAUK, CJ4/3963, Memo to Sir John Blelloch from Stephen Boys-Smith, NIO, 5 June 1981.

24   *Ibid.*

25   *Ibid.*

26   *Ibid.*

27   *Ibid.*

28   *Ibid.*, CJ4/4198, Draft letter from D. F. E. (Frances) Elliot to Mr D. McNamara, Liverpool, April 1981. Emphasis added.

29   *Ibid.*, Memo to secretary of state's private secretary from C. Davenport, Law and Order Division, Stormont House Annexe, 23 June 1981.

30   *Ibid.*, Letter to Don Concannon from Michael Alison, 10 August 1981.

31   The ULDP was founded on 2 June 1981.

32   David Blatherwick later served as ambassador to Ireland – from September 1991 to March 1995.

33   NAUK, CJ4/3963, Memo to David Blatherwick from Stephen Leach, Political Affairs Division, 4 August 1981.

34   *Ibid.*

35   It later transpired that the UVF was culpable; McKittrick *et al.*, *Lost Lives*, pp. 878–9.

36   NAUK, CJ4/4198, Memo to George Fergusson from C. Davenport, 22 September 1981.

37   *Ibid.*

38   NAUK, CJ4/3963, Memo to D. J. Wyatt from David Blatherwick, NIO, 19 October 1981.

39   Taylor, *Brits*, p. 199.

40   NAUK, CJ4/3963, Memo to D. J. Wyatt from David Blatherwick NIO, 19 October 1981.

41   *Ibid.*

42   *Ibid.*

43   *Ibid.* The Public Affairs Branch replaced Laneside.

44   *Ibid.*, Memo to D. J. Wyatt from P. W. J. Buxton, 20 October 1981.

45   *Ibid.*

46   *Ibid.*

47   Owen Carron was Bobby Sands' election agent for the April 1981 Fermanagh/south Tyrone by-election, which was caused by the death of Frank Maguire, MP. Sands was elected, but after he died on hunger strike Carron was elected on an anti-H-Block ticket. He lost his seat in the UK general election of 1983 because the SDLP stood a candidate in the constituency and split the nationalist vote, allowing Ken Maginnis to take the seat.

48   NAUK, CJ4/3963, Memo to D. J. Wyatt from C. Davenport, 20 October 1981.

49   *Ibid.*, Memo to D. J. Wyatt from Stephen Leach, Public Affairs Division, 21 October 1981.

50   *Ibid.*, CJ4/4198, Memo to D. J. Wyatt from David Blatherwick, 11 November 1981.

51   *Ibid.*, Notes of meeting with Billy Elliot and Mary McCurrie, ULDP, 19 November 1981.

52   *Ibid.*

53   *Ibid.*, Memo to D. J. Wyatt from David Blatherwick, 20 November 1981.

54   *Ibid.*, Memo to P. W. J. Buxton from Stephen Boys-Smith, 12 January 1982.

55   *Ibid.*

56   *Ibid.*

57   *Ibid.*

58   *Ibid.*

59   Dorril, Stephen, *The Silent Conspiracy: Inside the Intelligence Services in the 1990s* (Mandarin, London 1994), p. 484, cited on Powerbase website: http://powerbase.info/index.php/Harold_Doyne-Ditmas (accessed 12 April 2015).

60   NAUK, CJ4/4198, Memo to P. W. J. Buxton from R. A. Harrington, 13 January 1982.

61   *Ibid.*, Memo to Stephen Boys-Smith from D. J. Wyatt, 13 January 1982.

62   *Ibid.*

63   This phrase was taken from Sinn Féin's Danny Morrison, who said at its Ard-Fheis in October 1981: 'Who here really believes we can win the war through the ballot box? But will anyone here object if, with a ballot paper in this hand and an Armalite in the other, we take power in Ireland?' http://news.bbc.co.uk/hi/english/static/in_depth/northern_ireland/2001/provisional_ira/1981.stm (accessed 12 April 2016).

64   NAUK, CJ4/4198, Memo to Stephen Boys-Smith from D. J. Wyatt, 13 January 1982.

65   *Ibid.*, Newspaper cutting, *The Irish News*, 22 April 1982.

66   *Ibid.*, 29 April 1982.

67   The authorities were aware, by this time, that the UDA had infiltrated the prison service.

68   Cory, Judge Peter, *Cory Collusion Inquiry Report – Patrick Finucane* (The Stationery Office, London, April 2004), p. 60; de Silva, *The Report of the Patrick Finucane Review*, Volume I, p. 12, paragraph 53 and p. 303ff.

69   *Ibid.*, p. 304, paragraph 16.6–8.

70   *Ibid.*, p. 305, paragraph 16.14.

71   NAUK, CJ4/4198, Newspaper cutting, *The Irish News*, 29 April 1982.

72   *Ibid.*, CJ4/4225, Note for the Record, 4 May 1982.

73   *Ibid.*

74   NAUK, CJ4/4198, Newspaper cutting (unnamed and undated); the article is headed: 'UDA chiefs given bail after appeals from churchmen'.

75   De Silva, *The Report of the Patrick Finucane Review*, Volume I, p. 8, paragraph 29.

76   NAUK, CJ4/4198, Newspaper cutting (unnamed and undated); the article is headed: 'UDA chiefs given bail after appeals from churchmen'.

77   *The Irish Times*, 16 April 1983.

78   *Ibid.*, 26 and 28 February 1986.

79   NAUK., CJ4/4198, Several documents removed and retained under Section 3 (4) of the Public Records Act 1958.

80   *Ibid.*, Letter and paper on loyalist groups from D. F. J. R. Hill to David Snoxill, RID of FCO, 24 June 1982.

81   *Ibid.*

82    *Ibid.*, CJ4/4815, Letter and note to Paul Coulson, NIO, from Chief Superintendent R. J. K. Sinclair, RUC Headquarters, 7 September 1982.

83    *Ibid.*

84    McKittrick *et al.*, *Lost Lives*, p. 1553.

85    De Silva, *The Report of the Patrick Finucane Review*, Volume I, p. 108, paragraph 6.55.

86    *Ibid.*, p. 38, paragraph 1.70.

87    *Ibid.*, p. 11, paragraph 49.

88    *Ibid.*, Volume II, Additional documents relating to Brian Nelson, Nelson's statement to Stevens investigation, 15 January 1990, pp. 50–1. Some punctuation has been added to the original.

89    Brian Fitzsimons was later to die in the Chinook Helicopter crash over the Mull of Kintyre, Scotland, in 1994.

90    De Silva, *The Report of the Patrick Finucane Review*, Vol. II, Loose minute from Stormont House Annexe, 29 September 1989, p. 323.

**CONCLUSION**

1    Cadwallader, *Lethal Allies*, p. 163.

2    *The Irish Times*, 27 August 1975.

3    *Ibid.*, 28 April 2003.

4    It was technically possible for the UN to deploy peacekeepers to Northern Ireland under the Charter of the United Nations. The UN Charter gives the Security Council primary responsibility for the maintenance of international peace and security. In fulfilling this responsibility, the Council may establish a UN peacekeeping operation, providing the guiding principles of such an operation are adhered to. These principles require the *consent of the parties* to any dispute (in this case the Irish and British government disputing the ability of the British to protect the civilian population from sectarian murders and attacks); *impartiality* (by the peacekeepers); and *the non-use of force except in self-defence*. Chapter VII of the UN Charter contains provisions related to 'Action with Respect to the Peace, Breaches of the Peace and Acts of Aggression'. The Council may invoke Chapter VII of the charter when authorising the deployment of UN peacekeeping operations into volatile settings where the state is unable to maintain security and public order. http://www.un.org/en/peacekeeping/operations/principles.shtml (accessed on 12 August 2015).

# BIBLIOGRAPHY

Anderson, D., *14 May Days: The Inside Story of the Loyalist Strike of 1974* (Gill & Macmillan, Dublin, 1994)

Anderson, D. and Killingray D., *Policing and Decolonisation* (Routledge, New York, 1992)

Barron, Justice H., *Interim Report on the Report of the Independent Commission of Inquiry into the Dublin and Monaghan Bombings* (Joint Oireachtas Committee on Justice, Equality, Defence and Women's Rights, Dublin, 2003)

Barron, Justice H., *Interim Report on the Report of the Independent Commission of Inquiry into the Dublin Bombings of December 1972 and January 1973* (Joint Oireachtas Committee on Justice, Equality, Defence and Women's Rights, Dublin, 2004)

Barron, Justice H., *Interim Report on the Report of the Bombing of Kay's Tavern, Dundalk* (Joint Oireachtas Committee on Justice, Equality, Defence and Women's Rights, Dublin, 2006)

Bew, P. and Gillespie, G., *Northern Ireland: A Chronology of the Troubles 1968–1999* (2nd edn; Gill & Macmillan, Dublin, 1999)

Boulton, D., *The UVF 1966–73: An Anatomy of Loyalist Rebellion* (Torc Books, Dublin, 1973)

Bourke, R., *Peace in Ireland: The War of Ideas* (Pimlico, London, 2003)

Cadwallader, A., *Lethal Allies: British Collusion in Ireland* (Mercier Press, Cork, 2013)

Cohen, S., *States of Denial: Knowing about Atrocities and Suffering* (Polity Press, Cambridge, 2001)

Cory, Judge P., *Cory Collusion Inquiry Report – Patrick Finucane* (The Stationery Office, London, 2004)

Curtis, L., *Ireland: The Propaganda War* (Pluto Press, London, 1984)

Dickson, B., 'The Detention of Suspected Terrorists in Northern Ireland and Great Britain', *University of Richmond Law Review*, Vol. 43, No. 3, 2009, pp. 927–966

De Silva, The Rt Hon. Sir D., *The Report of the Patrick Finucane Review* (The Stationery Office, London, 2012)

Dillon, M., *The Dirty War* (Routledge, New York, 1990)

Dillon, M., *The Shankill Butchers: A Case Study of Mass Murder* (Arrow Books, London, 1990)

Dillon, M., *The Trigger Men* (Mainstream Publishing, Edinburgh, 2004)

Dorril, S., *The Silent Conspiracy: Inside the Intelligence Services in the 1990s* (Mandarin, London, 1994)

Dorril, S., *MI6: Fifty Years of Special Operations* (Fourth Estate, London, 2000)

Fisk, R., *The Point of No Return* (André Deutsch Ltd, London, 1975)

MacAirt, C., *The McGurk's Bar Bombing* (Frontline Noir, Edinburgh, 2012)

McGovern, Mark, 'State Violence and the Colonial Roots of Collusion in Northern Ireland', in *Race and Class*, Vol. 57, No. 2 (Sage, October–December 2015), pp. 3–23

McKittrick, D., Kelters, S., Feeney, B., Thornton, C. and McVea, D., *Lost Lives: The Stories of the Men, Women and Children Who Died as a Result of the Northern Ireland Troubles* (2nd edn; Mainstream Publishing Company, Edinburgh, 2007)

Moore, C., *The Kincora Scandal: Political Cover-up and Intrigue in Northern Ireland* (Marino, Dublin, 1996)

Murray, R., *The SAS in Ireland* (revd edition; Mercier Press, Cork, 2004)

Newsinger, J., *British Counter-Insurgency: From Palestine to Northern Ireland* (Palgrave, Basingstoke, 2002)

O'Callaghan, E., *Belfast Days: A 1972 Teenage Diary* (Merrion Press, Newbridge, 2014)

O'Callaghan, M. and O'Donnell, C., 'The Northern Ireland Government, The Paisleyite Movement and Ulster Unionism in 1966', in *Irish Political Studies*, Vol. 21, No. 2, June 2006, pp. 203–22

Pat Finucane Centre, *The Hidden History of the UDR: The Secret Files Revealed* (pamphlet, August 2014)

Rolston, B., *Children of the Revolution: The Lives of Sons and Daughters of Activists in Northern Ireland* (Guildhall Press, Derry, 2011)

Ross, F. S., *Smashing H-Block: The Rise and Fall of the Popular Campaign against Criminalization, 1976–1982* (Liverpool University Press, Liverpool, 2011)

Routledge, P., *Public Servant, Secret Agent: The Elusive Life and Violent Death of Airey Neave* (Fourth Estate, London, 2002)

Shirlow, P., *The End of Ulster Loyalism?* (Manchester University Press, Manchester, 2012)

Taylor, P., *Brits: The War against the IRA* (Bloomsbury, London, 2002)

Taylor, P., *Loyalists* (revd edn; Bloomsbury, London, 2000)

Taylor, P., *Provos: The IRA and Sinn Fein* (Bloomsbury, London, 1997)

Travers, S. and Fetherstonhaugh, N., *The Miami Showband Massacre* (Hachette Ireland, Dublin, 2008)

Urwin, M., *Counter-Gangs: A History of Undercover Military Units in Northern Ireland 1971–1976* (Spinwatch, Justice for the Forgotten and The Pat Finucane Centre, 2013) http://www.spinwatch.org/index.php/issues/northern-ireland/item/5448-counter-gangs-a-history-of-undercover-military-units-in-northern-ireland-1971-1976

Whelan, K., *The Tree of Liberty: Radicalism, Catholicism and the Construction of Irish Identity 1760–1830* (University of Notre Dame, South Bend, 1997)

Wood, I., *Crimes of Loyalty: A History of the UDA* (Edinburgh University Press, Edinburgh, 2006)

# INDEX